MCSE™
Exchange 2000
Design

William R. Baldwin

MCSE™ Exchange 2000 Design Exam Cram
©2001 The Coriolis Group. All rights reserved.

Limits of Liability and Disclaimer of Warranty

Trademarks

The Coriolis Group, LLC
14455 N. Hayden Road
Suite 220
Scottsdale, Arizona 85260

(480)483-0192
FAX (480)483-0193
www.coriolis.com

Library of Congress Cataloging-in-Publication Data
Baldwin, William. 1971-
    MCSE Exchange 2000 Design / by William Baldwin.
        p.   cm. -- (Exam cram)
    Includes index.
    ISBN 1-58880-032-6
    1. Electronic data processing personnel--Certification.   2. Microsoft software--Examinations--Study guides.   3. Microsoft Exchange Server (Computer file)   I. Title.   II. Series.
QA76.3. B38   2001
005.7'13769--dc21
                                            2001028861
                                            CIP

Publisher
Steve Sayre

Acquisitions Editor
Lee Anderson

Product Marketing Manager
Brett Woolley

Project Editor
Sean Tape

Technical Reviewer
J. Peter Bruzzese

Production Coordinator
Todd Halvorsen

Cover Designer
Laura Wellander

Layout Designer
April Nielsen

Printed in the United States of America
10 9 8 7 6 5 4 3 2 1

The Coriolis Group, LLC • 14455 North Hayden Road, Suite 220 • Scottsdale, Arizona 85260

A Note from Coriolis

Our goal has always been to provide you with the best study tools on the planet to help you achieve your certification in record time. Time is so valuable these days that none of us can afford to waste a second of it, especially when it comes to exam preparation.

Over the past few years, we've created an extensive line of *Exam Cram* and *Exam Prep* study guides, practice exams, and interactive training. To help you study even better, we have now created an e-learning and certification destination called **ExamCram.com**. (You can access the site at **www.examcram.com**.) Now, with every study product you purchase from us, you'll be connected to a large community of people like yourself who are actively studying for their certifications, developing their careers, seeking advice, and sharing their insights and stories.

We believe that the future is all about collaborative learning. Our **ExamCram.com** destination is our approach to creating a highly interactive, easily accessible collaborative environment, where you can take practice exams and discuss your experiences with others, sign up for features like "Questions of the Day," plan your certifications using our interactive planners, create your own personal study pages, and keep up with all of the latest study tips and techniques.

We hope that whatever study products you purchase from us—*Exam Cram* or *Exam Prep* study guides, *Personal Trainers, Personal Test Centers*, or one of our interactive Web courses—will make your studying fun and productive. Our commitment is to build the kind of learning tools that will allow you to study the way you want to, whenever you want to.

Visit ExamCram.com now to enhance your study program.

Help us continue to provide the very best certification study materials possible. Write us or email us at **learn@examcram.com** and let us know how our study products have helped you study. Tell us about new features that you'd like us to add. Send us a story about how we've helped you. We're listening!

Good luck with your certification exam and your career. Thank you for allowing us to help you achieve your goals.

ExamCram.com Connects You to the Ultimate Study Center!

Look for these other products from The Coriolis Group:

MCSE Exchange 2000 Design Exam Prep
by Michael Shannon and Deniss Suhanovs

MCSE Exchange 2000 Administration Exam Cram
by David V. Watts and Will Willis

Exchange 2000 Server On Site
by Göran Husman

Exchange 2000 .NET Server Black Book
by Evan Benjamin and Phillip Schein

For my wife Meredith and my son Zachary.
—William R. Baldwin

About the Author

Bill Baldwin is a professional technical trainer specializing in network operating systems and messaging; he is the president of WRBaldwin, Inc., in Cleveland, Ohio. He has worked with a "Baby Bell" planning a 250,000-seat Windows 2000/Exchange 2000 deployment and has written many technical publications since he began his career in 1989.

Bill has been a Microsoft Certified Systems Engineer (MCSE) since 1996, a Microsoft Certified Trainer (MCT) since 1997. He has been recognized by the Chauncey Group as a Certified Technical Trainer (CTT) since 1999, and he has held the CompTIA A+ certification as a Certified Service Technician since 1998.

After starting his technical career programming accounting software on UNIX systems, Bill worked as a technical trainer and writer for Case Western Reserve University (CWRU). At CWRU he taught classes on WordPerfect, Microsoft Office, Microsoft Windows, dBase, and Paradox, and he published six training manuals while employed there.

Working as the network administrator for a point-of-sale company in northeast Ohio, Bill migrated its systems from Novell Netware and MS Mail to Windows NT and Exchange 4.0. He also oversaw the messaging system's evolution to Exchange 5.5. As a lead consultant and project manager for a professional services company, he was involved in many aspects of information technology, including server migration and messaging system deployment. He led a team of engineers and was technical project manager for the company's largest account.

Bill has taught over one hundred Microsoft certification courses. In 1999, he formed his own training and consulting company and travels the United States teaching high-end Microsoft courses. He has written study guides on Windows 2000 and Exchange 2000 for the Coriolis Group. He has also written online and instructor-led training manuals on Windows 2000 and Exchange 2000 for ElementK Press.

Bill and his wife, Meredith, had their first child, Zachary, in 1999. They enjoy Cleveland Browns games, the outdoors, family gatherings, and amusement parks. Bill is an amateur racecar driver with the Sports Car Club of America (SCCA). He also enjoys attending the Cleveland Grand Prix every summer. You can reach him for comments, corrections, or criticism by email at wrbaldwin@yahoo.com. Also visit www.wrbaldwin.com for more information.

Acknowledgments

My list of acknowledgments is shorter than I had hoped, which made the book more difficult than I had hoped. It's good to be busy and my planned co-author and good friend John Roh was just that. Unfortunately, John was unable to participate in this book. His incredible knowledge of Exchange was used via email. John thanks for the sounding board. That's is about it from a content standpoint. I'd to thank the writers of the hundreds of white papers and the Exchange 2000 programmers; it's a great product.

I'd like to give a big thank you to the editors. Sean Tape, my Project Editor, did a wonderful job coordinating a very tight schedule. My Copy Editor, Sharon McCarson, made me look like I can actually write. Thanks Sharon for the countless corrections. Todd Halvorsen, the Production Coordinator, did a wonderful job with a tight schedule. Finally, Peter Bruzzese, the technical editor, provided great input without trying to have it written his way. Thanks Pete for all your suggestions, including the ones I implemented and the ones I didn't.

A giant thank you to my wife, Meredith. Your ability to put up with me is unmatched, and as I've said before, I'd never be able to accomplish such things without you. Hopefully, Zachary will read this someday. At the age of two, it's amazing that he can understand what it means when daddy has to work. Seeing you pop your head in my office and saying, "Daddy work?", makes this all worth while. I love you son.

Contents at a Glance

Chapter 1   Microsoft Certification Exams   1

Chapter 2   Integration with Windows 2000 Active Directory   23

Chapter 3   Designing an Installation Plan   49

Chapter 4   Planning for Exchange Administration   71

Chapter 5   Designing a Fault Tolerant Data Storage Topology   99

Chapter 6   Designing a Routing Group Topology   125

Chapter 7   Planning for Server Roles and Placement   147

Chapter 8   Security Planning for Exchange 2000   169

Chapter 9   Designing Public Folder Usage and Implementation   187

Chapter 10   Planning for Internet Connectivity   207

Chapter 11   Migrating from and Coexisting with Exchange 5.5   229

Chapter 12   Planning for Clients   269

Chapter 13   Designing an Instant Messaging Solution   285

Chapter 14   Sample Test   299

Chapter 15   Answer Key   327

Table of Contents

Introduction xix

Self-Assessment xxxi

Chapter 1
Microsoft Certification Exams 1
   Assessing Exam-Readiness   2
   The Exam Situation   3
   Exam Layout and Design: New Case Study Format   4
      Multiple-Choice Question Format   5
      Build-List-and-Reorder Question Format   6
      Create-a-Tree Question Format   8
      Drag-and-Connect Question Format   11
      Select-and-Place Question Format   12
   Microsoft's Testing Formats   13
   Strategies for Different Testing Formats   15
      The Case Study Exam Strategy   15
      The Fixed-Length and Short-Form Exam Strategy   16
      The Adaptive Exam Strategy   17
   Question-Handling Strategies   18
   Mastering the Inner Game   19
   Additional Resources   20

Chapter 2
Integration with Windows 2000 Active Directory 23
   Active Directory Basics   24
      Active Directory Objects   24
      The Schema   26
   The Logical Structure of Active Directory   27
      Domains   27
      Organizational Units and Containers   27

Trees and Forests   28

Lightweight Directory Access Protocol (LDAP)   30

What's in a Name?   31

Server Functions   34

The Physical Structure of AD   37

Exchange 2000 in AD   37

Practice Questions   40

Need to Know More?   47

Chapter 3
Designing an Installation Plan 49

Preparing Windows 2000   50

Hardware Requirements   50

Internet Information Services (IIS)   51

Active Directory   51

ForestPrep   53

DomainPrep   53

Installing Exchange 2000   55

Administrative Groups   55

Routing Groups   55

Components and Services   56

Mixed/Native Mode   59

Unattended Installation   59

Administrative Tools   60

Verifying an Exchange 2000 Installation   61

Folders and Shares   61

Services   62

Practice Questions   63

Need to Know More?   70

Chapter 4
Planning for Exchange Administration 71

Administrative Models   72

Centralized Model   72

Distributed Model   73

Hybrid Model   74

Administrative Roles   75

Administrative Tools   77

 Exchange System Manager   77

 Active Directory Users and Computers   79

 Advanced Configuration Tools   79

 Custom Consoles   79

Administrative Groups   80

 How Many Administrative Groups Should You Create?   81

 When Should You Create Administrative Groups?   81

Delegating Administrative Control   81

 Delegation Wizard and Roles   82

 Advanced Security   83

 Delegating Control over Recipients   84

Address Lists   85

 Filter Rules   85

 Controlling Access to Address Lists   86

 All Address Lists   87

 Global Address Lists   87

 Offline Address Lists   88

 Recipient Update Service   88

Policies   88

 Recipient Policies   88

 System Policies   89

Practice Questions   91

Need to Know More?   97

Chapter 5
Designing a Fault Tolerant Data Storage Topology 99

Stores   100

 Mailbox Store   100

 Public Folder Store   100

 Database Files   101

 Data in the Stores   101

 Designing a Store Topology   103

Storage Groups and Transaction Logs   103

 Transaction Logs   103

 Log Files   104

 Circular Logging   105

 Designing a Storage Group Topology   106

Extensible Storage Engine   107
    Single Instance Storage   107
    Mounting and Dismounting Stores   107
Placement of Databases and Logs   108
    Performance   108
    Data Recovery   109
    Hardware   110
Full-Text Indexing   110
Backing Up and Restoring Data   111
    Backup   111
    Verify   114
    Restore   115
Practice Questions   117
Need to Know More?   124

Chapter 6
Designing a Routing Group Topology 125
Routing Groups   126
    First Routing Group   126
    Multiple Routing Groups   127
Mixed Mode versus Native Mode   128
Connectors   129
    Routing Group Connectors   130
    Bridgehead Servers   131
    Security   131
    SMTP Connectors   132
    X.400 Connectors   133
    Public Folder Referrals   133
    Other Connectors   134
    Costs and Link States   134
    Routing Topology Designs   135
Routing Topology Design Considerations   137
    Existing Network Infrastructure   137
    Existing Messaging Systems   137
    Planning for Growth and Change   138
Practice Questions   139
Need to Know More?   146

Chapter 7

Planning for Server Roles and Placement 147

    Server Roles   148

        Mailbox Servers   148

        Public Folder Servers   150

        Front-End/Back-End Servers   150

        Connector Servers   152

        Outlook Web Access (OWA) Server   153

        Active Directory Servers   153

        Other Exchange Server Roles   155

    Server Placement   155

        Mailbox Servers   155

        Public Folder Servers   155

        Front-End/Back-End Servers   156

        Perimeter Networks   156

        Using a Single Firewall   158

    Practice Questions   159

    Need to Know More?   168

Chapter 8

Security Planning for Exchange 2000 169

    Why Do You Need Security?   170

        Internal Threats   170

        External Threats   170

    Virus Protection   171

        Client-Side Protection   171

        Server-Side Protection   172

    TCP/IP Security   172

        TCP/IP Filtering   172

        IPSec   174

        SSL   175

    Remote Authentication   176

    PKI   176

        Certificate Server   176

        KM Server   177

    Secure Messaging   177

        Client-Side Security   177

        Service-Side Security   177

Practice Questions 179

Need to Know More? 186

Chapter 9
Designing Public Folder Usage and Implementation 187

Public Folder Trees 188

All Public Folders 189

General-Purpose Trees 189

Replication 190

Replication Configuration 192

Connectors and Referrals 192

Active Directory 193

Accessing Data 194

Permissions 196

Types of Permissions 196

Inheritance 197

Practice Questions 199

Need to Know More? 206

Chapter 10
Planning for Internet Connectivity 207

Internet Information Services (IIS) 208

Virtual Servers 209

Internet Email 211

Outgoing Mail 211

Incoming Mail 212

Remote Client Connectivity 213

Outlook 9X/2000 213

Outlook Express 213

Outlook Web Access (OWA) 214

Authentication 214

Anonymous Access 214

Basic Authentication 214

Windows Integrated Authentication 214

Secure Communications 215

Virtual Private Network 215

Certificates and SSL 215

Connection Control 216

Network News Transfer Protocol (NNTP)   216

Practice Questions   219

Need to Know More?   228

Chapter 11
Migrating from and Coexisting with Exchange 5.5 229

Overview   230

    Migrating the Exchange Directory   230

    Migrating the Exchange Messaging System   231

    Coexistence   231

Migrating Pre-Windows 2000 Domains to Active Directory   231

    Performing an In-Place Upgrade   231

    The Active Directory Migration Tool   232

Migrating and Synchronizing Data from Exchange 5.5 Organizations
to Active Directory   235

    The Active Directory Connector   235

    ADC Connection Agreements   238

    Resource Mailboxes   242

    Active Directory Cleanup Wizard   242

Upgrading to Exchange 2000   243

    Upgrading Exchange Server 5.5 to Exchange 2000   244

    Moving Mailboxes from Pre-Exchange 2000 Servers to
Exchange 2000 Servers   246

Coexistence with Pre-Exchange 2000 Systems   249

    Directory Synchronization and Access   249

    Message Routing   251

    Public Folder Replication and Access   251

    Other Coexistence Scenarios   252

The Exchange Server Migration Tool   254

Practice Questions   257

Need to Know More?   267

Chapter 12
Planning for Clients 269

Outlook 2000   270

Outlook Express   271

Outlook Web Access (OWA)   272

    Browser Support   273

    Authentication   273

Chat Clients   275
Instant Messaging Clients   275
Practice Questions   277
Need to Know More?   283

Chapter 13
Designing an Instant Messaging Solution 285
Instant Messaging   286
Exchange 2000 Instant Messaging   287
Instant Messaging Architecture   287
    Server Roles   287
    Domains   288
Instant Messaging (RVP) Virtual Server   290
MSN Messenger   291
Practice Questions   292
Need to Know More?   298

Chapter 14
Sample Test 299

Chapter 15
Answer Key 327

Index 341

Introduction

Welcome to *MCSE Exchange 2000 Design Exam Cram*! Whether this is your first or your fifteenth *Exam Cram* book, you'll find information here and in Chapter 1 that will help ensure your success as you pursue knowledge, experience, and certification. This book aims to help you get ready to take—and pass—the Microsoft certification Exam 70-225, titled "Designing and Deploying a Messaging Infrastructure with Microsoft Exchange 2000 Server." This Introduction explains Microsoft's certification programs in general and talks about how the *Exam Cram* series can help you prepare for Microsoft's Windows 2000 certification exams.

Exam Cram books help you understand and appreciate the subjects and materials you need to pass Microsoft certification exams. *Exam Cram* books are aimed strictly at test preparation and review. They do not teach you everything you need to know about a topic. Instead, I present and dissect the questions and problems I've found that you're likely to encounter on a test. I've worked to bring together as much information as possible about Microsoft certification exams.

Nevertheless, to completely prepare yourself for any Microsoft test, I recommend that you begin by taking the Self-Assessment included in this book immediately following this Introduction. This tool will help you evaluate your knowledge base against the requirements for an MCSE under both ideal and real circumstances.

Based on what you learn from that exercise, you might decide to begin your studies with some classroom training or some background reading. On the other hand, you might decide to pick up and read one of the many study guides available from Microsoft or third-party vendors on certain topics, including The Coriolis Group's *Exam Prep* series. I also recommend that you supplement your study program with visits to **ExamCram.com** to receive additional practice questions, get advice, and track the Windows 2000 MCSE program.

I also strongly recommend that you install, configure, and fool around with the software that you'll be tested on, because nothing beats hands-on experience and familiarity when it comes to understanding the questions you're likely to encounter on a certification test. Book learning is essential, but hands-on experience is the best teacher of all!

The Microsoft Certified Professional (MCP) Program

The MCP Program currently includes the following separate tracks, each of which boasts its own special acronym (as a certification candidate, you need to have a high tolerance for alphabet soup of all kinds):

➤ *MCP (Microsoft Certified Professional)*—This is the least prestigious of all the certification tracks from Microsoft. Passing one of the major Microsoft exams qualifies an individual for the MCP credential. Individuals can demonstrate proficiency with additional Microsoft products by passing additional certification exams.

➤ *MCP+SB (Microsoft Certified Professional + Site Building)*—This certification program is designed for individuals who are planning, building, managing, and maintaining Web sites. Individuals with the MCP+SB credential will have demonstrated the ability to develop Web sites that include multimedia and searchable content and Web sites that connect to and communicate with a back-end database. It requires one MCP exam, plus two of these three exams: "70-055: Designing and Implementing Web Sites with Microsoft FrontPage 98," "70-057: Designing and Implementing Commerce Solutions with Microsoft Site Server, 3.0, Commerce Edition," and "70-152: Designing and Implementing Web Solutions with Microsoft Visual InterDev 6.0."

➤ *MCSE (Microsoft Certified Systems Engineer)*—Anyone who has a current MCSE is warranted to possess a high level of networking expertise with Microsoft operating systems and products. This credential is designed to prepare individuals to plan, implement, maintain, and support information systems, networks, and internetworks built around Microsoft Windows 2000 and its BackOffice Server 2000 family of products.

To obtain an MCSE, an individual must pass four core operating system exams, one optional core exam, and two elective exams. The operating system exams require individuals to prove their competence with desktop and server operating systems and networking/internetworking components.

For Windows NT 4 MCSEs, the Accelerated exam, "70-240: Microsoft Windows 2000 Accelerated Exam for MCPs Certified on Microsoft Windows NT 4.0," is an option. This free exam covers all of the material tested in the Core Four exams. The hitch in this plan is that you can take the test only once. If you fail, you must take all four core exams to recertify. The Core Four exams are: "70-210: Installing, Configuring and Administering Microsoft Windows 2000 Professional," "70-215: Installing, Configuring and Administering Microsoft Windows 2000 Server," "70-216: Implementing and

Administering a Microsoft Windows 2000 Network Infrastructure," and "70-217: Implementing and Administering a Microsoft Windows 2000 Directory Services Infrastructure."

To fulfill the fifth core exam requirement, you can choose from three design exams: "70-219: Designing a Microsoft Windows 2000 Directory Services Infrastructure," "70-220: Designing Security for a Microsoft Windows 2000 Network," or "70-221: Designing a Microsoft Windows 2000 Network Infrastructure." You are also required to take two elective exams. An elective exam can fall in any number of subject or product areas, primarily BackOffice Server 2000 components. The two design exams that you don't select as your fifth core exam also qualify as electives. If you are on your way to becoming an MCSE and have already taken some exams, visit **www.microsoft.com/ trainingandservices/** for information about how to complete your MCSE certification.

In September 1999, Microsoft announced its Windows 2000 track for MCSE and also announced retirement of Windows NT 4.0 MCSE core exams on 12/31/2000. Individuals who wish to remain certified MCSEs after 12/31/2001 must "upgrade" their certifications on or before 12/31/2001. For more detailed information than is included here, visit **www.microsoft.com/ trainingandservices/**.

New MCSE candidates must pass seven tests to meet the MCSE requirements. It's not uncommon for the entire process to take a year or so, and many individuals find that they must take a test more than once to pass. The primary goal of the *Exam Prep* and *Exam Cram* test preparation books is to make it possible, given proper study and preparation, to pass all Microsoft certification tests on the first try. Table 1 shows the required and elective exams for the Windows 2000 MCSE certification.

➤ *MCSD (Microsoft Certified Solution Developer)*—The MCSD credential reflects the skills required to create multitier, distributed, and COM-based solutions, in addition to desktop and Internet applications, using new technologies. To obtain an MCSD, an individual must demonstrate the ability to analyze and interpret user requirements; select and integrate products, platforms, tools, and technologies; design and implement code, and customize applications; and perform necessary software tests and quality assurance operations.

To become an MCSD, you must pass a total of four exams: three core exams and one elective exam. Each candidate must choose one of these three desktop application exams—"70-016: Designing and Implementing Desktop Applications with Microsoft Visual C++ 6.0," "70-156: Designing and

Table 1 MCSE Windows 2000 Requirements

Core

If you have not passed these 3 Windows NT 4 exams	
Exam 70-067	Implementing and Supporting Microsoft Windows NT Server 4.0
Exam 70-068	Implementing and Supporting Microsoft Windows NT Server 4.0 in the Enterprise
Exam 70-073	Microsoft Windows NT Workstation 4.0
then you must take these 4 exams	
Exam 70-210	Installing, Configuring, and Administering Microsoft Windows 2000 Professional
Exam 70-215	Installing, Configuring, and Administering Microsoft Windows 2000 Server
Exam 70-216	Implementing and Administering a Microsoft Windows 2000 Network Infrastructure
Exam 70-217	Implementing and Administering a Microsoft Windows 2000 Directory Services Infrastructure
If you have already passed exams 70-067, 70-068, and 70-073, you may take this exam	
Exam 70-240	Microsoft Windows 2000 Accelerated Exam for MCPs Certified on Microsoft Windows NT 4.0

5th Core Option

Choose 1 from this group	
Exam 70-219	Designing a Microsoft Windows 2000 Directory Services Infrastructure
Exam 70-220	Designing Security for a Microsoft Windows 2000 Network
Exam 70-221	Designing a Microsoft Windows 2000 Network Infrastructure
Exam 70-226	Designing Highly Available Web Solutions with Microsoft Windows 2000 Server Technologies

Elective*

Choose 2 from this group	
Exam 70-019	Designing and Implementing Data Warehouse with Microsoft SQL Server 7.0
Exam 70-056	Implementing and Supporting Web Sites Using Microsoft Site Server 3.0
Exam 70-080	Implementing and Supporting Microsoft Internet Explorer 5.0 by Using the Internet Explorer Administration Kit
Exam 70-085	Implementing and Supporting Microsoft SNA Server 4.0
Exam 70-086	Implementing and Supporting Microsoft Systems Management Server 2.0
Exam 70-222	Migrating from Microsoft Windows NT 4.0 to Microsoft Windows 2000
Exam 70-223	Installing, Configuring, and Administering Microsoft Clustering Services by Using Microsoft Windows 2000 Advanced Server
Exam 70-224	Installing, Configuring, and Administering Microsoft Exchange 2000 Server
▶ Exam 70-225	Designing and Deploying a Messaging Infrastructure with Microsoft Exchange 2000 Server
Exam 70-227	Installing, Configuring, and Administering Microsoft Internet Security and Acceleration (ISA) Server 2000 Enterprise Edition
Exam 70-228	Installing, Configuring, and Administering Microsoft SQL Server 2000 Enterprise Edition
Exam 70-229	Designing and Implementing Databases with Microsoft SQL Server 2000 Enterprise Edition
Exam 70-244	Supporting and Maintaining a Microsoft Windows NT Server 4.0 Network

This is not a complete listing—you can still be tested on some earlier versions of these products. However, we have included mainly the most recent versions so that you may test on these versions and thus be certified longer. We have not included any tests that are scheduled to be retired.

* 5th Core Option exams may also be used as electives, but can only be counted once toward a certification. You cannot receive credit for an exam as both a core and an elective in the same track.

Implementing Desktop Applications with Microsoft Visual FoxPro 6.0," or "70-176: Designing and Implementing Desktop Applications with Microsoft Visual Basic 6.0"—*plus* one of these three distributed application exams—"70-015: Designing and Implementing Distributed Applications with Microsoft Visual C++ 6.0," "70-155: Designing and Implementing Distributed Applications with Microsoft Visual FoxPro 6.0," or "70-175: Designing and Implementing Distributed Applications with Microsoft Visual Basic 6.0." The third core exam is "70-100: Analyzing Requirements and Defining Solution Architectures." Elective exams cover specific Microsoft applications and languages, including Visual Basic, C++, the Microsoft Foundation Classes, Access, SQL Server, Excel, and more.

➤ *MCDBA (Microsoft Certified Database Administrator)*—The MCDBA credential reflects the skills required to implement and administer Microsoft SQL Server databases. To obtain an MCDBA, an individual must demonstrate the ability to derive physical database designs, develop logical data models, create physical databases, create data services by using Transact-SQL, manage and maintain databases, configure and manage security, monitor and optimize databases, and install and configure Microsoft SQL Server.

To become an MCDBA, you must pass a total of three core exams and one elective exam. The required core exams are "70-028: Administering Microsoft SQL Server 7.0," "70-029: Designing and Implementing Databases with Microsoft SQL Server 7.0," and "70-215: Installing, Configuring and Administering Microsoft Windows 2000 Server."

The elective exams that you can choose from cover specific uses of SQL Server and include "70-015: Designing and Implementing Distributed Applications with Microsoft Visual C++ 6.0," "70-019: Designing and Implementing Data Warehouses with Microsoft SQL Server 7.0," "70-155: Designing and Implementing Distributed Applications with Microsoft Visual FoxPro 6.0," "70-175: Designing and Implementing Distributed Applications with Microsoft Visual Basic 6.0," and two exams that relate to Windows 2000: "70-216: Implementing and Administering a Microsoft Windows 2000 Network Infrastructure," and "70-087: Implementing and Supporting Microsoft Internet Information Server 4.0."

If you have taken the three core Windows NT 4 exams on your path to becoming an MCSE, you qualify for the Accelerated exam (it replaces the Network Infrastructure exam requirement). The Accelerated exam covers the objectives of all four of the Windows 2000 core exams. In addition to taking the Accelerated exam, you must take only the two SQL exams—Administering and Database Design.

➤ *MCT (Microsoft Certified Trainer)*—Microsoft Certified Trainers are deemed able to deliver elements of the official Microsoft curriculum, based on technical knowledge and instructional ability. Thus, it is necessary for an individual seeking MCT credentials (which are granted on a course-by-course basis) to pass the related certification exam for a course and complete the official Microsoft training in the subject area, and to demonstrate an ability to teach.

This teaching skill criterion may be satisfied by proving that one has already attained training certification from Novell, Banyan, Lotus, the Santa Cruz Operation, or Cisco, or by taking a Microsoft-sanctioned workshop on instruction. Microsoft makes it clear that MCTs are important cogs in the Microsoft training channels. Instructors must be MCTs before Microsoft will allow them to teach in any of its official training channels, including Microsoft's affiliated Certified Technical Education Centers (CTECs) and its online training partner network. As of January 1, 2001, MCT candidates must also possess a current MCSE.

Microsoft has announced that the MCP+I and MCSE+I credentials will not be continued when the MCSE exams for Windows 2000 are in full swing because the skill set for the Internet portion of the program has been included in the new MCSE program. Therefore, details on these tracks are not provided here; go to **www.microsoft.com/trainingandservices/** if you need more information.

Once a Microsoft product becomes obsolete, MCPs typically have to recertify on current versions. (If individuals do not recertify, their certifications become invalid.) Because technology keeps changing and new products continually supplant old ones, this should come as no surprise. This explains why Microsoft has announced that MCSEs have 12 months past the scheduled retirement date for the Windows NT 4 exams to recertify on Windows 2000 topics. (Note that this means taking at least two exams, if not more.)

The best place to keep tabs on the MCP program and its related certifications is on the Web. The URL for the MCP program is **www.microsoft.com/trainingandservices-/**. But Microsoft's Web site changes often, so if this URL doesn't work, try using the Search tool on Microsoft's site with either "MCP" or the quoted phrase "Microsoft Certified Professional" as a search string. This will help you find the latest and most accurate information about Microsoft's certification programs.

Taking a Certification Exam

Once you've prepared for your exam, you need to register with a testing center. Each computer-based MCP exam costs $100, and if you don't pass, you may retest for an additional $100 for each additional try. In the United States and

Canada, tests are administered by Prometric and by Virtual University Enterprises (VUE). Here's how you can contact them:

➤ *Prometric*—You can sign up for a test through the company's Web site at **www.prometric.com**. Or, you can register by phone at 800-755-3926 (within the United States or Canada) or at 410-843-8000 (outside the United States and Canada).

➤ *Virtual University Enterprises*—You can sign up for a test or get the phone numbers for local testing centers through the Web page at **www.vue.com/ms/**.

To sign up for a test, you must possess a valid credit card, or contact either company for mailing instructions to send them a check (in the U.S.). Only when payment is verified, or a check has cleared, can you actually register for a test.

To schedule an exam, call the number or visit either of the Web pages at least one day in advance. To cancel or reschedule an exam, you must call before 7 P.M. pacific standard time the day before the scheduled test time (or you may be charged, even if you don't appear to take the test). When you want to schedule a test, have the following information ready:

➤ Your name, organization, and mailing address.

➤ Your Microsoft Test ID. (Inside the United States, this means your Social Security number; citizens of other nations should call ahead to find out what type of identification number is required to register for a test.)

➤ The name and number of the exam you wish to take.

➤ A method of payment. (As I've already mentioned, a credit card is the most convenient method, but alternate means can be arranged in advance, if necessary.)

Once you sign up for a test, you'll be informed as to when and where the test is scheduled. Try to arrive at least 15 minutes early. You must supply two forms of identification—one of which must be a photo ID—to be admitted into the testing room.

All exams are completely closed-book. In fact, you will not be permitted to take anything with you into the testing area, but you will be furnished with a blank sheet of paper and a pen or, in some cases, an erasable plastic sheet and an erasable pen. I suggest that you immediately write down on that sheet of paper all the information you've memorized for the test. In *Exam Cram* books, this information appears on a tear-out sheet inside the front cover of each book. You will have some time to compose yourself, record this information, and take a sample orientation exam before you begin the real thing. I suggest you take the orientation test before taking your first exam, but because they're all more or less identical in layout, behavior, and controls, you probably won't need to do this more than once.

When you complete a Microsoft certification exam, the software will tell you whether you've passed or failed.

If you need to retake an exam, you'll have to schedule a new test with Prometric or VUE and pay another $100.

 The first time you fail a test, you can retake the test the next day. However, if you fail a second time, you must wait 14 days before retaking that test. The 14-day waiting period remains in effect for all retakes after the second failure.

Tracking MCP Status

As soon as you pass any Microsoft exam (except Networking Essentials), you'll attain Microsoft Certified Professional (MCP) status. Microsoft also generates transcripts that indicate which exams you have passed. You can view a copy of your transcript at any time by going to the MCP secured site and selecting Transcript Tool. This tool will allow you to print a copy of your current transcript and confirm your certification status.

Once you pass the necessary set of exams, you'll be certified. Official certification normally takes anywhere from six to eight weeks, so don't expect to get your credentials overnight. When the package for a qualified certification arrives, it includes a Welcome Kit that contains a number of elements (see Microsoft's Web site for other benefits of specific certifications):

➤ A certificate suitable for framing, along with a wallet card and lapel pin.

➤ A license to use the MCP logo, thereby allowing you to use the logo in advertisements, promotions, and documents, and on letterhead, business cards, and so on. Along with the license comes an MCP logo sheet, which includes camera-ready artwork. (Note: Before using any of the artwork, individuals must sign and return a licensing agreement that indicates they'll abide by its terms and conditions.)

➤ A subscription to *Microsoft Certified Professional Magazine*, which provides ongoing data about testing and certification activities, requirements, and changes to the program.

Many people believe that the benefits of MCP certification go well beyond the perks that Microsoft provides to newly anointed members of this elite group. I've starting to see more job listings that request or require applicants to have an MCP, MCSE, and so on, and many individuals who complete the program can qualify for increases in pay and/or responsibility. As an official recognition of hard work and broad knowledge, one of the MCP credentials is a badge of honor in many IT organizations.

How to Prepare for an Exam

Preparing for any Exchange 2000 Server-related test (including "Designing and Deploying a Messaging Infrastructure with Microsoft Exchange 2000 Server") requires that you obtain and study materials designed to provide comprehensive information about the product and its capabilities that will appear on the specific exam for which you are preparing. The following list of materials will help you study and prepare:

➤ The Exchange 2000 Server product CD includes comprehensive online documentation and related materials; it should be a primary resource when you are preparing for the test.

➤ The exam preparation materials, practice tests, and self-assessment exams on the Microsoft Training & Services page at **www.microsoft.com/trainingandservices/default.asp?PageID=mcp**. The Testing Innovations link offers samples of the new question types found on the Windows 2000 MCSE exams. Find the materials, download them, and use them!

➤ The exam preparation advice, practice tests, questions of the day, and discussion groups on the **ExamCram.com** e-learning and certification destination Web site (**www.examcram.com**).

In addition, you'll probably find any or all of the following materials useful in your quest for Exchange 2000 Design expertise:

➤ *Microsoft training kits*—Microsoft Press offers a training kit that specifically targets Exam 70-225. For more information, visit: **http://mspress. microsoft.com/findabook/list/series_ak.htm**. This training kit contains information that you will find useful in preparing for the test.

➤ *Microsoft TechNet CD*—This monthly CD-based publication delivers numerous electronic titles that include coverage of Directory Services Design and related topics on the Technical Information (TechNet) CD. Its offerings include product facts, technical notes, tools and utilities, and information on how to access the Seminars Online training materials for Directory Services Design. A subscription to TechNet costs $299 per year, but it is well worth the price. Visit **www.microsoft.com/technet/** and check out the information under the "TechNet Subscription" menu entry for more details.

➤ *Study guides*—Several publishers—including The Coriolis Group—offer Windows 2000 titles. The Coriolis Group series includes the following:

   ➤ *The Exam Cram series*—These books give you information about the material you need to know to pass the tests.

➤ *The Exam Prep series*—These books provide a greater level of detail than the *Exam Cram* books and are designed to teach you everything you need to know from an exam perspective. Each book comes with a CD that contains interactive practice exams in a variety of testing formats.

Together, the two series make a perfect pair.

➤ *Multimedia*—These Coriolis Group materials are designed to support learners of all types—whether you learn best by reading or doing:

➤ *The Exam Cram Personal Trainer*—Offers a unique, personalized self-paced training course based on the exam.

➤ *The Exam Cram Personal Test Center*—Features multiple test options that simulate the actual exam, including Fixed-Length, Random, Review, and Test All. Explanations of correct and incorrect answers reinforce concepts learned.

➤ *Classroom training*—CTECs, online partners, and third-party training companies (like Wave Technologies, Learning Tree, Data-Tech, and others) all offer classroom training on Windows 2000. These companies aim to help you prepare to pass Exam 70-225. Although such training runs upwards of $350 per day in class, most of the individuals lucky enough to partake find it to be quite worthwhile.

➤ *Other publications*—There's no shortage of materials available about Exchange 2000 Design. The resource sections at the end of each chapter should give you an idea of where I think you should look for further discussion.

By far, this set of required and recommended materials represents a nonpareil collection of sources and resources for Exchange 2000 Design and related topics. I anticipate that you'll find that this book belongs in this company

About this Book

Each topical *Exam Cram* chapter follows a regular structure, along with graphical cues about important or useful information. Here's the structure of a typical chapter:

➤ *Opening hotlists*—Each chapter begins with a list of the terms, tools, and techniques that you must learn and understand before you can be fully conversant with that chapter's subject matter. I follow the hotlists with one or two introductory paragraphs to set the stage for the rest of the chapter.

➤ *Topical coverage*—After the opening hotlists, each chapter covers a series of topics related to the chapter's subject title. Throughout this section, I highlight topics or concepts likely to appear on a test using a special Exam Alert layout, like this:

This is what an Exam Alert looks like. Normally, an Exam Alert stresses concepts, terms, software, or activities that are likely to relate to one or more certification test questions. For that reason, I think any information found offset in Exam Alert format is worthy of unusual attentiveness on your part. Indeed, most of the information that appears on The Cram Sheet appears as Exam Alerts within the text.

Pay close attention to material flagged as an Exam Alert; although all the information in this book pertains to what you need to know to pass the exam, I flag certain items that are really important. You'll find what appears in the meat of each chapter to be worth knowing, too, when preparing for the test. Because this book's material is very condensed, I recommend that you use this book along with other resources to achieve the maximum benefit.

In addition to the Exam Alerts, I have provided tips that will help you build a better foundation for Exchange 2000 Design knowledge. Although the information may not be on the exam, it is certainly related and will help you become a better test-taker.

This is how tips are formatted. Keep your eyes open for these, and you'll become an Exchange 2000 guru in no time!

➤ *Practice questions*—Although I talk about test questions and topics throughout the book, a section at the end of each chapter presents a series of mock test questions and explanations of both correct and incorrect answers.

➤ *Details and resources*—Every chapter ends with a section titled "Need to Know More?". This section provides direct pointers to Microsoft and third-party resources offering more details on the chapter's subject. In addition, this section tries to rank or at least rate the quality and thoroughness of the topic's coverage by each resource. If you find a resource you like in this collection, use it, but don't feel compelled to use all the resources. On the other hand, I recommend only resources I use on a regular basis, so none of my recommendations will be a waste of your time or money (but purchasing them all at once probably represents an expense that many network administrators and would-be MCPs and MCSEs might find hard to justify).

The bulk of the book follows this chapter structure slavishly, but there are a few other elements that I'd like to point out. Chapter 14 includes a sample test that provides a good review of the material presented throughout the book to ensure you're ready for the exam. Chapter 15 is an answer key to the sample test that appears in Chapter 14. In addition, you'll find a handy index.

Finally, the tear-out Cram Sheet attached next to the inside front cover of this *Exam Cram* book represents a condensed and compiled collection of facts and tips that I think you should memorize before taking the test. Because you can dump this information out of your head onto a piece of paper before taking the exam, you can master this information by brute force—you need to remember it only long enough to write it down when you walk into the test room. You might even want to look at it in the car or in the lobby of the testing center just before you walk in to take the test.

How to Use this Book

I've structured the topics in this book to build on one another. Therefore, some topics in later chapters make more sense after you've read earlier chapters. That's why I suggest you read this book from front to back for your initial test preparation. If you need to brush up on a topic or you have to bone up for a second try, use the index or table of contents to go straight to the topics and questions that you need to study. Beyond helping you prepare for the test, I think you'll find this book useful as a tightly focused reference to some of the most important aspects of Exchange 2000.

Given all the book's elements and its specialized focus, I've tried to create a tool that will help you prepare for—and pass—Microsoft Exam 70-225. Please share your feedback on the book with us, especially if you have ideas about how I can improve it for future test-takers. I'll consider everything you say carefully, and I'll respond to all suggestions.

Send your questions or comments to us at **learn@examcram.com**. Please remember to include the title of the book in your message; otherwise, I'll be forced to guess which book you're writing about. And I don't like to guess—I want to *know*! Also, be sure to check out the Web pages at **www.examcram.com**, where you'll find information updates, commentary, and certification information.

Thanks, and enjoy the book!

Self-Assessment

The reason I included a Self-Assessment in this *Exam Cram* book is to help you evaluate your readiness to tackle MCSE certification. It should also help you understand what you need to know to master the topic of this book—namely, Exam 70-225, "Designing and Deploying a Messaging Infrastructure with Microsoft Exchange 2000 Server." But before you tackle this Self-Assessment, let's talk about concerns you may face when pursuing an MCSE for Windows 2000, and what an ideal MCSE candidate might look like.

MCSEs in the Real World

In the next section, I describe an ideal MCSE candidate, knowing full well that only a few real candidates will meet this ideal. In fact, my description of that ideal candidate might seem downright scary, especially with the changes that have been made to the program to support Windows 2000. But take heart: Although the requirements to obtain an MCSE may seem formidable, they are by no means impossible to meet. However, be keenly aware that it does take time, involves some expense, and requires real effort to get through the process.

Increasing numbers of people are attaining Microsoft certifications, so the goal is within reach. You can get all the real-world motivation you need from knowing that many others have gone before, so you will be able to follow in their footsteps. If you're willing to tackle the process seriously and do what it takes to obtain the necessary experience and knowledge, you can take—and pass—all the certification tests involved in obtaining an MCSE. In fact, I've designed *Exam Preps*, the companion *Exam Crams*, *Exam Cram Personal Trainers*, and *Exam Cram Personal Test Centers* to make it as easy on you as possible to prepare for these exams. I've also greatly expanded our Web site, **www.examcram.com**, to provide a host of resources to help you prepare for the complexities of Windows 2000.

Besides MCSE, other Microsoft certifications include:

➤ MCSD, which is aimed at software developers and requires one specific exam, two more exams on client and distributed topics, plus a fourth elective exam drawn from a different, but limited, pool of options.

➤ Other Microsoft certifications, whose requirements range from one test (MCP) to several tests (MCP+SB, MCDBA).

The Ideal Windows 2000 MCSE Candidate

Just to give you some idea of what an ideal MCSE candidate is like, here are some relevant statistics about the background and experience such an individual might have. Don't worry if you don't meet these qualifications, or don't come that close—this is a far from ideal world, and where you fall short is simply where you'll have more work to do.

➤ Academic or professional training in network theory, concepts, and operations. This includes everything from networking media and transmission techniques through network operating systems, services, and applications.

➤ Three-plus years of professional networking experience, including experience with Ethernet, token ring, modems, and other networking media. This must include installation, configuration, upgrade, and troubleshooting experience.

Note: The Windows 2000 MCSE program is much more rigorous than the previous NT MCSE program; therefore, you'll really need some hands-on experience. Some of the exams require you to solve real-world case studies and network design issues, so the more hands-on experience you have, the better.

➤ Two-plus years in a networked environment that includes hands-on experience with Windows 2000 Server, Windows 2000 Professional, Windows NT Server, Windows NT Workstation, and Windows 95 or Windows 98. A solid understanding of each system's architecture, installation, configuration, maintenance, and troubleshooting is also essential.

➤ Knowledge of the various methods for installing Windows 2000, including manual and unattended installations.

➤ A thorough understanding of key networking protocols, addressing, and name resolution, including TCP/IP, IPX/SPX, and NetBEUI.

➤ A thorough understanding of NetBIOS naming, browsing, and file and print services.

➤ Familiarity with key Windows 2000-based TCP/IP-based services, including HTTP (Web servers), DHCP, WINS, DNS, plus familiarity with one or more of the following: Internet Information Server (IIS), Index Server, and Proxy Server.

➤ An understanding of how to implement security for key network data in a Windows 2000 environment.

➤ Working knowledge of NetWare 3.x and 4.x, including IPX/SPX frame formats, NetWare file, print, and directory services, and both Novell and Microsoft client software. Working knowledge of Microsoft's Client Service For NetWare (CSNW), Gateway Service For NetWare (GSNW), the NetWare Migration Tool (NWCONV), and the NetWare Client For Windows (NT, 95, and 98) is essential.

➤ A good working understanding of Active Directory. The more you work with Windows 2000, the more you'll realize that this new operating system is quite different than Windows NT. New technologies like Active Directory have really changed the way that Windows is configured and used. I recommend that you find out as much as you can about Active Directory and acquire as much experience using this technology as possible. The time you take learning about Active Directory will be time very well spent!

Fundamentally, this boils down to a bachelor's degree in computer science, plus three years' experience working in a position involving network design, installation, configuration, and maintenance. I believe that well under half of all certification candidates meet these requirements, and that, in fact, most meet less than half of these requirements—at least, when they begin the certification process. But because all the people who already have been certified have survived this ordeal, you can survive it too—especially if you heed what our Self-Assessment can tell you about what you already know and what you need to learn.

Put Yourself to the Test

The following series of questions and observations is designed to help you figure out how much work you must do to pursue Microsoft certification and what kinds of resources you may consult on your quest. Be absolutely honest in your answers, or you'll end up wasting money on exams you're not yet ready to take. There are no right or wrong answers, only steps along the path to certification. Only you can decide where you really belong in the broad spectrum of aspiring candidates.

Two things should be clear from the outset, however:

➤ Even a modest background in computer science will be helpful.

➤ Hands-on experience with Microsoft products and technologies is an essential ingredient to certification success.

Educational Background

1. Have you ever taken any computer-related classes? [Yes or No]

   If Yes, proceed to question 2; if No, proceed to question 4.

2. Have you taken any classes on computer operating systems? [Yes or No]

   If Yes, you will probably be able to handle Microsoft's architecture and system component discussions. If you're rusty, brush up on basic operating system concepts, especially virtual memory, multitasking regimes, user mode versus kernel mode operation, and general computer security topics.

   If No, consider some basic reading in this area. I strongly recommend a good general operating systems book, such as *Operating System Concepts, 5th Edition*, by Abraham Silberschatz and Peter Baer Galvin (John Wiley & Sons, 1998, ISBN 0-471-36414-2). If this title doesn't appeal to you, check out reviews for other, similar titles at your favorite online bookstore.

3. Have you taken any networking concepts or technologies classes? [Yes or No]

   If Yes, you will probably be able to handle Microsoft's networking terminology, concepts, and technologies (brace yourself for frequent departures from normal usage). If you're rusty, brush up on basic networking concepts and terminology, especially networking media, transmission types, the OSI Reference Model, and networking technologies such as Ethernet, token ring, FDDI, and WAN links.

   If No, you might want to read one or two books in this topic area. The two best books that I know of are *Computer Networks, 3rd Edition*, by Andrew S. Tanenbaum (Prentice-Hall, 1996, ISBN 0-13-349945-6) and *Computer Networks and Internets, 2nd Edition*, by Douglas E. Comer (Prentice-Hall, 1998, ISBN 0-130-83617-6).

   Skip to the next section, "Hands-on Experience."

4. Have you done any reading on operating systems or networks? [Yes or No]

   If Yes, review the requirements stated in the first paragraphs after questions 2 and 3. If you meet those requirements, move on to the next section. If No, consult the recommended reading for both topics. A strong background will help you prepare for the Microsoft exams better than just about anything else.

Hands-on Experience

The most important key to success on all of the Microsoft tests is hands-on experience, especially with Windows 2000 Server and Professional, plus the many add-on services and BackOffice components around which so many of the Microsoft certification exams revolve. If I leave you with only one realization after taking this Self-Assessment, it should be that there's no substitute for time spent installing, configuring, and using the various Microsoft products upon which you'll be tested repeatedly and in depth.

5. Have you installed, configured, and worked with:

➤ Windows 2000 Server? [Yes or No]

If Yes, make sure you understand basic concepts as covered in Exam 70-215. You should also study the TCP/IP interfaces, utilities, and services for Exam 70-216, plus implementing security features for Exam 70-220.

 You can download objectives, practice exams, and other data about Microsoft exams from the Training and Certification page at **www.microsoft.com/trainingandservices/default.asp?PageID= mcp/**. Use the "Exams" link to obtain specific exam information.

If you haven't worked with Windows 2000 Server, you must obtain one or two machines and a copy of Windows 2000 Server. Then, learn the operating system and whatever other software components on which you'll also be tested.

In fact, I recommend that you obtain two computers, each with a network interface, and set up a two-node network on which to practice. With decent Windows 2000-capable computers selling for about $500 to $600 apiece these days, this shouldn't be too much of a financial hardship. You may have to scrounge to come up with the necessary software, but if you scour the Microsoft Web site you can usually find low-cost options to obtain evaluation copies of most of the software that you'll need.

➤ Windows 2000 Professional? [Yes or No]

If Yes, make sure you understand the concepts covered in Exam 70-210.

If No, you will want to obtain a copy of Windows 2000 Professional and learn how to install, configure, and maintain it. You can use *MCSE Windows 2000 Professional Exam Cram* to guide your activities and studies, or work straight from Microsoft's test objectives if you prefer.

For any and all of these Microsoft exams, the Resource Kits for the topics involved are a good study resource. You can purchase softcover Resource Kits from Microsoft Press (search for them at **http://mspress.microsoft.com/**), but they also appear on the TechNet CDs (**www.microsoft.com/technet**). Along with *Exam Crams* and *Exam Preps*, I believe that Resource Kits are among the best tools you can use to prepare for Microsoft exams.

6. For any specific Microsoft product that is not itself an operating system (for example, SQL Server), have you installed, configured, used, and upgraded this software? [Yes or No]

If the answer is Yes, skip to the next section. If it's No, you must get some experience. Read on for suggestions on how to do this.

Experience is a must with any Microsoft product exam, be it something as simple as FrontPage 2000 or as challenging as SQL Server 7.0. For trial copies of other software, search Microsoft's Web site using the name of the product as your search term. Also, search for bundles like "BackOffice" or "Small Business Server."

 If you have the funds, or your employer will pay your way, consider taking a class at a Certified Training and Education Center (CTEC) or at an Authorized Academic Training Partner (AATP). In addition to classroom exposure to the topic of your choice, you get a copy of the software that is the focus of your course, along with a trial version of whatever operating system it needs, with the training materials for that class.

Before you even think about taking any Microsoft exam, make sure you've spent enough time with the related software to understand how it may be installed and configured, how to maintain such an installation, and how to troubleshoot that software when things go wrong. This will help you in the exam, and in real life!

Testing Your Exam-Readiness

Whether you attend a formal class on a specific topic to get ready for an exam or use written materials to study on your own, some preparation for the Microsoft certification exams is essential. At $100 a try, pass or fail, you want to do everything you can to pass on your first try. That's where studying comes in.

I have included a practice exam in this book, so if you don't score that well on the test, you can study more and then tackle the test again. I also have exams that you can take online through the **ExamCram.com** Web site at **www.examcram.com**. If you still don't hit a score of at least 70 percent after these tests, you'll want to investigate the other practice test resources I mention in this section.

For any given subject, consider taking a class if you've tackled self-study materials, taken the test, and failed anyway. The opportunity to interact with an instructor and fellow students can make all the difference in the world, if you can afford that privilege. For information about Microsoft classes, visit the Training and Certification page at **www.microsoft.com/education/partners/ctec.asp** for Microsoft Certified Education Centers or **www.microsoft.com/aatp/default.htm** for Microsoft Authorized Training Providers.

If you can't afford to take a class, visit the Training and Certification page anyway, because it also includes pointers to free practice exams and to Microsoft Certified Professional Approved Study Guides and other self-study tools. And even if you can't afford to spend much at all, you should still invest in some low-cost practice exams from commercial vendors.

7. Have you taken a practice exam on your chosen test subject? [Yes or No]

If Yes, and you scored 70 percent or better, you're probably ready to tackle the real thing. If your score isn't above that threshold, keep at it until you break that barrier.

If No, obtain all the free and low-budget practice tests you can find and get to work. Keep at it until you can break the passing threshold comfortably.

 When it comes to assessing your test readiness, there is no better way than to take a good-quality practice exam and pass with a score of 70 percent or better. When preparing myself, I shoot for 80-plus percent, just to leave room for the "weirdness factor" that sometimes shows up on Microsoft exams.

Assessing Readiness for Exam 70-225

In addition to the general exam-readiness information in the previous section, there are several things you can do to prepare for the Designing and Deploying a Messaging Infrastructure with Microsoft Exchange 2000 Server exam. As you're getting ready for Exam 70-225, visit the Exam Cram Windows 2000 Resource Center at **www.examcram.com/studyresource/w2kresource/**. Another valuable resource is the Exam Cram Insider newsletter. Sign up at **www.examcram.com** or send a blank email message to **subscribe-ec@mars.coriolis.com**. I also suggest that you join an active MCSE mailing list. One of the better ones is managed by Sunbelt Software. Sign up at **www.sunbelt-software.com** (look for the Subscribe button).

You can also cruise the Web looking for "braindumps" (recollections of test topics and experiences recorded by others) to help you anticipate topics you're likely to encounter on the test. The MCSE mailing list is a good place to ask where the useful braindumps are, or you can check Shawn Gamble's list at **www. commandcentral.com**.

 You can't be sure that a braindump's author can provide correct answers. Thus, use the questions to guide your studies, but don't rely on the answers in a braindump to lead you to the truth. Double-check everything you find in any braindump.

Microsoft exam mavens also recommend checking the Microsoft Knowledge Base (available on its own CD as part of the TechNet collection, or on the Microsoft Web site at **http://support.microsoft.com/support/**) for "meaningful technical support issues" that relate to your exam's topics. Although I've not sure exactly what the quoted phrase means, I have also noticed some overlap between technical support questions on particular products and troubleshooting questions on the exams for those products.

Onward, through the Fog!

Once you've assessed your readiness, undertaken the right background studies, obtained the hands-on experience that will help you understand the products and technologies at work, and reviewed the many sources of information to help you prepare for a test, you'll be ready to take a round of practice tests. When your scores come back positive enough to get you through the exam, you're ready to go after the real thing. If you follow my assessment regime, you'll not only know what you need to study, but when you're ready to make a test date at Prometric or VUE. Good luck!

Microsoft Certification Exams

Terms you'll need to understand:

✓ Case study

✓ Multiple-choice question format

✓ Build-list-and-reorder question format

✓ Create-a-tree question format

✓ Drag-and-connect question format

✓ Select-and-place question format

✓ Fixed-length tests

✓ Simulations

✓ Adaptive tests

✓ Short-form tests

Techniques you'll need to master:

✓ Assessing your exam-readiness

✓ Answering Microsoft's varying question types

✓ Altering your test strategy depending on the exam format

✓ Practicing (to make perfect)

✓ Making the best use of the testing software

✓ Budgeting your time

✓ Guessing (as a last resort)

Exam-taking is not something that most people anticipate eagerly, no matter how well prepared they may be. In most cases, familiarity helps offset test anxiety. In plain English, this means you probably won't be as nervous when you take your fourth or fifth Microsoft certification exam as you'll be when you take your first one.

Whether it's your first exam or your tenth, understanding the details of taking the new exams (how much time to spend on questions, the environment you'll be in, and so on) and the new exam software will help you concentrate on the material rather than on the setting. Likewise, mastering a few basic exam-taking skills should help you recognize—and perhaps even outfox—some of the tricks and snares you're bound to find in some exam questions.

This chapter, besides explaining the exam environment and software, describes some proven exam-taking strategies that you should be able to use to your advantage.

Assessing Exam-Readiness

I strongly recommend that you read through and take the Self-Assessment included with this book (it appears just before this chapter, in fact). This will help you compare your knowledge base to the requirements for obtaining an MCSE, and it will also help you identify parts of your background or experience that may be in need of improvement, enhancement, or further learning. If you get the right set of basics under your belt, obtaining Microsoft certification will be that much easier.

Once you've gone through the Self-Assessment, you can remedy those topical areas where your background or experience may not measure up to an ideal certification candidate. But you can also tackle subject matter for individual tests at the same time, so you can continue making progress while you're catching up in some areas.

Once you've worked through an *Exam Cram*, have read the supplementary materials, and have taken the practice test, you'll have a pretty clear idea of when you should be ready to take the real exam. Although I strongly recommend that you keep practicing until your scores top the 75 percent mark, 80 percent would be a good goal to give yourself some margin for error in a real exam situation (where stress will play more of a role than when you practice). Once you hit that point, you should be ready to go. But if you get through the practice exam in this book without attaining that score, you should keep taking practice tests and studying the materials until you get there. You'll find more pointers on how to study and prepare in the Self-Assessment. But now, on to the exam itself!

The Exam Situation

When you arrive at the testing center where you scheduled your exam, you'll need to sign in with an exam coordinator. He or she will ask you to show two forms of identification, one of which must be a photo ID. After you've signed in and your time slot arrives, you'll be asked to deposit any books, bags, or other items you brought with you. Then, you'll be escorted into a closed room.

All exams are completely closed book. In fact, you will not be permitted to take anything with you into the testing area, but you will be furnished with a blank sheet of paper and a pen or, in some cases, an erasable plastic sheet and an erasable pen. Before the exam, you should memorize as much of the important material as you can, so you can write that information on the blank sheet as soon as you are seated in front of the computer. You can refer to this piece of paper anytime you like during the test, but you'll have to surrender the sheet when you leave the room.

You will have some time to compose yourself, to record this information, and to take a sample orientation exam before you begin the real thing. I suggest you take the orientation test before taking your first exam, but because they're all more or less identical in layout, behavior, and controls, you probably won't need to do this more than once.

Typically, the room will be furnished with anywhere from one to half a dozen computers, and each workstation will be separated from the others by dividers designed to keep you from seeing what's happening on someone else's computer. Most test rooms feature a wall with a large picture window. This permits the exam coordinator to monitor the room, to prevent exam-takers from talking to one another, and to observe anything out of the ordinary that might go on. The exam coordinator will have preloaded the appropriate Microsoft certification exam—for this book, that's Exam 70-225—and you'll be permitted to start as soon as you're seated in front of the computer.

All Microsoft certification exams allow a certain maximum amount of time in which to complete your work (this time is indicated on the exam by an on-screen counter/clock, so you can check the time remaining whenever you like). All Microsoft certification exams are computer generated. In addition to multiple choice, you'll encounter select and place (drag and drop), create a tree (categorization and prioritization), drag and connect, and build list and reorder (list prioritization) on most exams. Although this may sound quite simple, the questions are constructed not only to check your mastery of basic facts and figures about Exchange 2000 Design, but they also require you to evaluate one or more sets of circumstances or requirements. Often, you'll be asked to give more than one answer to a question. Likewise, you might be asked to select the best or most effective solution to a problem from a range of choices, all of which technically are correct. Taking the exam is quite an adventure, and it involves real thinking. This book shows you what to expect and how to deal with the potential problems, puzzles, and predicaments.

In the next section, you'll learn more about how Microsoft test questions look and how they must be answered.

Exam Layout and Design: New Case Study Format

The format of Microsoft's Exchange 2000 exams is different from that of its previous exams. The Design exam (70-225) consists entirely of a series of case studies, and the questions can be of six types. In the Admin exam (70-224), the same six types of questions can appear, but you are not likely to encounter complex multiquestion case studies.

For the Design exam, each case study or "testlet" presents a detailed problem that you must read and analyze. Figure 1.1 shows an example of what a case study looks like. You must select the different tabs in the case study to view the entire case.

Following each case study is a set of questions related to the case study; these questions can be one of six types (which are discussed next). Careful attention to details provided in the case study is the key to success. Be prepared to toggle frequently between the case study and the questions as you work. Some of the case studies also include diagrams, which are called *exhibits*, that you'll need to examine closely to understand how to answer the questions.

Once you complete a case study, you can review all the questions and your answers. Also, once you move on to the next case study, you can return to the previous case study and make any changes.

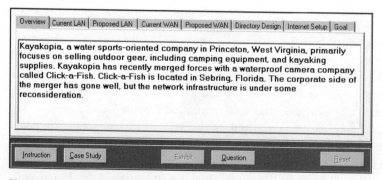

Figure 1.1   This is how case studies appear.

The six types of question formats are:

➤ Multiple choice, single answer

➤ Multiple choice, multiple answers

➤ Build list and reorder (list prioritization)

➤ Create a tree

➤ Drag and connect

➤ Select and place (drag and drop)

Note: Exam formats may vary by test center location. Although most design exams consist entirely of a series of case studies or testlets, a test-taker may occasionally encounter a strictly multiple-choice test. You may want to call the test center or visit ExamCram.com to see if you can find out which type of test you'll encounter.

Multiple-Choice Question Format

Some exam questions require you to select a single answer, whereas others ask you to select multiple correct answers. The following multiple-choice question requires you to select a single correct answer. Following the question is a brief summary of each potential answer and why it is either right or wrong.

Question 1

> You have two domains (**north** and **south**) connected to an empty root domain, **wrbaldwin.com**. This forest consists of a second tree **msbaldwin.com**. **msbaldwin.com** is the forest root. If you were to install the first installation of Exchange 2000 into the **north** domain, in which domain would you have to modify the schema?
>
> ○ a. **north.wrbaldwin.com**
>
> ○ b. **south.wrbaldwin.com**
>
> ○ c. **msbaldwin.com**
>
> ○ d. **wrbaldwin.com**

The correct answer is c because only one Schema Master is present in the forest, and it is in the forest root. Answers a and d are misleading because they try to make you believe that either each domain has its own schema or each tree does. Answer b is just for filler and could not possible be the answer.

This sample question format corresponds closely to the Microsoft certification exam format—the only difference on the exam is that questions are not followed by answer keys. To select an answer, you would position the cursor over the radio button next to the answer. Then, click the mouse button to select the answer.

Let's examine a question where one or more answers are possible. This type of question provides checkboxes rather than radio buttons for marking all appropriate selections.

Question 2

> You have two domains (**north** and **south**) connected to an empty root domain, **wrbaldwin.com**. This forest consists of a second tree, **msbaldwin.com**. **msbaldwin.com** is the forest root. If you were to install the first installation of Exchange 2000 into the **north** domain, which of the following groups would you have to be a member of? [Check all correct answers]
>
> ❏ a. MSBALDWIN\Enterprise Admins
>
> ❏ b. MSBALDWIN\Domain Admins
>
> ❏ c. MSBALDWIN\Schema Admins
>
> ❏ d. WRBALDWIN\Enterprise Admins
>
> ❏ e. WRBALDWIN\Schema Admins
>
> ❏ f. NORTH\Domain Admins

Answers a, c, and f are correct. The first time Exchange 2000 is installed in a forest, the schema is modified; only members of Schema Admins can modify the schema. Also, you must be an administrator in the domain where Exchange is going to be installed and a member of Enterprise in the forest root domain, MSBALDWIN. Domain Admins in MSBALDWIN are not administrators in NORTH, and this is why answer b is wrong. Answers d and e are wrong, because those are not valid groups outside the forest root domain, MSBALDWIN.

For this particular question, three answers are required. Microsoft sometimes gives partial credit for partially correct answers. For Question 2, you have to check the boxes next to items a, c, and f to obtain credit for a correct answer. Notice that picking the right answers also means knowing why the other answers are wrong!

Build-List-and-Reorder Question Format

Questions in the build-list-and-reorder format present two lists of items—one on the left and one on the right. To answer the question, you must move items from the list on the right to the list on the left. The final list must then be reordered into a specific order.

These questions can best be characterized as "From the following list of choices, pick the choices that answer the question. Arrange the list in a certain order." To give you practice with this type of question, some questions of this type are included in this study guide. Here's an example of how they appear in this book; for a sample of how they appear on the test, see Figure 1.2.

Question 3

From the following list of famous people, pick those that have been elected president of the United States. Arrange the list in the order that they served.

Thomas Jefferson

Ben Franklin

Abe Lincoln

George Washington

Andrew Jackson

Paul Revere

The correct answer is:

George Washington

Thomas Jefferson

Andrew Jackson

Abe Lincoln

On an actual exam, the entire list of famous people would initially appear in the list on the right. You would move the four correct answers to the list on the left, and then reorder the list on the left. Notice that the answer to the question did not include all items from the initial list. However, this may not always be the case.

To move an item from the right list to the left list, first select the item by clicking on it, and then click on the Add button (left arrow). Once you move an item from one list to the other, you can move the item back by first selecting the item and then clicking on the appropriate button (either the Add button or the Remove button). Once items have been moved to the left list, you can reorder an item by selecting the item and clicking on the up or down button.

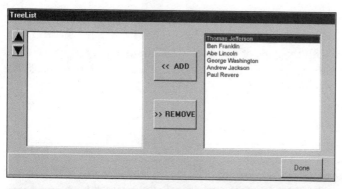

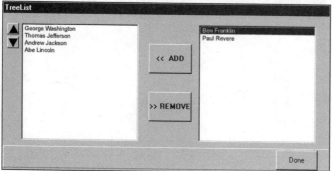

Figure 1.2 This is how build-list-and-reorder questions appear.

Create-a-Tree Question Format

Questions in the create-a-tree format also present two lists—one on the left side of the screen and one on the right side of the screen. The list on the right consists of individual items, and the list on the left consists of nodes in a tree. To answer the question, you must move items from the list on the right to the appropriate node in the tree.

These questions can best be characterized as simply a matching exercise. Items from the list on the right are placed under the appropriate category in the list on the left. Here's an example of how they appear in this book; for a sample of how they appear on the test, see Figure 1.3.

Question 4

> The calendar year is divided into four seasons:
>
> > Winter
> >
> > Spring
> >
> > Summer
> >
> > Fall
>
> Identify the season when each of the following holidays occurs:
>
> > Christmas
> >
> > Fourth of July
> >
> > Labor Day
> >
> > Flag Day
> >
> > Memorial Day
> >
> > Washington's Birthday
> >
> > Thanksgiving
> >
> > Easter

The correct answer is:

> Winter
> > Christmas
> > Washington's Birthday
>
> Spring
> > Flag Day
> > Memorial Day
> > Easter
>
> Summer
> > Fourth of July
> > Labor Day
>
> Fall
> > Thanksgiving

In this case, all the items in the list were used. However, this may not always be the case.

To move an item from the right list to its appropriate location in the tree, you must first select the appropriate tree node by clicking on it. Then, you select the item to be moved and click on the Add button. If one or more items have been added to a tree node, the node will be displayed with a "+" icon to the left of the node name. You can click on this icon to expand the node and view the item(s) that have been added. If any item has been added to the wrong tree node, you can remove it by selecting it and clicking on the Remove button.

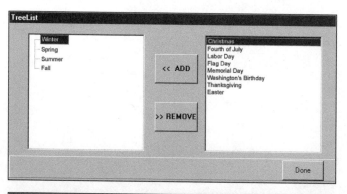

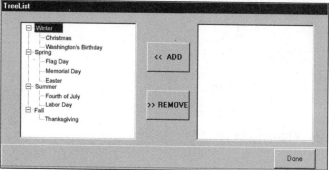

Figure 1.3   This is how create-a-tree questions appear.

Drag-and-Connect Question Format

Questions in the drag-and-connect format present a group of objects and a list of "connections." To answer the question, you must move the appropriate connections between the objects.

This type of question is best described using graphics. Here's an example.

Question 5

The following objects represent the different states of water:

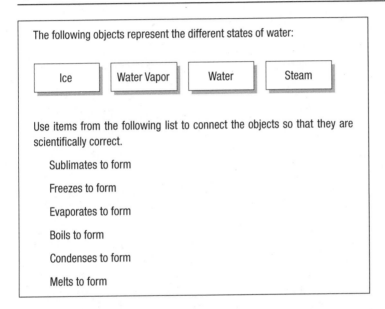

Ice   Water Vapor   Water   Steam

Use items from the following list to connect the objects so that they are scientifically correct.

Sublimates to form

Freezes to form

Evaporates to form

Boils to form

Condenses to form

Melts to form

The correct answer is:

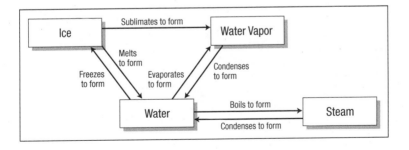

For this type of question, it's not necessary to use every object, and each connection can be used multiple times.

Select-and-Place Question Format

Questions in the select-and-place (drag-and-drop) format present a diagram with blank boxes, and a list of labels that need to be dragged to correctly fill in the blank boxes. To answer the question, you must move the labels to their appropriate positions on the diagram.

This type of question is best described using graphics. Here's an example.

Question 6

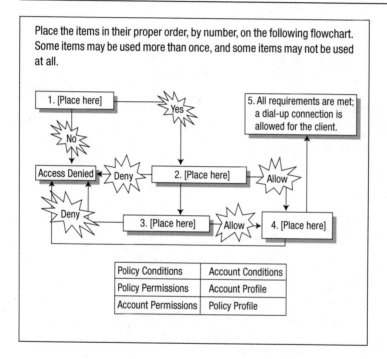

The correct answer is:

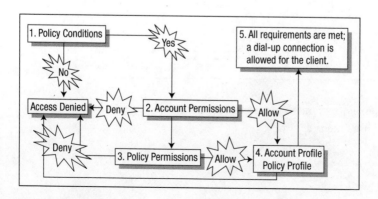

Microsoft's Testing Formats

Currently, Microsoft uses four different testing formats:

➤ Case study

➤ Fixed length

➤ Adaptive

➤ Short form

As I mentioned earlier, the case study approach is used with Microsoft's Design exams, such as the one covered by this book. These exams consist of a set of case studies that you must analyze to enable you to answer questions related to the case studies. Such exams include one or more case studies (tabbed topic areas), each of which is followed by 5 to 20 questions. The question types for Design exams and for the Exchange 2000 Admin exam are multiple choice, build list and reorder, create a tree, drag and connect, and select and place. Depending on the test topic, some exams are totally case-based, whereas others are not.

Other Microsoft exams employ advanced testing capabilities that might not be immediately apparent. Although the questions that appear are primarily multiple choice, the logic that drives them is more complex than older Microsoft tests, which use a fixed sequence of questions, called a *fixed-length test*. Some questions employ a sophisticated user interface, which Microsoft calls a *simulation*, to test your knowledge of the software and systems under consideration in a more or less "live" environment that behaves just like the original. The Testing Innovations link at **www.microsoft.com/trainingandservices/default.asp?PageID=mcp** includes a downloadable practice simulation.

For some exams, Microsoft has turned to a well-known technique, called *adaptive testing*, to establish a test-taker's level of knowledge and product competence. Adaptive exams look the same as fixed-length exams, but they discover the level of difficulty at which an individual test-taker can correctly answer questions. Test-takers with differing levels of knowledge or ability therefore see different sets of questions; individuals with high levels of knowledge or ability are presented with a smaller set of more difficult questions, whereas individuals with lower levels of knowledge are presented with a larger set of easier questions. Two individuals may answer the same percentage of questions correctly, but the test-taker with a higher knowledge or ability level will score higher because his or her questions are worth more.

Also, the lower-level test-taker will probably answer more questions than his or her more-knowledgeable colleague. This explains why adaptive tests use ranges of values to define the number of questions and the amount of time it takes to complete the test.

Adaptive tests work by evaluating the test-taker's most recent answer. A correct answer leads to a more difficult question (and the test software's estimate of the test-taker's knowledge and ability level is raised). An incorrect answer leads to a less difficult question (and the test software's estimate of the test-taker's knowledge and ability level is lowered). This process continues until the test targets the test-taker's true ability level. The exam ends when the test-taker's level of accuracy meets a statistically acceptable value (in other words, when his or her performance demonstrates an acceptable level of knowledge and ability), or when the maximum number of items has been presented (in which case, the test-taker is almost certain to fail).

Microsoft also introduced a short-form test for its most popular tests. This test delivers 25 to 30 questions to its takers, giving them exactly 60 minutes to complete the exam. This type of exam is similar to a fixed-length test, in that it allows readers to jump ahead or return to earlier questions, and to cycle through the questions until the test is done. Microsoft does not use adaptive logic in this test, but claims that statistical analysis of the question pool is such that the 25 to 30 questions delivered during a short-form exam conclusively measure a test-taker's knowledge of the subject matter in much the same way as an adaptive test. You can think of the short-form test as a kind of "greatest hits exam" (that is, the most important questions are covered) version of an adaptive exam on the same topic.

Note: Some of the Microsoft exams can contain a combination of adaptive and fixed-length questions.

Microsoft tests can come in any one of these forms. Whatever you encounter, you must take the test in whichever form it appears; you can't choose one form over another. If anything, it pays more to prepare thoroughly for an adaptive exam than for a fixed-length or a short-form exam: The penalties for answering incorrectly are built into the test itself on an adaptive exam, whereas the layout remains the same for a fixed-length or short-form test, no matter how many questions you answer incorrectly.

The biggest difference between an adaptive test and a fixed-length or short-form test is that on a fixed-length or short-form test, you can revisit questions after you've read them over one or more times. On an adaptive test, you must answer the question when it's presented and will have no opportunities to revisit that question thereafter.

Strategies for Different Testing Formats

Before you choose a test-taking strategy, you must know if your test is case study-based, fixed length, short form, or adaptive. When you begin your exam, you'll know right away if the test is based on case studies. The interface will consist of a tabbed window that allows you to easily navigate through the sections of the case.

If you are taking a test that is not based on case studies, the software will tell you that the test is adaptive, if in fact the version you're taking is an adaptive test. If your introductory materials fail to mention this, you're probably taking a fixed-length test (50 to 70 questions). If the total number of questions involved is 25 to 30, you're taking a short-form test. Some tests announce themselves by indicating that they will start with a set of adaptive questions, followed by fixed-length questions.

You'll be able to tell for sure if you are taking an adaptive, fixed-length, or short-form test by the first question. If it includes a checkbox that lets you mark the question for later review, you're taking a fixed-length or short-form test. If the total number of questions is 25 to 30, it's a short-form test; if more than 30, it's a fixed-length test. Adaptive test questions can be visited (and answered) only once, and they include no such checkbox.

The Case Study Exam Strategy

Most test-takers find that the case study type of test used for the Design exam is the most difficult to master. When it comes to studying for a case study test, your best bet is to approach each case study as a standalone test. The biggest challenge you'll encounter is that you'll feel that you won't have enough time to get through all of the cases that are presented.

Each case provides a lot of material that you'll need to read and study before you can effectively answer the questions that follow. The trick to taking a case study exam is to first scan the case study to get the highlights. Make sure you read the overview section of the case so that you understand the context of the problem at hand. Then, quickly move on and scan the questions.

As you are scanning the questions, make mental notes to yourself so that you'll remember which sections of the case study you should focus on. Some case studies may provide a fair amount of extra information that you don't really need to answer the questions. The goal with this scanning approach is to avoid having to study and analyze material that is not completely relevant.

When studying a case, carefully read the tabbed information. It is important to answer each and every question. You will be able to toggle back and forth from case to questions, and from question to question within a case testlet. However, once you leave the case and move on, you may not be able to return to it. You may want to take notes while reading useful information so you can refer to them when you tackle the test questions. It's hard to go wrong with this strategy when taking any kind of Microsoft certification test.

The Fixed-Length and Short-Form Exam Strategy

A well-known principle when taking fixed-length or short-form exams is to first read over the entire exam from start to finish while answering only those questions you feel absolutely sure of. On subsequent passes, you can dive into more complex questions more deeply, knowing how many such questions you have left.

Fortunately, the Microsoft exam software for fixed-length and short-form tests makes the multiple-visit approach easy to implement. At the top-left corner of each question is a checkbox that permits you to mark that question for a later visit.

Note: Marking questions makes review easier, but you can return to any question by clicking the Forward or Back button repeatedly.

As you read each question, if you answer only those you're sure of and mark for review those that you're not sure of, you can keep working through a decreasing list of questions as you answer the trickier ones in order.

 There's at least one potential benefit to reading the exam over completely before answering the trickier questions: Sometimes, information supplied in later questions sheds more light on earlier questions. At other times, information you read in later questions might jog your memory about Exchange 2000 Design facts, figures, or behavior that helps you answer earlier questions. Either way, you'll come out ahead if you defer those questions about which you're not absolutely sure.

Here are some question-handling strategies that apply to fixed-length and short-form tests. Use them if you have the chance:

➤ When returning to a question after your initial read-through, read every word again—otherwise, your mind can fall quickly into a rut. Sometimes, revisiting a question after turning your attention elsewhere lets you see something you missed, but the strong tendency is to see what you've seen before. Try to avoid that tendency at all costs.

➤ If you return to a question more than twice, try to articulate to yourself what you don't understand about the question, why answers don't appear to make sense, or what appears to be missing. If you chew on the subject awhile, your subconscious might provide the details you lack, or you might notice a "trick" that points to the right answer.

As you work your way through the exam, another counter that Microsoft provides will come in handy—the number of questions completed and questions outstanding. For fixed-length and short-form tests, it's wise to budget your time by making sure that you've completed one-quarter of the questions one-quarter of the way through the exam period, and three-quarters of the questions three-quarters of the way through.

If you're not finished when only five minutes remain, use that time to guess your way through any remaining questions. Remember, guessing is potentially more valuable than not answering, because blank answers are always wrong, but a guess may turn out to be right. If you don't have a clue about any of the remaining questions, pick answers at random, or choose all a's, b's, and so on. The important thing is to submit an exam for scoring that has an answer for every question.

 At the very end of your exam period, you're better off guessing than leaving questions unanswered.

The Adaptive Exam Strategy

If there's one principle that applies to taking an adaptive test, it could be summed up as "Get it right the first time." You cannot elect to skip a question and move on to the next one when taking an adaptive test, because the testing software uses your answer to the current question to select whatever question it plans to present next. Nor can you return to a question once you've moved on, because the software gives you only one chance to answer the question. You can, however, take notes, because sometimes information supplied in earlier questions will shed more light on later questions.

Also, when you answer a question correctly, you are presented with a more difficult question next, to help the software gauge your level of skill and ability. When you answer a question incorrectly, you are presented with a less difficult question, and the software lowers its current estimate of your skill and ability. This continues until the program settles into a reasonably accurate estimate of what you know and can do, and takes you on average through somewhere between 15 and 30 questions as you complete the test.

The good news is that if you know your stuff, you'll probably finish most adaptive tests in 30 minutes or so. The bad news is that you must really, really know your stuff to do your best on an adaptive test. That's because some questions are so convoluted, complex, or hard to follow that you're bound to miss one or two, at a minimum, even if you do know your stuff. So the more you know, the better you'll do on an adaptive test, even accounting for the occasionally weird or unfathomable questions that appear on these exams.

 Because you can't always tell in advance if a test is fixed length, short form, or adaptive, you will be best served by preparing for the exam as if it were adaptive. That way, you should be prepared to pass no matter what kind of test you take. But if you do take a fixed-length or short-form test, remember the tips from the preceding section. They should help you improve on what you could do on an adaptive test.

If you encounter a question on an adaptive test that you can't answer, you must guess an answer immediately. Because of how the software works, you may suffer for your guess on the next question if you guess right, because you'll get a more difficult question next!

Question-Handling Strategies

For those questions that take only a single answer, usually two or three of the answers will be obviously incorrect, and two of the answers will be plausible—of course, only one can be correct. Unless the answer leaps out at you (if it does, reread the question to look for a trick; sometimes those are the ones you're most likely to get wrong), begin the process of answering by eliminating those answers that are most obviously wrong.

Almost always, at least one answer out of the possible choices for a question can be eliminated immediately because it matches one of these conditions:

➤ The answer does not apply to the situation.

➤ The answer describes a nonexistent issue, an invalid option, or an imaginary state.

After you eliminate all answers that are obviously wrong, you can apply your retained knowledge to eliminate further answers. Look for items that sound correct but refer to actions, commands, or features that are not present or not available in the situation that the question describes.

If you're still faced with a blind guess among two or more potentially correct answers, reread the question. Try to picture how each of the possible remaining answers would alter the situation. Be especially sensitive to terminology; sometimes the choice of words ("remove" instead of "disable") can make the difference between a right answer and a wrong one.

Only when you've exhausted your ability to eliminate answers, but remain unclear about which of the remaining possibilities is correct, should you guess at an answer. An unanswered question offers you no points, but guessing gives you at least some chance of getting a question right; just don't be too hasty when making a blind guess.

Note: If you're taking a fixed-length or a short-form test, you can wait until the last round of reviewing marked questions (just as you're about to run out of time, or out of unanswered questions) before you start making guesses. You will have the same option within each case study testlet (but once you leave a testlet, you may not be allowed to return to it). If you're taking an adaptive test, you'll have to guess to move on to the next question if you can't figure out an answer some other way. Either way, guessing should be your technique of last resort!

Numerous questions assume that the default behavior of a particular utility is in effect. If you know the defaults and understand what they mean, this knowledge will help you cut through many Gordian knots.

Mastering the Inner Game

In the final analysis, knowledge breeds confidence, and confidence breeds success. If you study the materials in this book carefully and review all the practice questions at the end of each chapter, you should become aware of those areas where additional learning and study are required.

After you've worked your way through the book, take the practice exam in the back of the book. Taking this test will provide a reality check and help you identify areas to study further. Make sure you follow up and review materials related to the questions you miss on the practice exam before scheduling a real exam. Only when you've covered that ground and feel comfortable with the whole scope of the practice exam should you set an exam appointment. Only if you score 80 percent or better should you proceed to the real thing (otherwise, obtain some additional practice tests so you can keep trying until you hit this magic number).

If you take a practice exam and don't score at least 80 to 85 percent correct, you'll want to practice further. Microsoft provides links to practice exam providers and also offers self-assessment exams at **www.microsoft.com/trainingandservices/**. You should also check out **ExamCram.com** for downloadable practice questions.

Armed with the information in this book and with the determination to augment your knowledge, you should be able to pass the certification exam. However, you need to work at it, or you'll spend the exam fee more than once before you finally pass. If you prepare seriously, you should do well. I am confident that you can do it!

The next section covers other sources you can use to prepare for the Microsoft certification exams.

Additional Resources

A good source of information about Microsoft certification exams comes from Microsoft itself. Because its products and technologies—and the exams that go with them—change frequently, the best place to go for exam-related information is online.

If you haven't already visited the Microsoft Certified Professional site, do so right now. The MCP home page resides at **www.microsoft.com/trainingandservices** (see Figure 1.4).

Note: This page might not be there by the time you read this, or may be replaced by something new and different, because things change regularly on the Microsoft site. Should this happen, please read the sidebar titled "Coping with Change on the Web."

Coping with Change on the Web

Sooner or later, all the information we've shared with you about the Microsoft Certified Professional pages and the other Web-based resources mentioned throughout the rest of this book will go stale or be replaced by newer information. In some cases, the URLs you find here might lead you to their replacements; in other cases, the URLs will go nowhere, leaving you with the dreaded "404 File not found" error message. When that happens, don't give up.

There's always a way to find what you want on the Web if you're willing to invest some time and energy. Most large or complex Web sites—and Microsoft's qualifies on both counts—offer a search engine. On all of Microsoft's Web pages, a Search button appears along the top edge of the page. As long as you can get to Microsoft's site (it should stay at **www.microsoft.com** for a long time), use this tool to help you find what you need.

The more focused you can make a search request, the more likely the results will include information you can use. For example, you can search for the string

```
"training and certification"
```

to produce a lot of data about the subject in general, but if you're looking for the preparation guide for Exam 70-225, "Designing and Deploying a Messaging Infrastructure with Microsoft Exchange 2000 Server," you'll be more likely to get there quickly if you use a search string similar to the following:

```
"Exam 70-225" AND "preparation guide"
```

Likewise, if you want to find the Training and Certification downloads, try a search string such as this:

```
"training and certification" AND "download page"
```

Finally, feel free to use general search tools—such as **www.search.com**, **www.altavista.com**, and **www.excite.com**—to look for related information. Although Microsoft offers great information about its certification exams online, there are plenty of third-party sources of information and assistance that need not follow Microsoft's party line. Therefore, if you can't find something where the book says it lives, intensify your search.

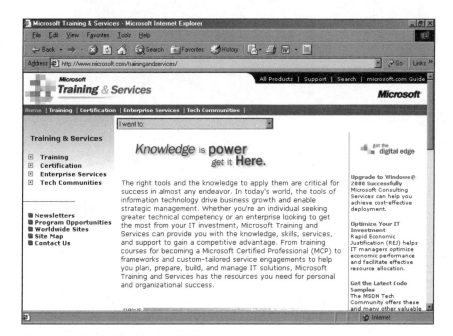

Figure 1.4   The Microsoft Certified Professional home page.

Integration with Windows 2000 Active Directory

Terms you'll need to understand:

- ✓ Security principal
- ✓ Contact
- ✓ User account
- ✓ Computer account
- ✓ Security group
- ✓ Distribution group
- ✓ Global group
- ✓ Domain local group
- ✓ Universal group
- ✓ Schema
- ✓ Domain
- ✓ Domain controller
- ✓ Mixed mode
- ✓ Native mode

- ✓ Organizational Unit (OU)
- ✓ Tree
- ✓ Forest
- ✓ Light Directory Access Protocol (LDAP)
- ✓ User Principal Name (UPN)
- ✓ Global Catalog server
- ✓ Flexible Single Master Operation (FSMO)
- ✓ Site
- ✓ Site link
- ✓ Subnet
- ✓ Mailbox-enabled

Techniques you'll need to master:

- ✓ Planning groups for use with Exchange 2000 and Active Directory
- ✓ Creating objects in Active Directory

- ✓ Delegating control in Active Directory

Before diving into the wonderful world of Exchange 2000 design, it's important to understand Windows 2000 Active Directory. You will then learn how Active Directory and Exchange 2000 work together and, in some cases, as one. First, a bit of Exchange history.

In previous versions of Exchange (4.0, 5.0, and 5.5), Exchange maintained a separate directory from the operating system. Exchange mailboxes could be linked to a domain user, but the two were separate objects in different databases. Exchange 4.0/5.x maintained up to three databases per server. The public information store (pub.edb) held public folders. The private information store (priv.edb) held mailboxes. The directory (dir.edb) held the names and attributes associated with the folders and mailboxes in the public and private information stores.

If you are familiar with Exchange 4.0/5.x, one fundamental difference you will notice with Exchange 2000 is that Exchange 2000 no longer maintains a directory of its own. Exchange 2000 now shares a directory with Windows 2000. For example, in Exchange 4.0/5.x, you may have a mailbox called Zachary Baldwin that is linked to a domain user called zbaldwin. In Exchange 2000, you would simply have a single object in Active Directory, Zachary Baldwin. Zachary Baldwin would be a mailbox-enabled user object with a logon name of zbaldwin. You will learn more about this integration later in the "Exchange 2000 in AD" section of this chapter. First, we review some Active Directory basics.

Active Directory Basics

Active Directory is the Windows 2000 Directory Service. Think of a directory as a very detailed phonebook. The directory contains objects (users, groups, computers, and so on) and their corresponding attributes (user name, password, phone number, and so on). The directory is used to organize and manage resources. Windows 2000 Active Directory is a replacement for Windows NT 4 Directory Service (NTDS).

If you are familiar with Windows NT 4, realize that Windows 2000 Active Directory is an upgrade of Windows NT 4 NTDS. Windows 2000 Active Directory is not a fresh rewrite; it is an extension of NTDS and therefore can coexist with NTDS. For example, NTDS servers (known as *domain controllers*) can exist in a Windows 2000 Active Directory domain. Also, Active Directory domains can interact with NTDS domains.

Active Directory Objects

Windows 2000 Active Directory is a collection of objects. Each object is defined by a collection of attributes. There are too many types of objects and attributes to list, and many are not relevant.

You should know the four basic types of objects: users, contacts, computers, and groups. You should also know there are many objects that are never seen. Most of these objects define settings for programs like Exchange 2000.

Before discussing the details of some of the Active Directory objects, you will need to understand the concept of *security principals*. In Windows NT 4 NTDS Directory, all objects were security principals; however, in Windows 2000 Active Directory, many objects are not. A security principal is defined as an object that has a security ID (SID) attribute. This SID is unique and is used for granting and restricting access to resources. For example, if you were to give Zachary Baldwin permission to read the file readme.txt on a Windows 2000 computer, the access control list (ACL) for readme.txt would contain Zachary's SID. When Zachary tries to access readme.txt, this SID is used to grant Zachary permission.

In the previous example, if you were to rename the Zachary Baldwin account, it would still have access to readme.txt. A security principal's SID does not change under normal circumstances. However, if you were to delete the Zachary Baldwin account and create a new account with the same name, it would not have access to readme.txt. The new account would have a different SID.

User objects are security principals. User objects define Active Directory users. Each user on the network will typically have a single user object (also known as a *user account*) defined for them. Each user account will contain attributes that define that account's identity, as well as information about the user. For backward compatibility with previous versions of NT and Exchange, user accounts are defined by many names. These names are described in detail later in the chapter (see the section titled "What's in a Name?").

Contacts are not security principals. Contacts contain similar attributes as user accounts (name, address, phone number). Contacts, however, do not have a SID and cannot be used to log on to a computer. Contacts are primarily used to define users who do not log on to the Active Directory. Contacts replace Exchange 4.0/5.x custom recipients.

Computer objects (also known as *computer accounts*) are security principals and represent computers on the network. Typically, every computer will have a single computer account associated with it. Exceptions to this include Windows 95, 98, and ME, which do not require a computer account. All Windows NT and Windows 2000 computers require computer accounts in Active Directory so that the computer can be authenticated. After the computer account is authenticated, a user must then log on and access Active Directory and the resources it protects with a valid Active Directory user account.

Group objects (also known as *groups*) are used for many purposes. First, there are two types of groups and three group scopes, meaning that there are six distinct kinds of groups. The group type dictates whether or not the object is a security principal. *Security groups* have SIDs and therefore are security principals. *Distribution groups* are similar to contacts in that they do not have SIDs and are therefore not security principals. Distribution groups replace Exchange 4.0/5.x distribution lists. The group scope is a bit more complicated, dictating both group membership (what types of objects the group can have as members) and group assignment. Group assignment, an often overlooked function of group scope, means that a group of a certain scope can be assigned permissions to resources either in the domain in which the group is defined or in any trusted domain. The valid scopes are global, domain local, and universal. Table 2.1 shows the restrictions on group scope.

The Schema

The Active Directory *schema* is a collection of object and attribute definitions. An object definition is called an *object class,* and an attribute definition is called an *attribute.* An object class is defined either by attributes that it *must* contain, or by attributes that it *may* contain. Object classes can also have a *parent* object class, and the *child* object class inherits the attributes from the parent. An attribute defines the type of data stored in Active Directory. Attributes must be defined before object classes and can be used in multiple object classes. Manipulating the schema is discouraged and therefore difficult. Fortunately, you should not need to know how to do this. Although object classes and attributes can be added to the schema, they can never be removed. The schema itself is an object in the Active Directory defined by an object class.

Table 2.1 Group scopes.		
Group Scope	**Membership**	**Assigned Permissions For**
Global	Users (own domain only)	Any trusted domain
	Global groups (own domain only)*	
Domain Local	Users (any trusted domain)	Own domain only
	Domain local groups (own domain only)*	
	Global groups (any trusted domain)	
	Universal groups (any trusted domain)*	
Universal*	Users (any trusted domain)	Any trusted domain
	Global groups (any trusted domain)	
	Universal groups (any trusted domain)	

Only available when Active Directory is in native mode. Native mode is described in "The Logical Structure of Active Directory" section, later in this chapter.

You should remember what object classes and attributes are and what functions they perform.

The Logical Structure of Active Directory

Active Directory is defined by both a physical and logical structure. The logical structure is the one that most relates to Exchange 2000.

Domains

A *domain* is defined as both a replication and security boundary. Active Directory data is stored in a database on computers designated as domain controllers. A domain controller for the WRBALDWIN domain would contain all objects in that domain. Additional domain controllers can be created for many reasons including fault tolerance and performance. All domain controllers in the WRBALDWIN domain would contain a full read/write copy of all objects in the WRBALDWIN domain. This set of objects is often called a *partition* in the database because the database will contain other information too. This partition should be loosely consistent on all domain controllers. If you stop making changes to all domain controllers, that partition will eventually replicate to all domain controllers in the domain. While the relationship between domains in Active Directory has been simplified, the basic concept of a domain has not changed much from Windows NT 4 to Windows 2000.

By default, Windows 2000 domains are initially in mixed mode. A Windows 2000 mixed-mode domain may contain Windows NT domain controllers and Windows 2000 domain controllers. Once a domain is switched to native mode, it should no longer contain Windows NT domain controllers. Switching to native mode is a one-way process; a domain cannot be switched back (see Figure 2.1).

 Microsoft will typically refer to Windows NT as "pre-Windows 2000" in the user interface. On the test and in most documentation, both terms may be used. Remember that "pre-Windows 2000" usually means Windows NT, but can also refer to Windows 95, 98, and ME, depending on the context.

Organizational Units and Containers

Organizational Units (OUs) and containers are new to Windows 2000. OUs and containers help organize objects in Active Directory. Each object in Active Directory exists in the root of Active Directory (not advisable), in an OU, or in a

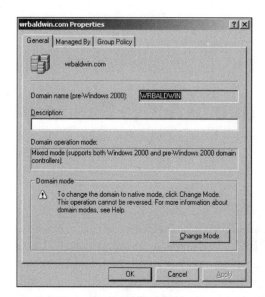

Figure 2.1   Switching to native mode.

container. Containers are in Active Directory by default and cannot be deleted or created. Administrators, however, typically create OUs. OUs can be nested, but a container cannot contain an OU. OUs can be used to, among other things, organize, delegate control, and deploy group policies. OUs cannot be used to restrict access to resources. Containers and OUs can be distinguished in Active Directory Users and Computers by their folder icon (see Figure 2.2).

Trees and Forests

A *tree* is one or more domains with contiguous DNS name space. A *forest* is one or more trees with non-contiguous DNS name space. For example, **wrbaldwin.com** and **support.wrbaldwin.com** could be two domains within the same tree, but

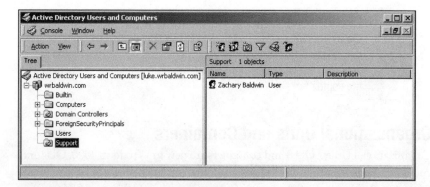

Figure 2.2   Active Directory Users and Computers.

examcram.com would have to be a separate tree because its name space is not contiguous with **wrbaldwin.com**. When Active Directory is installed, you must either join a forest or create a new one. When you join a forest, you must either join a tree or create a new one. When you join a tree, you must either join a domain or create a new one.

Care must be taken when creating a new forest. The first domain in the forest (the forest root) will be the keystone for all other domains. The forest root domain can never be uninstalled without reinstalling the entire forest. After the forest root has been created, additional domains can be added as either child domains or as new trees. Each new domain can also contain child domains. When diagramming domains, trees, and forests, triangles are used to represent domains. The forest root is typically drawn higher than the roots of other trees (see Figure 2.3).

Finally, there are several design issues to take into consideration when dealing with forests. One of the primary issues is administration. All Windows 2000/NT computers contain a local group that is also called Administrators (see Figure 2.4). Administrators have control over the local computer.

All domains contain a domain local group called Administrators (see Figure 2.5). Administrators have control over the domain. All domains have a global group called Domain Admins.

The Domain Admins group is a member of both Administrators groups. This means Domain Admins have control over both the domain and the local computers. The forest root (and only the forest root) has a group called Enterprise Admins. The Enterprise Admins group is a member of each Administrators group in each domain in the forest. However, Enterprise Admins is not a member of the Administrators groups on the local computers in the forest. Therefore, Enterprise Admins have control over all domains in the forest, but not necessarily the local computers. Table 2.2 summarizes administrative groups.

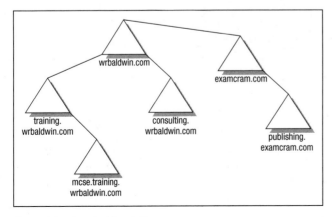

Figure 2.3 A typical forest diagram.

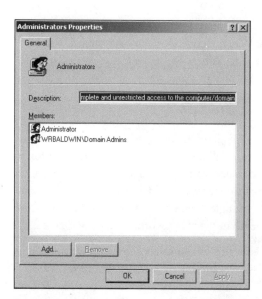

Figure 2.4 Members of an Administrators group on a local computer.

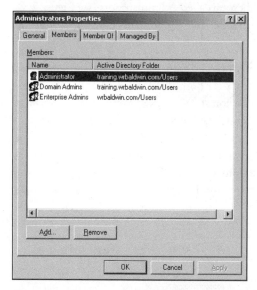

Figure 2.5 Members of an Administrators group in a child domain.

Lightweight Directory Access Protocol (LDAP)

Lightweight Directory Access Protocol (LDAP) is a standard protocol used to access the contents of the Active Directory. LDAP clients with the appropriate permissions can use LDAP to search, add to, and modify the Active Directory. An LDAP distinguished name will uniquely identify an object in the Active Directory.

Table 2.2 Administrative groups.			
Name	Scope	Member of	Control Over
Administrators	Local*	N/A	Own Computer
Administrators	Domain Local*	N/A	Own Domain
Domain Admins	Global	Administrators (Local)	All Computers in Domain
		Administrators (Domain Local)	Own Domain
Enterprise Admins	Universal**	Administrators (Domain Local)	All Domains in Forest

*Local groups are defined on computers; Domain Local groups are defined in domains.

**Enterprise Admins is a Universal group when the forest root is in native mode. In mixed mode, Enterprise Admins is a Global group.

For example, a user account named Zachary Baldwin located in the Support Organizational Unit in the **wrbaldwin.com** domain would have the following distinguished name:

```
dc=com, dc=wrbaldwin, ou=support, cn=zachary baldwin
```

There are a few important points to remember about distinguished names. First, this order does not matter. The following example would also be valid:

```
cn=zachary baldwin, ou=support, dc=wrbaldwin, dc=com
ou=support, cn=zachary baldwin, dc=com, dc=wrbaldwin
```

Also, when a container is referred to instead of an Organizational Unit, cn= is used instead of ou=. For example, if the Zachary Baldwin user account was in the Users container, its distinguished name would be:

```
dc=com, dc=wrbaldwin, cn=users, cn=zachary baldwin
```

What's in a Name?

Distinguished names are rarely used. You will have to understand them and occasionally use them, but they normally do not show up in the user interface of the basic tools like Active Directory Users and Computers. There will be many more names in Active Directory you will have to become familiar with.

The Relative Distinguished Name (cn=Zachary Baldwin) is the name you will see in Active Directory Users and Computers (see Figure 2.2). The Relative Distinguished Name is called the Full Name in the user interface (see Figure 2.6). The Full Name must be unique in the Organizational Unit.

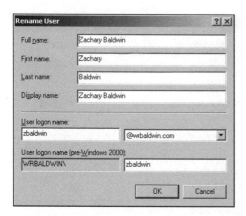

Figure 2.6   User account names.

The User Principal Name (UPN) is a combination of the User Logon Name (**zbaldwin**) and a UPN suffix (**@wrbaldwin.com**), as shown in Figure 2.6. The UPN can be used to log on to Windows 2000 computers only. When a user logs on using a UPN (**zbaldwin@yahoo.com**), he or she does not have to specify a domain name (see Figure 2.7). Therefore, UPNs must be unique for all user accounts in the entire forest. A common misconception is that the UPN suffix (**@wrbaldwin.com**) identifies the user's domain; it's not always true. Administrators can add additional UPN suffixes using Active Directory Domains and Trusts. For example, Zachary's UPN could be **zbaldwin@examcram.com**, even though he is in the **wrbaldwin.com** domain. A final note on UPNs: They look a lot like email addresses. Although it's good practice to make a user's UPN match his or her email address, the UPN and email address are two separate attributes and could be different.

Before learning about pre-Windows 2000 logon names, you need to understand the difference between a NetBIOS name and a host name. NetBIOS names remain in Windows 2000 for backward compatibility with pre-Windows 2000

Figure 2.7   User Principal Name (UPN).

computers and domains. NetBIOS names are not compatible with the Internet. A NetBIOS name can be up to 16 characters long (the 16th character is used to determine the type of name) and are by default the same as the host name. For example, a computer with a NetBIOS name of LUKE would have a host name of **luke** (NetBIOS names are typically uppercase and host names are typically lower-case). Of course, there's more: The host name is just part of the computer's fully qualified domain name (FQDN). A computer's FQDN identifies that computer uniquely throughout the scope of the Internet. If **luke** were in the **wrbaldwin.com** DNS domain, its FQDN would be **luke.wrbaldwin.com**. Domains also have NetBIOS name and FQDNs. By default, if a domain's FQDN is **wrbaldwin.com**, its NetBIOS name would be WRBALDWIN; **training.wrbaldwin.com** would be TRAINING. Of course, to complicate things, using the first part of the FQDN for the NetBIOS name is only the default and can be changed.

Why would a domain have a different NetBIOS name than the first part of its FQDN? A good example would be companies migrating from Windows NT and Exchange 5.5 to Windows 2000 and Exchange 2000 (a large portion of what this book is about). Windows NT domains did not have FQDNs and many of them had names like CORPNT, DOMAIN, EASTDOMAIN, and so on. Upgrading to Windows 2000, most companies will choose to use their identity, like **wrbaldwin.com**. They may even use a subdomain like **ad.wrbaldwin.com**. In either case, it's not likely that their Windows NT NetBIOS domain names match.

The User Logon Name (pre-Windows 2000; see Figure 2.6) is the NetBIOS type logon name. In Windows NT (and Windows 2000), this is in the form DOMAIN_NAME\Logon_Name, for example, WRBALDWIN\zbaldwin. This name is used when logging on to a Windows computer and a NetBIOS domain name is specified (see Figure 2.8).

Figure 2.8   User Logon Name (pre-Windows 2000).

When you log on to a domain, you either use a UPN or a pre-Windows 2000 Logon Name. This is a very important point to remember.

Server Functions

Let's look at a forest with three domains: **wrbaldwin.com**, **training.wrbaldwin.com**, and **consulting.wrbaldwin.com**. Each domain has at least one domain controller. Assume the TRAINING domain (remember TRAINING is the NetBIOS name for **training.wrbaldwin.com**) has two domain controllers. Each of these domain controllers has an Active Directory database, and in that database, each domain controller has a read/write copy of the TRAINING domain objects. This means these domain controllers can authenticate computers and users, change TRAIN-ING objects, and answer queries for TRAINING information. What if a user is searching Active Directory for objects outside the TRAINING domain, in, for example, the CONSULTING domain? It wouldn't make sense to query at least one domain controller in every domain in the forest. Because of this, and other reasons, at least one domain controller in the forest is designated as a *Global Catalog server*. A domain controller designated as a Global Catalog server contains a full copy of its own objects and a partial copy of all the objects in all other domains. This partial copy includes all objects and a subset of their attributes. For example, the Global Catalog server would contain all user accounts' first and last names, but not their middle initials. By default, the first domain controller in the forest is the only Global Catalog server. Any domain controller can be a Global Catalog server, and there is no limit to the number of Global Catalog servers. Figure 2.9 shows the contents of the databases of four domain controllers in the WRBALDWIN and TRAINING domains. One domain controller in each domain is designated a Global Catalog server.

The placement of Global Catalog servers can have tremendous impact on design. The first issue has been discussed; users will query a Global Catalog server when they search for objects outside their domain. The second issue has a much greater impact. Every time a user logs on with an account from a native-mode domain, the domain controller that authenticates the user queries a Global Catalog server. If a Global Catalog server is not available, the user will not be authenticated and must log on with cached credentials, if possible. The domain controller queries a Global Catalog server to find all universal groups of which the user account is a member. Universal groups can contain users from any native-mode domain, and universal groups can be used to control access to resources in any domain. Because of this, domain controllers must add universal group membership to a user access token when that user logs on.

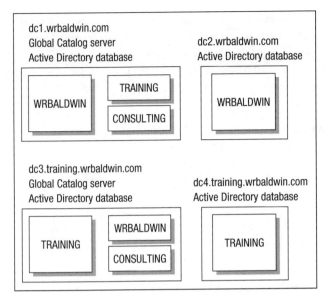

Figure 2.9 Active Directory database contents.

 Exchange 2000 requires access to at least one Global Catalog server. This is true even in a mixed-mode domain and in single-domain forests.

Global Catalog servers are comparable to *Flexible Single Master Operations (FSMOs)*. Certain domain controllers are designated operations masters, or FMSOs, for certain roles in the forest and domain. In addition to objects and partial objects (Global Catalog information), the Active Directory database contains the schema and Configurations information. These are often referred to as partitions of the database. For example, a domain controller in the TRAINING domain that is not a Global Catalog server contains a TRAINING partition, a schema partition, and a Configuration partition. On this domain controller, the TRAINING partition is read/write, but the schema partition and parts of the Configuration partition are read-only. The read/write copy of the schema partition is located on the domain controller designated the Schema Master. So, to make changes to the schema, you must have access to the Schema Master. The portion of the Configuration partition that is read-only is the domain naming information. The read/write copy of the domain naming portion of the Configuration partition is located on the domain controller designated the Domain Naming Master. So, to add a domain to the forest, you must have access to the Domain Naming Master. By default, the domain controller designated as the Schema Master and Domain

Naming Master is the first domain controller in the forest. These are both designated as forest roles, meaning there are only one Schema Master and Domain Naming Master per forest. Figure 2.10 shows the contents of the databases of four domain controllers in the WRBALDWIN and TRAINING domains. *DC1 is the only Global Catalog server.*

 Microsoft has intentionally made the schema difficult to modify. Typically, only the setup programs of Active Directory-integrated applications like Exchange 2000 should modify the schema. The roadblock Microsoft built was to make the schema read-only, even on the Schema Master. A checkbox in Active Directory schema allows the schema to be modified. Additionally, only members of Schema Admins can modify the schema. The Schema Admins group is only in the forest root, and by default only the Administrator account in the forest root is a member.

In addition to the two forest FSMOs, there are three domain FSMOs. By default, the first domain controller in each domain in the forest is the PDC Emulator, RID Master, and Infrastructure Master. Although these are not partitions in the database, they are roles performed by one and only one domain controller in each domain.

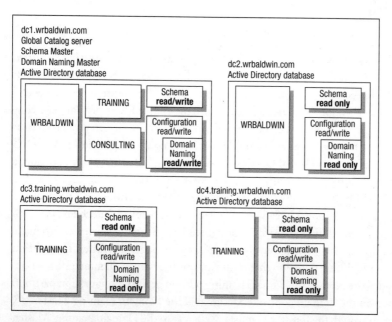

Figure 2.10   Active Directory database contents.

The Physical Structure of AD

The physical structure of a network will have a great impact on the design of both Exchange and Active Directory. Unlike the logical structure, however, Exchange 2000 will maintain its own configuration call routing groups. Routing groups are discussed in Chapter 6. I'll give you a brief overview of Active Directory sites, subnets, and site links. Active Directory sites are used to control replication traffic, client authentication, and DFS (Distributed File System). DFS is out of the scope of this book.

By default, all domain controllers in the forest are in the same site. Domain controllers within the same site will form a replication ring and will replicate, via partners, every five minutes. Additional sites can be created and domain controllers can be moved to these sites. Administrators can control replication between sites by modifying the site links that join the sites. Site links will control replication cost, interval, and schedule.

Because all client computers don't have accounts in Active Directory, there is no way to move client computer accounts into a specific site. Therefore, to control which domain controllers with which a client computer will try to authenticate first, you must create *subnets*. A subnet is a range of IP addresses. Once a subnet is associated with a site, all client computers in that subnet will attempt to authenticate with domain controllers in their site first. If no domain controller is available in their site, they will attempt to authenticate with domain controllers in other sites.

Exchange 2000 in AD

When Exchange 2000 is installed into a forest, there is a change made to that forest's schema (also known as extending the schema). New object classes and attributes are added to the schema to accommodate Exchange 2000. There are over 100 new object classes and over 500 new attributes added. This process is done only when the first Exchange 2000 Server is installed. These new object classes and attributes all start with "ms-Exch" and can be viewed using Active Directory schema (see Figure 2.11) or ADSIEdit.

Exchange extends the schema for two purposes. First, Exchange settings will be stored in the Configuration partition of the Active Directory database. Because the Configuration partition is replicated to all domain controllers in the forest, Exchange settings will be available forest-wide. The second reason to extend the schema is to store recipient information in the domain partition. After Exchange 2000 is installed, many objects (such as user accounts) can now be mailbox-enabled. For now, notice the difference between the property page of a user before Exchange 2000 is installed (Figure 2.12), after Exchange 2000 is installed (Figure 2.13), and finally, after the user is mailbox-enabled (Figure 2.14).

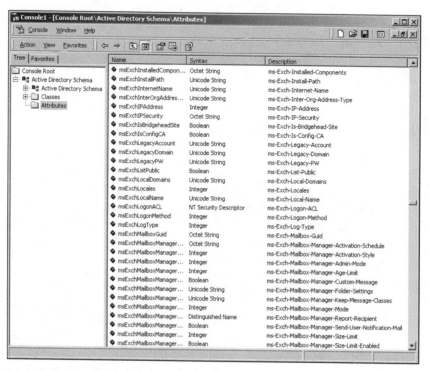

Figure 2.11 Active Directory schema.

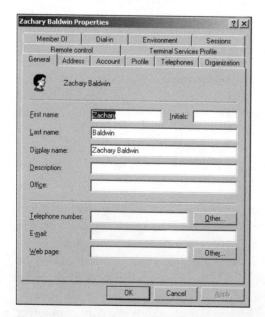

Figure 2.12 User account property page before Exchange 2000 is installed.

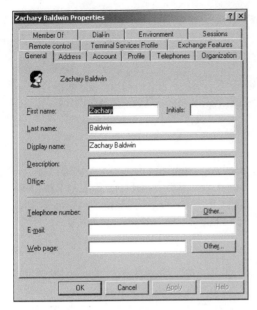

Figure 2.13   User account property page after Exchange 2000 is installed.

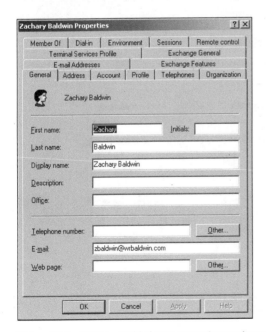

Figure 2.14   Mailbox-enabled user account property page.

Practice Questions

Case Study

WRBaldwin, Inc., will be deploying Exchange 2000 within one year. Before deploying Exchange 2000, WRBaldwin must deploy Windows 2000 and Active Directory.

Company Profile

WRBaldwin is a medium-sized consulting company based in Atlanta, GA. Its core business has always been professional services and staff extension. WRBaldwin has recently expanded into training in its Atlanta and Tampa locations. This business accounts for 15% of total sales but is currently losing money.

Business Plan

WRBaldwin would like to expand its training business to all six locations. WRBaldwin is not concerned with the training business making money, but it would like to break even. Internally, the training department is referred to as WRB Training. WRBaldwin would like the consulting and training business to collaborate but remain separate entities.

Existing IT Environment: Network Diagram

Figure 2.15 shows WRBaldwin's network diagram.

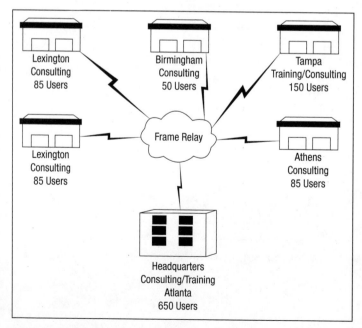

Figure 2.15 Network diagram.

Company Commentary

CIO: As we expand training to the other locations, I'll be hiring IT staff to handle the training computers. I feel that because the training computers may be exposed to students, it's important to have these in their own domain.

Director of Consulting IT: As we deploy Active Directory, I'm concerned with additional traffic on our frame relay connections. I'd like to control replication between sites and prevent users from having to cross the frame to get logged on. We should be ready to deploy Active Directory in about six months.

Director of Training IT: We have discussed the possibility of making the training department its own forest. Unfortunately, this will not be the case. The TRAINING domain will be a subdomain of the **wrbaldwin.com** domain. I will have full control over **training.wrbaldwin.com**, but the admins in **wrbaldwin.com** will also have administrative rights in my domain. We are ready to deploy Active Directory now.

Question 1

If the training department deploys Active Directory as **training.wrbaldwin.com** before consulting deploys **wrbaldwin.com**, which of the following will have to be done when the corporate headquarters installs Active Directory? [Check all correct answers]

❑ a. During the installation of the **wrbaldwin.com** domain, it will have to join the **training.wrbaldwin.com** forest.

❑ b. After installing **wrbaldwin.com**, use Ntdsutil.exe to merge forests.

❑ c. After installing **wrbaldwin.com**, reinstall **training.wrbaldwin.com**.

❑ d. After installing **wrbaldwin.com**, use Active Directory Domains and Trusts to merge forests.

❑ e. After installing **wrbaldwin.com**, reinstall the **training.wrbaldwin.com**. Use Movetree.exe to move the accounts from the old **training.wrbaldwin.com** domain to the new **training.wrbaldwin.com** domain. Decommission the old **training.wrbaldwin.com** domain.

Answer c is correct. The only way for training to be a child domain under **wrbaldwin.com** is to install training after **wrbaldwin.com**. Answer a is incorrect because when Active Directory is installed for the first time, that domain becomes the root of the forest (or forest root). Additional domains can be added as children or as additional trees, but the forest root (in this case, **training.wrbaldwin.com**) can never have a parent domain. Domains can only become parents by adding children to them. Answer b is incorrect because the Ntdsutil.exe tool cannot be used to merge forests. Answer d is incorrect because

Active Directory Domains and Trusts cannot be used to merge forests. Answer e is incorrect because the Movetree.exe utility can be use to move accounts between domain in the same forest only.

Question 2

After WRBaldwin, Inc., deploys Active Directory to both consulting and training, it needs to promote one of its member servers in the **training.wrbaldwin.com** domain to a domain controller to relieve the overloaded domain controllers. Members of which of the following groups can add a replica domain controller to the **training.wrbaldwin.com** domain? [Check all correct answers]

- ❑ a. WRBALDWIN\Administrators
- ❑ b. WRBALDWIN\Domain Admins
- ❑ c. WRBALDWIN\Enterprise Admins
- ❑ d. TRAINING\Administrators
- ❑ e. TRAINING\Domain Admins
- ❑ f. TRAINING\Server Operators

Answers c, d, and e are correct. Only members of the Administrators group in those local domains have permissions to add additional domain controllers. The WRBALDWIN\Enterprise Admins group is a universal group (global group in mixed mode) that is a member of the Administrators group in all domains in the forest. The TRAINING\Domain Admins group is a global group that is a member of the Administrators group in its own domain. Answer a is incorrect because members of the WRBALDWIN\Administrators group only have permissions in the WRBALDWIN domain. Because Administrators is a local group, it can only be assigned rights and permissions in its own domain. Answer b is incorrect because members of the WRBALDWIN\Domain Admins group only have permissions in the WRBALDWIN domain. Because Domain Admins is a global group, it can be assigned rights and permissions in any domain in the forest, but by default it does not have permissions in any other domains. Answer f is incorrect because members of the Server Operators have limited rights in the domain. Adding domain controllers is not one of them.

Question 3

While planning for the WRBaldwin, Inc., Active Directory deployment, an architect suggests using **wrbaldwintraining.wrbaldwin.com** instead of **training.wrbaldwin.com**. What would the default NetBIOS name for the **wrbaldwintraining.wrbaldwin.com** domain be?

○ a. WRBALDWINTRAINING

○ b. WRBALDWINTRAININ

○ c. WRBALDWINTRAINI

○ d. WRBALDWINTRAIN

○ e. WRBALDWIN

Answer c is correct. NetBIOS names are a maximum of 16 characters. The last character, however, is a hex code defining the type of NetBIOS name. The default NetBIOS name is generated by taking the first 15 characters of the first part of the fully qualified domain name (FQDN).

Question 4

After WRBaldwin finishes the Active Directory deployment, you install the first Exchange 2000 computer on a domain controller in **training.wrbaldwin.com**. Which group or groups must you be a member of? [Check all correct answers]

❏ a. WRBALDWIN\Administrators

❏ b. WRBALDWIN\Domain Admins

❏ c. WRBALDWIN\Enterprise Admins

❏ d. WRBALDWIN\Schema Admins

❏ e. TRAINING\Administrators

Answers c, d, and e are correct. Because this is the first installation of Exchange 2000 in the forest, Exchange will modify the schema. Only members of Schema Admins can modify the schema. You must also be a member of the Administrators of the domain for which you are installing Exchange and a member of Enterprise Admins of the forest root to run the forest prep section of the setup. Answers a and b are incorrect because WRBALDWIN\Administrators and WRBALDWIN\Domain Admins cannot modify the schema and have not administrator rights in TRAINING.

Question 5

> WRBaldwin, Inc., is deciding whether or not to complicate Active Directory with Organizational Units (OUs). Which of the following are valid reasons for creating OUs in Active Directory? [Check all correct answers]
>
> ❏ a. Delegation of Control
>
> ❏ b. Controlling access to resources
>
> ❏ c. Deploying software
>
> ❏ d. Organization of accounts
>
> ❏ e. Assigning group policies
>
> ❏ f. Increase logon efficiency

Answers a, c, d, and e are correct. By organizing accounts into Organizational Units (OUs), you can delegate control of an OU to administrators. Then administrators do not have to be a member of the Administrators group and can be given only the control they need. You can use group policies to deploy software to accounts in a specific OU. Organizing accounts into OUs can make it easier for administrators to find and manage users. Group policies can be used to control a user's desktop, folder redirection, logon scripts, software deployment, and more. You can deploy group policies to accounts in specific OUs. Answer b is incorrect because OUs cannot be used to control access to resources. Security groups, NTFS, and shared folder permissions should be used. Answer f is incorrect because organizing accounts into OUs will not improve logon efficiency. If multiple group policies are deployed, it could slow logon time.

Question 6

After WRBaldwin, Inc., deployed Active Directory and created OUs, a member of the Domain Admins group attempts to delegate administrative control to an OU. In Active Directory Users and Computers, they would like to use the Security tab of the OU to assign permissions. They do not see a Security tab on the property page of the OU. How can they view the Security tab?

○ a. From the View menu, select Advanced Features.

○ b. From the View menu, select Filter Options. In the Filter Options property page, select Advanced Features.

○ c. Log on as a member of Administrators.

○ d. Log on as member of Enterprise Admins.

○ e. You must use the Delegation of Control Wizard.

Answer a is correct. By default, the Security and Object tabs are hidden. The Advanced Features option will make these tabs and additional folders visible. Answer b is incorrect because the Filter Options settings are used to configure which columns are displayed in the Contents pane of the Microsoft Management Console. Answers c and d are incorrect because members of the Administrators group have the right to view the Security tab; there is no need to have additional permissions. Answer e is incorrect. Although using the Delegation of Control Wizard is recommended, it is not required.

Question 7

You are planning the WRBaldwin, Inc., Active Directory deployment. You need to identify the critical components of AD. It has several roles that are single mastered. Some of these roles are per domain and other are per forest.

Per forest

Per domain

Match the following roles with the correct type (Note: some items may be used only once or not at all):

Domain Naming Master

Enterprise Master

Infrastructure Master

PDC Emulator

RID Master

Schema Master

SID Master

Tree Master

The answer is:

>   Per forest

>   Domain Naming Master

>   Schema Master

>   Per domain

>   Infrastructure Master

>   PDC Emulator

>   RID Master

There are five operations masters (flexible single master operation, or FSMO). Two are per forest (meaning only one for the entire forest) and three are per domain (meaning one for every domain in the forest). Certain domain controllers in the forest or domain hold the operation master roles. These roles can be changed. By default, the first domain controller in the forest holds the two per-forest roles and the first domain controller in each domain holds the three per-domain roles.

Need to Know More?

 MCSE Training Kit: Designing a Microsoft Windows 2000 Directory Services Infrastructure. Microsoft Press, Redmond, WA, 1998. ISBN 0-7356-1132-7. This title focuses on the design aspect of Active Directory as opposed to the nuts and bolts.

 Scheil, Dennis, and Diana Bartley. *MSCE Windows 2000 Directory Services Design Exam Cram.* The Coriolis Group, Scottsdale, AZ, 1999. ISBN 1-57610-714-0. Features detailed coverage of Active Directory security, auditing, and integration with existing applications.

 Wood, Adam. *Windows 2000 Active Directory Black Book.* The Coriolis Group, Scottsdale, AZ, 1999. ISBN 1-57610-256-4. This book provides immediate solutions to the challenges of working with the most important feature of Windows 2000.

 Read the *Windows 2000 Server Resource Kit Deployment Planning Guide* section on Active Directory.

 Search **www.microsoft.com/technet** and the Windows 2000 Server Help file using the terms at the beginning of the chapter.

Designing an
Installation Plan

Terms you'll need to understand:

✓ Active Directory

✓ Internet Information Services (IIS)

✓ Network News Transfer
  Protocol (NNTP)

✓ Configuration

✓ Schema

✓ Setup.exe /ForestPrep

✓ Setup.exe /DomainPrep

✓ Windows 2000
  Administrative Tools

✓ Adminpak.msi

✓ Administrative groups

✓ Exchange System Manager

✓ Routing groups

✓ Exchange Organization

✓ Native mode

✓ Mixed mode

✓ Unattended mode installation

✓ Exchange Advanced Security

Techniques you'll need to master:

✓ Designing an installation plan

✓ Preparing a forest for Exchange

✓ Preparing a domain for Exchange

✓ Verifying an Exchange
  2000 installation

The Exchange 2000 Design exam (70-225) objectives do not specifically focus on hands-on implementation. The exam's focus is on planning and design. There are topics on deployment, but these topics look at deployment from a higher level than the Exchange 2000 Admin exam (70-224). Think of the topics and questions in the Design exam as being geared toward project managers, CIOs, and network architects.

The focus of the exam, however, can shift from design to implementation and even administration. Although the exam's overall focus is on design, many of the questions may drill deep into very specific details. These details may be ones you've studied for and that you might even see on the Admin exam. Installation of Exchange 2000 is certainly an example of one of these topics. In the Design exam, case studies are based on the deployment of Exchange 2000, and to deploy, at some point we must install.

This chapter will focus on installing Exchange 2000 where no messaging system already exists. Of course, in real life and on the exam, this is not usually the case. Actually, most of the case studies on the exam will likely focus on migrating from Exchange 5.5 to Exchange 2000. This chapter will touch on the topic of migrating from Exchange 5.5 to Exchange 2000, but it is discussed in greater detail in Chapter 11.

Preparing Windows 2000

Before installing Exchange 2000, Windows 2000 with Active Directory must exist. Although Exchange 2000 does not have to be installed on a Windows 2000 domain controller, it does have to be installed on a computer that is a member of a Windows 2000 domain. You will have to analyze an organization's requirements before determining whether it is better to install Exchange 2000 on a member server or a domain controller.

Hardware Requirements

When analyzing the requirements of an organization, you also have to determine hardware requirements. Both Windows 2000 and Exchange 2000 have minimum and recommended hardware requirements (see Table 3.1).

Table 3.1 Exchange 2000 hardware requirements.	
Minimum	**Recommended**
Pentium-compatible 133MHz	Pentium-compatible 300MHz
128MB RAM	256MB RAM
500MB free hard disk space	2GB free hard disk space

Table 3.2 Example of Exchange 2000 server requirements.	
Metric	**Server Type**
<999 Mailboxes	Small server
1000-1999 Mailboxes	Medium server
>2000 Mailboxes	Large server

These requirements mean little when dealing with design. When network architects create designs, they use more general requirements based on types of servers. Table 3.2 shows an example of design guidelines.

Determining the actual server requirements of a small, medium, or large server would be done in the lab. There are many advantages to this approach, the most notable being that hardware is consistently declining in price. By the time the project is actually deployed, you may want to reclassify the details behind the server types. You may be told that a single Global Catalog server can only service requests from a maximum of three small servers. If you wanted to deploy only small servers to a location with 5,500 users, how many Global Catalog servers would you need in that location? Dividing 5,500 by 999 gives you six Exchange 2000 servers and therefore two Global Catalog servers.

 In case study questions, you will see more general requirements based on types of servers (see Table 3.2) not specific hardware.

Internet Information Services (IIS)

A major change from Exchange 5.5 to Exchange 2000 is the way Exchange handles Internet message transport. All Exchange 2000 Internet messages are now handled by *Internet Information Services (IIS)*. For this reason, IIS must be installed on a Windows 2000 server before Exchange 2000 is installed. The requirement that will catch most people off guard on the test is that all protocols handled for Exchange 2000 by IIS must be installed before Exchange 2000 can be installed. In a default Windows 2000 installation, all protocols except *Network News Transfer Protocol (NNTP)* are installed (see Table 3.3). Therefore, before installing Exchange 2000 on a default installation of Windows 2000, you must install NNTP. Memorize Table 3.3 and remember that NNTP is the only one not installed by default.

Active Directory

As you saw in Chapter 2, Exchange 2000 is fully integrated with Windows 2000 and Active Directory. For this reason, Exchange 2000 planning really begins before

Table 3.3   Internet Information Services protocols.

Protocol	Function(s)	TCP Port
Simple Mail Transfer Protocol (SMTP)	Send Internet email	25
Hypertext Transfer Protocol (HTTP)	Transfer Web pages	80
Post Office Protocol v3 (POP3)*	Retrieve Internet email	110
Internet Message Access Protocol v4 (IMAP4)*	Retrieve Internet email	143
	Advanced access to folders	
Network News Transfer Protocol (NNTP)	Send/Retrieve newsgroups	119

POP3 and IMAP4 are added to IIS after Exchange 2000 is installed.

Active Directory is installed. The design of the Active Directory forest where Exchange 2000 will be installed will have a great impact on Exchange 2000.

Before installing Exchange 2000, pre-Windows 2000 security should be considered. During installation of Active Directory, each domain has the option to support permissions compatible with pre-Windows 2000 computers. This option comes into effect when pre-Windows 2000 computers (Windows NT 4 servers, for example) need anonymous access to group membership and other group information. One reason for setting this option is the need to support Windows NT 4 Remote Access Service (RAS) servers. When a remote access client attempts to log on to a Windows NT 4 RAS server, the RAS queries Active Directory to see if the user is allowed to access the network via RAS. Windows NT 4 RAS servers use anonymous access for this query.

Using permissions compatible with pre-Windows 2000 computers allows everyone (specifically, the Everyone group) to view hidden membership of distribution lists. During Exchange 2000 installation, you will be warned if pre-Windows 2000 permissions are present (see Figure 3.1). There are two solutions to this problem. One option is to remove the Everyone group from the pre-Windows 2000 security group. You will then have to add users and computers who need pre-Windows 2000 access. Your second option is to upgrade the pre-Windows 2000 computers and/or applications to Windows 2000.

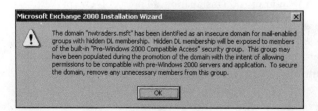

Figure 3.1   Pre-Windows 2000 security warning.

ForestPrep

As discussed in Chapter 2, when the first Exchange 2000 server of the forest is installed, the Active Directory schema will be modified. Only members of Schema Admins can modify the schema. You may not want the person installing Exchange 2000 to be a member of Schema Admins. Also, the Schema modification can take up to an hour to perform. Using Setup.exe with the /ForestPrep switch, a member of Schema Admin can modify the schema and prepare the forest for Exchange without installing an Exchange 2000 server. When using Setup.exe /ForestPrep, consider the following:

➤ To run ForestPrep, a user must be a member of both Schema Admins and Enterprise Admins. Both groups are located in forest root only.

➤ If Exchange 2000 is installed in the forest before ForestPrep is run, ForestPrep will be run during installation. This will only occur during the installation of the first Exchange 2000 server in the forest.

➤ After the forest has been prepped, you should wait for the new schema to replicate before installing Exchange 2000.

➤ The forest can be prepared soon after Active Directory is deployed, even if Exchange 2000 will not be deployed yet.

➤ You should prepare the forest on the Schema Master.

➤ Preparing the forest will take a long time and will task the Schema Master during the process. The forest should be prepared during offpeak hours.

➤ If you misspell /ForestPrep, the standard setup will run.

➤ You will have to either join or create an organization. The organization name can never be changed (see Figure 3.2).

➤ You will need to specify an Exchange 2000 Administrator Account; this account will be granted administrative rights to Exchange 2000.

DomainPrep

The /DomainPrep switch is similar to the /ForestPrep switch. DomainPrep performs pre-installing tasks on the domain where it is run. There are no options with DomainPrep (see Figure 3.3). A member of Domain Admins must run DomainPrep, and if Exchange 2000 is installed in the domain before DomainPrep is run, DomainPrep will be run during installation. This only occurs during the installation of the first Exchange 2000 server in the domain. DomainPrep performs the following tasks:

➤ The user account EUSER_EXSTOREVENTS is created in the domain. This user is used by the script event host and has limited access.

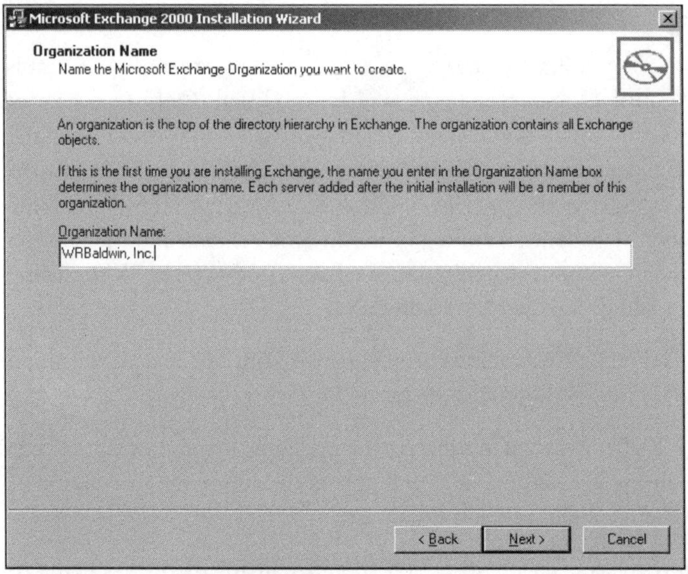

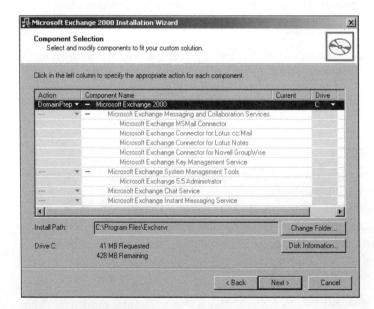

Figure 3.2 ForestPrep Wizard (Organization Name).

➤ The domain local group Exchange Enterprise Servers is created in the domain. This group will contain all computers in the domain running Exchange 2000.

➤ The global group Exchange Domain Servers is created in the domain. This group will contain all computers in the domain running Exchange 2000.

Figure 3.3 DomainPrep Wizard.

➤ The Exchange Enterprise Servers and Exchange Domain Servers are granted permissions in the domain.

Installing Exchange 2000

As mentioned before, proper planning is required before installing the first Exchange 2000 server. Running ForestPrep and DomainPrep will not only save time, but will also facilitate better planning. After ForestPrep and DomainPrep have been run, it is again important to plan and perhaps perform certain steps before Exchange 2000 is installed. These actions will differ depending on whether the Exchange 2000 installation is new or an upgrade from Exchange 5.5.

Administrative Groups

Administrative groups in Exchange 2000 are similar to Exchange 5.5 sites. Each Exchange server belongs to one, and only one, administrative group. Administrative groups can be used to define which actions users and groups can perform. Permissions can be assigned to administrative groups to control such tasks as creating and managing servers or routing groups.

As with Exchange 5.5 servers and sites, Exchange 2000 servers cannot be moved between administrative groups. If you are upgrading from Exchange 5.5 or if your Exchange 2000 installation is joining an Exchange 5.5 organization, your administrative groups will be based on your Exchange 5.5 sites. A solution to the potential problem is to create Exchange 5.5 sites based on the administrative group structure you desire in Exchange 2000. When you install Exchange 2000 Servers, have them join the appropriate administrative groups.

If you are creating a new organization, Exchange 2000 Setup will create an administrative group called First Administrative Group and put the first server in it. If you want to create a different administrative group or groups, you can do so before installing the first Exchange 2000 server. After ForestPrep has been run, you can install the *Exchange System Manager* using the Exchange Setup program. You can then use the Exchange System Manager to create administrative groups. When you install Exchange 2000 servers, have them join the appropriate administrative groups.

Routing Groups

One of the differences between Exchange 5.5 and Exchange 2000 is the addition of routing groups. In Exchange 5.5, sites were used as both routing and administrative boundaries. Exchange 2000 allows servers in the same administrative group to belong to different routing groups. However, the reverse is not true; servers in the same routing group must belong to the same administrative group. Routing groups actually belong to administrative groups and servers belong to routing groups. Servers can be moved to different routing groups, but only if they stay within the same administrative group. Once Exchange 2000 is switched to native mode, routing groups are still members of administrative groups, but the rules change. In native mode, servers can be moved to routing groups in different administrative groups. Exchange 2000 Setup will create a routing group named First Routing Group in the First Administrative Group. When the first Exchange 2000 server is installed, it will become a member of this group (see Figure 3.4).

 When Exchange 2000 is in mixed mode, servers can be moved to different routing groups, but only if they stay within the same administrative group. In native mode, servers can be moved to routing groups in different administrative groups. Mixed mode is explained in the "Mixed/Native Mode" section later in this chapter.

 In the Exchange System Manager, administrative groups and routing groups are not displayed by default. In the Properties page of the organization, you can configure which of these should be displayed (see Figure 3.5).

Components and Services

When the Exchange 2000 Setup program is run, you will have to decide which components will be installed. The list of available components vary depending on which version of Exchange 2000 you install. Exchange 2000 Server provides basic components needed to install Exchange. Exchange 2000 Server Enterprise adds the Chat component (see Table 3.4) and additional scalability. The following are only available with Exchange 2000 Server Enterprise:

➤ Databases over 16GB in size

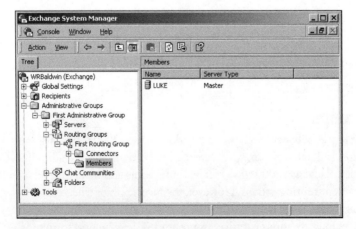

Figure 3.4   First Administrative Group and First Routing Group.

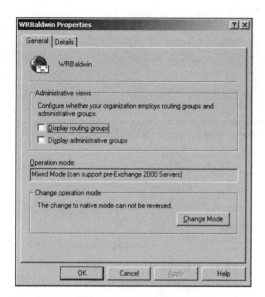

Figure 3.5 Properties page of an organization.

Table 3.4	Exchange 2000 service components.
Version	**Component**
Both	Microsoft Exchange Messaging and Collaboration Services
Both	Microsoft Exchange MSMail Connector
Both	Microsoft Exchange Connector for Lotus cc:Mail
Both	Microsoft Exchange Connector for Lotus Notes
Both	Microsoft Exchange Connector for Novell GroupWise
Both	Microsoft Key Management Service
Both	Microsoft Exchange System Management Tools
Both	Microsoft Exchange 5.5 Administrator
Enterprise only	Microsoft Exchange Chat Service
Both	Microsoft Exchange Instant Messaging Service

➤ Multiple databases on a single server

➤ Active/active clustering

➤ Front-end/back-end server configurations

Based on which components are installed, several services can be installed to support Exchange 2000. As with all Windows 2000-based services, these services can be started and stopped using the Services console. You can also install a service, then use the Services console to disable the service to prevent it from starting. This can also be useful as a diagnostic tool. Finally, most services are dependent on another service. This means if Service B is dependent on Service A, Service B will only start if Service A has started. Also if Service A is stopped, Service B will also be stopped. Table 3.5 lists Microsoft Exchange 2000 services and their dependencies.

Table 3.5   Exchange 2000 services and dependencies.

Services	Dependencies
Microsoft Exchange Chat	None
Microsoft Exchange Connectivity Controller	Event Log Microsoft Exchange System Attendant
Microsoft Exchange Connector for Lotus cc:Mail	Event Log Microsoft Exchange Information Store
Microsoft Exchange Connector for Lotus Notes	Event Log Microsoft Exchange Connectivity Controller Microsoft Exchange Information Store
Microsoft Exchange Connector for Novell GroupWise	Event Log Microsoft Exchange Connectivity Controller Microsoft Exchange Information Store Microsoft Exchange Router for Novell GroupWise
Microsoft Exchange Directory Synchronization	Microsoft Exchange MTA Stacks
Microsoft Exchange Event	Microsoft Exchange Information Store
Microsoft Exchange IMAP4	IIS Admin Service Microsoft Exchange Information Store
Microsoft Exchange Information Store	IIS Admin Service Microsoft Exchange System Attendant
Microsoft Exchange MTA Stacks	IIS Admin Service Microsoft Exchange System Attendant
Microsoft Exchange POP3	IIS Admin Service Microsoft Exchange Information Store
Microsoft Exchange Routing Engine	IIS Admin Service
Microsoft Exchange Router for Novell GroupWise	Event Log
Microsoft Exchange Site Replication	None

(continued)

Table 3.5 Exchange 2000 services and dependencies *(continued)*.	
Services	**Dependencies**
Microsoft Exchange System Attendant	Event Log
	NT LM Security Provider
	Remote Procedure Call (RPC)
	Remote Procedure Call (RPC) Locator
	Server
	Workstation
Microsoft Search	NT LM Security Support Provider
	Remote Procedure Call (RPC)
MS Mail Connector Interchange	Event Log
	Microsoft Exchange MTA Stacks
MS Schedule Plus Free-Busy Connector	Event Log
	Microsoft Exchange Information Store

Mixed/Native Mode

When Exchange 2000 is installed, it is running in mixed mode. Do not confuse Exchange 2000 mixed mode with Windows 2000 mixed mode. Windows 2000 mixed mode enables Windows 2000 Active Directory domain to have both Windows 2000 and Windows NT 4 domain controllers. Similarly, Exchange 2000 mixed mode allows Exchange 2000 to coexist with previous versions of Exchange.

 While in mixed mode, Exchange 2000 Servers must be in the same administrative group as the routing group object they belong to. Once Exchange 2000 is switched to native mode, servers can belong to routing groups in different administrative groups.

You should only switch an Exchange 2000 organization to mixed mode after all servers have been upgraded to Exchange 2000. You should also have no plan to install pre-Exchange 2000 Servers in the organization. Once you switch from mixed mode to native mode, the change cannot be reversed.

Unattended Installation

Exchange 2000 allows for the scripted unattended installation of Exchange 2000. Using the CreateUnattended switch with the Setup utility, a predefined installation file can be created. Typically, the reason for creating unattended installations is not to save time, but rather, to reduce mistakes. An unattended installation can be created and tested in a lab before releasing to production.

Note: Exchange 2000 does not support unattended installations of the first server in the forest unless ForestPrep and DomainPrep have been run. Exchange 2000 also does not support unattended installations of the first server in a domain unless DomainPrep has been run on that domain.

Administrative Tools

Because Exchange 2000 is fully integrated with Windows 2000, Windows 2000 tools are used for some of the Exchange 2000 administration. Some tools will be modified with additional Exchange 2000 extensions. In addition to the Windows 2000 tools, Exchange has its own tools for managing Exchange settings. The Exchange 2000 Setup program can install these tools and the Windows 2000 extensions. Using the Exchange 2000 Setup program, Exchange System Management Tools (which include the Windows 2000 extensions) can be installed on Windows 2000 computers, including those not running Exchange 2000 services and those running Windows 2000 Professional. After the Exchange System Management Tools are installed, the Microsoft Management Console (MMC) snap-ins can be added to an MMC console (see Figure 3.6).

Note: Before installing the Exchange System Management Tools on a computer, you should install the Windows 2000 Administrative Tools. These domain administration tools will be extended when the Exchange System Management Tools are installed. If the Windows 2000 Administrative Tools are installed after the Exchange System Management Tools, the Windows 2000 Administrative Tools will not be extended.

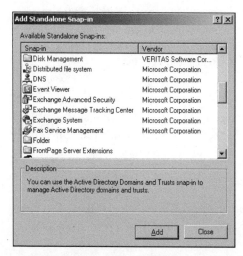

Figure 3.6 Exchange System Management Tools snap-ins.

The following is a list of tools used by Exchange 2000. These include Exchange System Management Tools and some of the Windows 2000 Administrative Tools.

➤ *Exchange System (Manager)*—Manages all aspects of Exchange 2000. This tool will modify information stored in the Configuration partition of a domain controller.

➤ *Exchange Advanced Security*—Allows users to secure authored messages via digital encryption and authenticate those messages with a digital signature.

➤ *Exchange Message Tracking Center*—Tracks messages in Exchange 2000.

➤ *Active Directory Users and Computers*—Is extended by the Exchange 2000 Setup program. Active Directory Users and Computers is used to manage objects in the Active Directory. With the Exchange 2000 extensions, Active Directory Users and Computers can be used to create and manage mailbox-enabled objects such as users, contacts, and groups.

➤ *ADSI Edit*—Is a low-level Active Directory management tool. ADSI Edit will enable you to configure advanced settings of Exchange 2000. Many of these settings are only available using ADSI Edit.

➤ *Active Directory Sites and Services*—Manages the topology of Active Directory. This includes domain controller replication. Because Exchange 2000 configuration is replicated between domain controllers, Active Directory Sites and Services controls replication of Exchange 2000 settings.

The Windows 2000 Administrative Tools can be installed by running Adminpak.msi from the systemroot\winnt\system32 folder of a computer running Windows 2000 Server or Advanced Server. These tools are installed by default on domain controllers. ADSI Edit is installed as part of the Support Tools located on the Windows 2000 Server or Advanced Server CD-ROM.

Verifying an Exchange 2000 Installation

It is typically not necessary to verify every aspect of an Exchange 2000 installation. Under normal circumstances, if the installation program completes, the installation was successful. However, a comprehensive installation plan should include verification of the installation.

Folders and Shares

One quick way to verify an installation is to check that all the appropriate folders exist on the server. Exchange 2000 Setup will also share specific folders. Table 3.6 shows Exchange 2000 folders. These folders are located under the Exchsrvr folder.

Table 3.6   Exchange 2000 folders and shares.

Folder	Description	Shared
Address	Dynamic-link libraries (DLLs) for email proxies	Yes
Bin	Exchange 2000 program files	No
CCMCdata	Storage for message in transit	No
Conndata	Used by the MSMail connector	No
Connect	Used by Exchange 2000 connectors	No
Dxadata	Used by MSMail for PC Networks	No
Exchweb	Used by Outlook Web Access (OWA)	No
ExchangeServer_*servername*	Used by Microsoft Search	No
Mtadata	Stores configuration information for the MTA	No
Res	Event Viewer and System Monitor logs	No
Schema	OLE DB schema	No
Srsdata	Used by Site Replication Service	No
Servername.log	Used for storage of message tracking logs	Yes

Services

Exchange 2000 services will log errors in the System event log if they fail to start. Exchange 2000 will also use the Application event log to log errors it may encounter. You should check both of these logs as well as the Directory Service event log after installation is complete. The Services snap-in is another useful tool for verifying that all the correct services have been installed and started. As seen earlier in this chapter, many services are dependent on both Exchange 2000 and Windows 2000 services. This means that the failure of an Exchange 2000 service to start may be caused by an error in a Windows 2000 service.

Practice Questions

Case Study

North Coast Training will be upgrading from Exchange 5.5 to Exchange 2000.

Company Profile

North Coast Training is a small training center in Cleveland, Ohio. Its core business has always been Instructor-Led Training (ILT). Recently, due to the popularity of the Internet, North Coast has expanded into the eLearning business. This business accounts for 5 percent of total sales but 20 percent of total profits. North Coast also publishes a line of training material.

Business Plan

North Coast recently opened its third training center in Cleveland and has plans to expand throughout the Midwest. North Coast has been very successful recently and is resisting the temptation to expand too fast. The company would like to focus on eLearning and publishing, but not lose focus on the ILT business.

Existing IT Environment: Network Diagram

Figure 3.7 shows North Coast Training's network diagram.

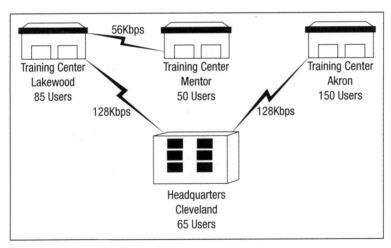

Figure 3.7   Network diagram.

Company Commentary

CIO: We have been growing faster than our IT department can handle. Our senior administrators spend too much time responding to help-desk issues. We need to better delegate control to junior administrators. My hope is to maintain the current senior administrators and hire more junior administrators.

Director of IT: We know the current leased lines are overtaxed and need upgrading. Until we get the funds for this upgrade, we've got to control traffic between locations. I'd like to see traffic reduced as much as possible.

Email Manager: Our slow links have caused us to abandon MAPI clients in Mentor. Mentor clients use POP3 to access the email servers. We're uncertain when the new links will be available, so I've been toying with the idea of using Outlook Web Access in Mentor.

Messaging System

North Coast upgraded from Exchange 5.0 to 5.5 just over a year ago. It has three Exchange Servers. There is a server in each site except Mentor. Mentor clients use POP3 to access the server in Lakewood. All other clients use Outlook 98 and MAPI. Because users transfer frequently from location to location, all three servers are in the same Exchange site, NCT. The organization name is North Coast Training.

Hardware

North Coast currently has three Exchange servers and three domain controllers (see Table 3.7). The IT department has determined that each Exchange Server should have at least 256MB of RAM. The Cleveland servers' RAM cannot be upgraded.

Table 3.7	Server configuration.			
Location	**Operating System**	**Service Pack**	**RAM**	**Function**
Cleveland	Windows NT 4 Server	SP5	128MB	Exchange
Cleveland	Windows NT 4 Server	SP6	256MB	PDC
Akron	Windows 2000 Server	SP1	384MB	Exchange
Akron	Windows NT 4	SP6	128MB	BDC
Lakewood	Windows 2000 Server	None	256MB	Exchange
Lakewood	Windows NT 4 Server	SP6	128MB	BDC

Exchange 2000 Requirements and Goals

North Coast would like to upgrade its Exchange environment to Exchange 2000. It would like to have a server in each location except Mentor. These servers should all be administrated by a single group of users in the IT staff. The current email system must be maintained during the upgrade.

Question 1

Before installing Exchange 2000, what is the first task that will need to be completed?

- ○ a.   Upgrade the Exchange server in Cleveland to Windows 2000.
- ○ b.   Upgrade the PDC in Cleveland to Windows 2000.
- ○ c.   Upgrade the Exchange server in Akron to Exchange 2000.
- ○ d.   Upgrade the BDC in Akron to Windows 2000.
- ○ e.   Upgrade the Exchange server in Lakewood to Exchange 2000.
- ○ f.   Upgrade the BDC in Lakewood to Windows 2000.

Answer b is correct. Exchange 2000 requires Active Directory. To upgrade the existing environment to Active Directory, the Windows NT 4 PDC should be upgraded to Windows 2000. This will migrate the NT 4 domain to Active Directory. Answer a is incorrect because this server cannot be upgraded to the 256MB RAM specified by IT for Exchange 2000. Answers c and e are incorrect because Exchange 2000 cannot be installed until Active Directory is in place. Answers d and f are incorrect because Windows NT 4 BDCs cannot be upgraded to Windows 2000 until the PDC is.

Question 2

> After the Exchange 2000 migration, the IT department will need access to Exchange from their desktops. They are currently running Windows NT 4 with Service Pack 4. What steps will they have to perform before they can manage Exchange 2000 from their desktops? Choose only the correct steps and place them in the correct order.
>
> Install Adminpak.msi
>
> Install Srvtools.msi
>
> Upgrade to Windows 2000 Professional
>
> Upgrade to Windows 2000 Server
>
> Install Exchange System Management Tools
>
> Install Exchange Messaging and Collaboration Tools
>
> Install Exchpak.msi

The correct answer is:

> Upgrade to Windows 2000 Professional
>
> Install Adminpak.msi
>
> Install Exchange System Management Tools

The users will need both the Exchange System Management Tools and the Windows 2000 Administrative Tools to administer Exchange 2000. Both these tools require Windows 2000, but do not specifically require Windows 2000 Server. Adminpak.msi is the Windows 2000 installer package for the Windows 2000 Administrative Tools.

Question 3

> The CIO is eager to convert the organization to native mode. When should North Coast's Exchange organization be switched from mixed mode to native mode?
>
> ○ a. After the first Exchange 2000 server is installed
>
> ○ b. After the last Exchange 2000 server is installed
>
> ○ c. After the Akron and Lakewood Exchange 5.5 servers are upgraded to Exchange 2000
>
> ○ d. When no pre-Exchange 2000 servers exist in the organization
>
> ○ e. When no pre-Windows 2000 servers exist in the forest

Answer d is correct. Exchange 2000 mixed mode supports both Exchange 2000 and pre-Exchange 2000 servers. An organization should be upgraded only when no pre-Exchange 2000 servers are present in the organization. Answers a, b, and c are incorrect because this is a guarantee that all pre-Exchange 2000 servers have been upgraded or decommissioned. Answer e is incorrect because pre-Windows 2000 servers refer to upgrading a Windows 2000 Active Directory domain to native mode.

Question 4

> How many routing groups should North Coast Training use in its design?
>
> ○ a. 0
>
> ○ b. 1
>
> ○ c. 2
>
> ○ d. 3
>
> ○ e. 4

Answer d is correct. The Director of IT specifically said, "I'd like to see traffic reduced as much as possible." By configuring a routing group for each location, traffic will be limited.

Question 5

How many administrative groups should North Coast Training use in its design?

- ○ a. 0
- ○ b. 1
- ○ c. 2
- ○ d. 3
- ○ e. 4

Answer b is correct. The Exchange 2000 Requirements and Goals state, "These servers should all be administrated by a single group of users in the IT staff." Using a single administrative group can facilitate this.

Question 6

You will be installing Exchange 2000 on a computer running Windows 2000 Server. Before installation, you would like to verify the Network News Transfer Protocol (NNTP) service has been installed. If you were to Telnet to the server from your workstation, which port should you Telnet to on the server?

- ○ a. 23
- ○ b. 25
- ○ c. 80
- ○ d. 110
- ○ e. 119

Answer e is correct. The NNTP uses port 119. Using Telnet to open port 119 will verify the NNTP service has been installed and is running on a Windows 2000 Server. Answer a is incorrect because port 23 is used for the Telnet service. Answer b is incorrect because port 25 is used for the Simple Mail Transfer Protocol (SMTP). Answer c is incorrect because port 80 is used for Hypertext Transfer Protocol (HTTP). Answer d is incorrect because port 110 is used for the Post Office Protocol version 3 (POP3).

Question 7

What is the minimum number of Global Catalog servers required by North Coast Training?

○ a. 0

○ b. 1

○ c. 2

○ d. 3

○ e. 4

Answer b is correct. A Global Catalog server is a domain controller that in addition to containing a full copy of its own domain partition, contains a partial copy of every other domain partition in the forest. Because this forest has a single domain, no Global Catalog servers are required for Windows 2000. However, Exchange 2000 requires at least one Global Catalog server. When Exchange 2000 starts, it queries DNS for the location of a Global Catalog server. If no Global Catalog servers are found, Exchange will not start. Answers a, c, d, and e are wrong because Exchange 2000 requires at least one Global Catalog server. While it is recommended to make all domain controllers in this design domain controllers, it is not required.

Need to Know More?

 Goncalves, Marcus. *Exchange 2000 Server Black Book.* The Coriolis Group, Scottsdale, AZ, 2000. ISBN 1-57610-641-1. Provides immediate solutions to the challenges of working with the most important features of Exchange 2000.

 Konkle, Joshua, Scott Schnoll, Michael Cooper, and David McAmis Schnoll. *Exchange 2000 Server: The Complete Reference.* McGraw-Hill Professional Publishing, 2000. ISBN 0072127392. This is a very good, very thick, everything-you-ever-wanted-to-know book. Great reference.

 Read *Microsoft Exchange 2000 Server Planning and Installation* located in the \Docs folder of the Exchange 2000 CD-ROM.

 Search **www.microsoft.com/technet** and the Windows 2000 Server Help file using the terms at the beginning of the chapter.

Planning for Exchange Administration

Terms you'll need to understand:

- ✓ Centralized administrative model
- ✓ Distributed administrative model
- ✓ Hybrid administrative model
- ✓ User management
- ✓ Server management
- ✓ Routing management
- ✓ Data management
- ✓ Exchange System Manager
- ✓ Microsoft Management Console (MMC)
- ✓ ADSI Edit
- ✓ Active Directory Tool
- ✓ Administrative groups
- ✓ Delegation of control
- ✓ Exchange Administration Delegation Wizard
- ✓ Exchange Administrator
- ✓ Exchange Full Administrator
- ✓ Exchange View Only Administrator
- ✓ Access control list (ACL)
- ✓ Address lists
- ✓ Filter rules
- ✓ All Address Lists
- ✓ Global Address Lists
- ✓ Offline Address Lists
- ✓ Recipient Update Service

Techniques you'll need to master:

- ✓ Categorizing a company into one of the administrative models
- ✓ Determining the number of administrative groups for an organization
- ✓ Determining when to create administrative groups for an organization
- ✓ Creating a delegation of control plan for Exchange System Manager and Active Directory Users and Computers
- ✓ Designing an address lists plan that includes address list membership, access, and management

Administration is a major factor in any Exchange 2000 deployment plan. This chapter will focus on designing such a plan based on an organization's administrative model. This model helps to determine administrative roles. You should have a clear understanding of the responsibilities of these roles.

Chapter 3 introduced administrative groups; this chapter will expand on that and discuss how to use security with these groups. This chapter will also talk in more detail about the administrative tools used to manage Exchange 2000. You will learn about address lists, including when and how they should be used. Finally, you will learn about policies. Policy planning will be one of the cornerstones of your administrative plan.

Administrative Models

As you start to construct your administrative plan, you need to analyze a company's *administrative model*. An administrative model describes how an organization's information services (IS) department is organized. More specifically, it answers who is responsible for what.

 You should be able to categorize a company in a case study into one of these administrative models: centralized, distributed, or hybrid.

Centralized Model

Many smaller companies have a *centralized administrative model*. In this model, a user, or centralized group of users, is responsible for all aspects of administration. With this model, there is no need to create additional administrative groups. Centralized administrative models are not limited to small companies; many medium to large companies are moving toward a centralized administrative model. This move by larger companies has been facilitated by the increase in bandwidth and remote administration capabilities. In a centralized administrative model, a single administrative group can contain all Exchange 2000 objects (see Figure 4.1).

This does not mean you cannot delegate control or that all administrators have access to every aspect of Exchange 2000. You can still use security to delegate control by assigning roles to users. The assignments, however, will be made over the entire organization.

Note: As you will see later in this chapter in the section titled "Delegating Administrative Control," you can delegate control over subsets of the organization even if you have a

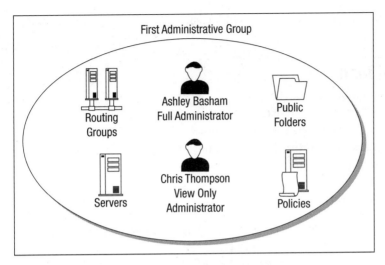

Figure 4.1   Example of a centralized administrative model.

single administrative group. This is more complicated than creating multiple administrative groups and delegating control to the administrative groups.

Distributed Model

As companies grow in size, centralized administration becomes more difficult. For many larger companies, it is most efficient to divide administration along geographic or organizational lines. Politics within the organization can be another reason for distributed administration, but this is strongly discouraged. With a *distributed administrative model*, multiple administrative groups can be created, and users or groups of users can be granted permission on these groups (see Figure 4.2). Although the creation of multiple administrative groups is not

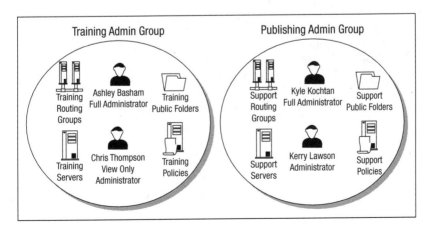

Figure 4.2   Example of a distributed administrative model.

specifically required, it will more easily facilitate the delegation of control to administrators.

Hybrid Model

Few organizations follow the centralized or distributed models exactly. Most companies require a combination of both models. In a *hybrid model*, a user or centralized group of users will have permissions to the entire organization, like the centralized model. In addition, administrative groups can be created and users can be granted permission to these administrative groups (see Figure 4.3).

 When a user or group is granted permission to an administrative group, the user or group has permissions to all objects in that administrative group. This inheritance is configured by default and can be modified. Permissions and inheritance are discussed in more detail in the section titled "Delegating Administrative Control."

There are many scenarios where administration can also be divided by specific areas in Exchange 2000. For example, an organization may have users responsible for policies and routing groups. They could still have users with permissions over the individual servers. Figure 4.4 shows an example of an organization with three administrative groups. Leah has permission over the entire organization, including all objects in all administrative groups. Jim and Kent have permissions over routing groups and policies for the entire organization, but do not have

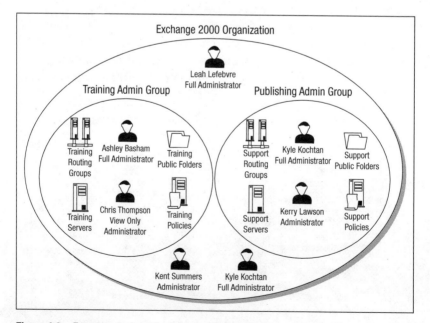

Figure 4.3 Example of a hybrid administrative model.

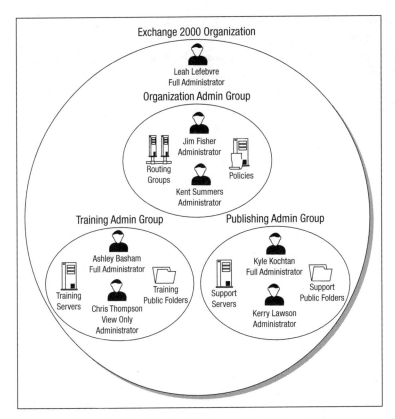

Figure 4.4   Example of a hybrid administrative model with three administrative groups.

permissions over the objects in the Training Admin Group or the Publishing Admin Group administrative groups.

When Exchange 2000 is in mixed mode, servers must belong to a routing group that is also a member of the same administrative group. When Exchange 2000 is in native mode, a server can belong to a routing group that belongs to a different administrative group. The Exchange organization in the example in Figure 4.4 would have to be in native mode.

Administrative Roles

After Exchange 2000 is deployed, users will handle the day-to-day operations. Depending on the size of the organization and the number of administrators, each user will play one or more administrative roles:

➤ *User management*—The user or users assigned to this role will be responsible for user/mailbox creation and maintenance. With previous versions of Exchange, this task may or may not have been performed by the same administrator responsible for Windows user management. Because Exchange 2000 mailboxes are now fully integrated with the same user or group of users, the same users or group of users will typically handle Exchange 2000 user management and Windows 2000 user management. As with Windows 2000 user management, it may be necessary to have certain administrators manage certain users. Organizational units should be created in Windows 2000 Active Directory. Then permission to administer certain users can be delegated for those organizational units. Users who have been delegated administrative control over an organizational unit will have administrative permissions to the users in that organizational unit.

➤ *Server management*—Server management typically entails management of policies and settings relating to the physical server. To give a user permission to manage a server, you must delegate control to an administrative group containing the server or servers you would like them to manage. Server managers typically use the Exchange System Manager Tool. This tool allows them to configure and monitor the servers.

Note: Exchange settings are stored in the Active Directory. Exchange Server Manager will need to contact a domain controller to run.

➤ *Routing management*—Router managers are responsible for message flow between servers in the organization. In previous versions of Exchange, sites controlled server management and routing. Because Exchange 2000 in mixed mode must support pre-Exchange 2000 servers, users who have been delegated control over an administrative group have permissions to both server management and routing. Once pre-Exchange 2000 servers are eliminated from the organization, Exchange 2000 can be switched to native mode. Once in native mode, routing groups can contain servers from several different administrative groups. In native mode, you can truly have separate users controlling routing.

➤ *Data management*—A data manager is responsible for the Exchange 2000 public and private stores. The public stores hold public folders and the private stores will hold the mailboxes. In a large organization, multiple public folder hierarchies and multiple private stores may be created. It is possible to delegate control to each of these stores. A data manager may also be responsible for data backup and recovery.

➤ *Real-time collaboration management*—A real-time collaboration manager is responsible for Instant Messaging and Chat. These services enable users to communicate instantly via Exchange. It is important for the user managing these services to have access to the network infrastructure for monitoring of network traffic.

Note: These roles are very high level. Many larger organizations further subdivide these roles into more specific roles. Also, many small organizations have a single user or small group of users who are assigned all these roles.

Administrative Tools

Whether a single administrator is playing all administrative roles or multiple groups are dividing the tasks, Exchange 2000 and Windows 2000 Management tools are required. This section will explain these tools in detail. Although most organizations will use these tools, Microsoft has also opened the door for organizations to write their own custom tools.

Exchange System Manager

The Exchange System Manager is the primary tool for managing Exchange 2000. This tool enables administrators to administer most aspects of Exchange 2000. This tool can be used to manage and monitor the following:

➤ Global Instant Messaging settings

➤ Global message delivery settings

➤ Recipient policies

➤ Address Lists

➤ Global Address Lists

➤ Offline Address Lists

➤ Administrative groups

➤ Servers

➤ Protocols

➤ Storage groups

➤ System policies

➤ Routing groups

➤ Chat

➤ Instant Messaging

➤ Public folders

➤ Message tracking

Exchange 2000 stores configuration information in the Configuration partition of Active Directory, and the Configuration partition is replicated to all domain controllers in the entire forest. Because the Exchange 2000 configuration is available on all domain controllers in the forest, Exchange System Manager does not have to contact a domain controller in its own domain, just one in its own forest.

Note: When the Exchange System Manager is launched, it will contact a DNS server and attempt to connect to a domain controller in its own subnet. If one is not available in its own subnet, it will try to find one in its own site. If one is not available in its own site, it will try other sites until it finds one.

The Exchange System Manager is a *Microsoft Management Console (MMC)* snap-in. When the Exchange System Manager snap-in is added to an MMC (see Figure 4.5), the user can choose which domain controller to connect to (see Figure 4.6).

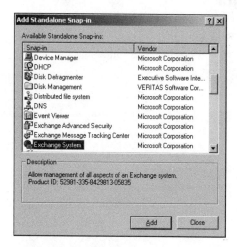

Figure 4.5   Exchange System Manager snap-in.

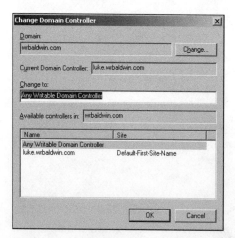

Figure 4.6   Change Domain Controller dialog box.

Active Directory Users and Computers

One major function *not* performed by Exchange System Manager is user and mailbox management. Exchange System Manager can manage recipient policies, but Active Directory Users and Computers handles creation of recipients such as users, contacts, and groups. Active Directory Users and Computers is the primary Windows 2000 tool used for user management and is extended for use with Exchange 2000.

Advanced Configuration Tools

Although Exchange System Manager and Active Directory Users and Computers can perform most system and recipient management, administrators often have to use more advanced tools. These tools are less refined and more complicated than Exchange System Manager and Active Directory Users and Computers. These tools can also cause damage to the system if not used properly.

➤ *ADSI Edit*—ADSI Edit is used to edit the Active Directory at a lower level than standard tools. Active Directory objects can be managed directly using ADSI Edit. ADSI Edit is not installed by default. The ADSI Edit snap-in is part of the Windows 2000 Support Tools. Among other tasks it can perform, ADSI Edit can, for example, change the way the Active Directory Display Name is generated. The name is typically arranged with the first name followed by the last name. Many companies want the last name to precede the first name. As you can see in Figure 4.7, ADSI Edit is quite extensive and finding settings like this are difficult.

➤ *Active Directory Tool*—The Active Directory Tool is one of the few tools that is not an MMC snap-in. This tool (ldp.exe) is installed as part of the Windows 2000 Support Tools. The Active Directory Tool is a basic LDAP client used to run LDAP queries against the Active Directory. Like ADSI Edit, the Active Directory Tool allows you to directly manipulate Active Directory objects.

Custom Consoles

The MMC supports the creation of custom consoles. It is often useful to give administrators a management console with only the containers and objects they need to use. Giving a user a subset of the Exchange System Manager discourages him from poking around where he doesn't belong. These simplified tools can also take the confusion out of administration. Figure 4.8 shows a custom Exchange Management Console that contains only the Routing Groups container. A routing manager could use this console.

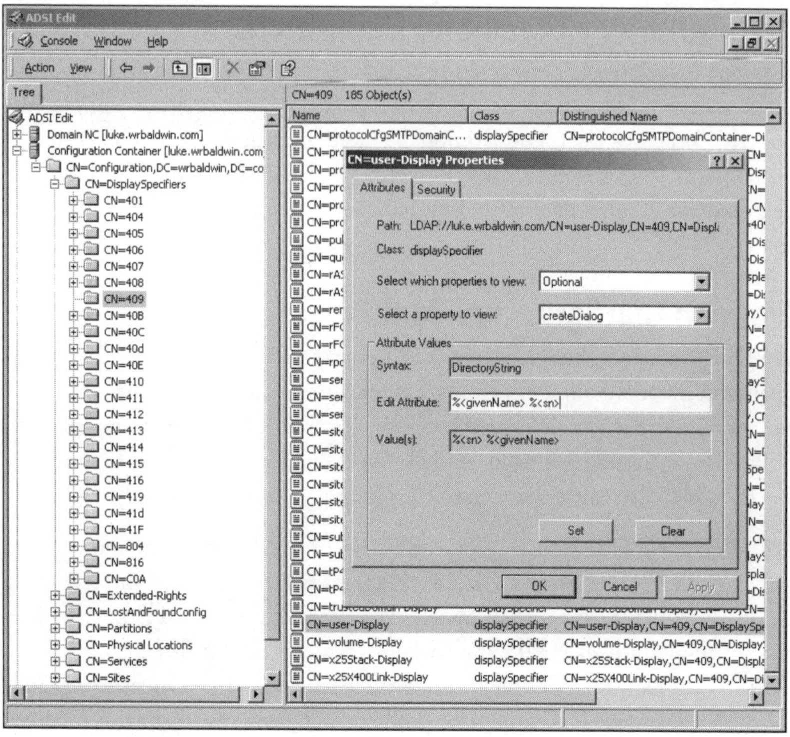

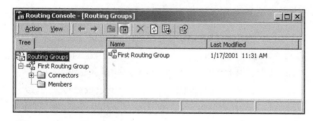

Figure 4.7 ADSI Edit.

Figure 4.8 Custom MMC console.

Administrative Groups

Although administrative groups can be used for organizing servers, their main purpose is delegation of control. Delegating control in Exchange 2000 begins with creating administrative groups. Each Exchange 2000 server belongs to one, and only one, administrative group. Users can be delegated control over one or more of these groups. A user with permissions to an administrative group will have permissions to the servers in that group. Exchange 2000 administrative groups are similar to pre-Exchange 2000 sites.

How Many Administrative Groups Should You Create?

Your administrative plan must include the number of administrative groups that will be created. Additional groups allow for more granularity; however, this will add complexity. The administrative model primarily influences the number of administrative groups.

When Should You Create Administrative Groups?

An important and often overlooked design issue involves deciding at what point you should create administrative groups. It is common to assume that the groups should be created just after the first server is installed. Although this can be acceptable, depending on the design, it may be beneficial to install administrative groups before the first Exchange 2000 server is even installed.

For a new Exchange 2000 installation, the first server in the organization becomes a member of the First Administrative Group. Servers cannot be moved between administrative groups and administrative groups can be renamed. Because the First Administrative Group cannot be renamed using the Exchange System Manager (administrative groups can be renamed using ADSI Edit), creating an administrative group prior to the installation of the first server in the organization may be a requirement for some new Exchange 2000 installations.

 To configure administrative groups prior to Exchange 2000 installation, run ForestPrep, then install the Exchange System Management Tools only. You can then use Exchange System Manager to create administrative groups.

When an Exchange 2000 server joins a pre-Exchange 2000 organization, there are two choices. It can either join a site from the pre-Exchange 2000 organization, or a new administrative group can be created using the method described above. When a pre-Exchange 2000 server is upgraded to Exchange 2000, it remains a member of its pre-Exchange 2000 site.

 Remember: Exchange 2000 in mixed mode sees pre-Exchange 2000 sites as administrative groups.

Delegating Administrative Control

Now that administrative groups have been created, it's time to use them by delegating control. Delegating control can be accomplished using two methods. The first method is easier, but limiting. The second method is more complicated but also more flexible.

Delegation Wizard and Roles

The *Exchange Administration Delegation Wizard* should not be confused with the Windows 2000 Delegation of Control wizard. Although both tools are used for delegating control, the Exchange tool accomplishes the task by assigning roles to users or groups. The Windows tool assigns permissions for objects to users or groups.

The Exchange Administration Delegation Wizard assigns one of three roles to a user or a group. The user or group that is assigned the role has the permissions associated with that role for all objects in the administrative group. The Exchange Administration Delegation Wizard can also be run on the organization (see Figure 4.9).

Delegating control at the organization level gives that user or group permission on the entire organization. The Exchange Delegation Wizard can assign the following roles:

➤ *Exchange Administrator*—Allows user or group to Full Administrator Exchange System information.

➤ *Exchange Full Administrator*—Allows user or group to Full Administrator Exchange System information and modify permissions.

➤ *Exchange View Only Administrator*—Allows user or group to Exchange System information.

Note: When you delegate control of an administrative group to a user or group, you must also assign that user or group as Exchange View Only Administrator of the organization. This will allow the user or group to drill down to the administrative group they have control over.

Figure 4.9   Delegate Control (Exchange Organization).

Advanced Security

Although the Exchange Administration Delegation Wizard is useful, it is far too limiting for configuring advanced security. The Exchange System Manager uses the same security model as Active Directory Users and Computers and therefore supports the use of a Security tab. The Security tab is on the Property page for most objects and containers in the Exchange System Manager. By default, the Security tab is hidden.

 To unhide the Security tab in the Exchange System Manager, add the DWORD value of ShowSecurityPage to the HKEY_CURRENT_USER\ Software\Microsoft\Exchange\EXAdmin key. The Value data should be set to 1.

Exchange 2000 advanced security can be used to delegate control for specific tasks such as sending and/or receiving email as a different user, creating routing groups, and creating public folders. Whereas most permissions can be modified using the Exchange System Manager, ADSI Edit has a slightly more extensive list of permissions. Using ADSI Edit is a bit more complicated, but an actual view of the permissions is given. For example, if you look at the *access control list (ACL)* for the top container in the Exchange System Manager, you'll see permissions have been inherited from a higher level (see Figure 4.10).

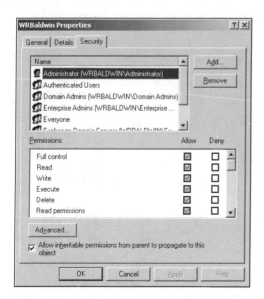

Figure 4.10   Access control list for WRBaldwin organization.

If the Exchange organization container is the top level, where did these permissions come from? Using ADSI Edit, you can see the WRBaldwin organization is a container, which is under the Microsoft Exchange container, which is under the Services container, which is in the Configuration partition of Active Directory (see Figure 4.11). Some permissions assigned to the WRBaldwin container were inherited from each of the parent containers.

Delegating Control over Recipients

Because recipients (users, contacts, and groups) are created using Active Directory Users and Computers, delegation of control is also performed with this tool. Like the Exchange System Manager, Active Directory Users and Computers has a wizard for delegation (see Figure 4.12).

Active Directory Users and Computers also has the Security tab hidden. Unlike the Exchange System Manager, you do not have to use the registry to unhide the Security tab. Selecting Advanced Options from the View menu will reveal the tab on the Property page of most objects and containers.

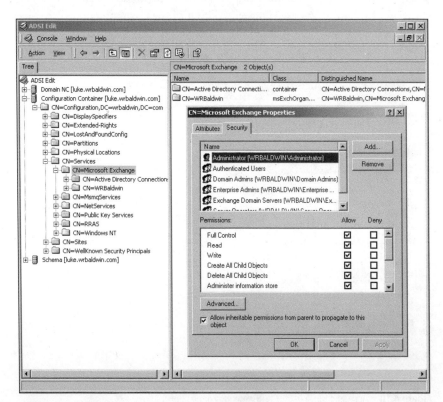

Figure 4.11 ADSI Edit.

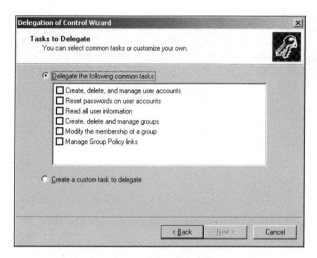

Figure 4.12 Active Directory Users and Computers Delegation of Control Wizard.

Note: When developing an administration design, it is important to consider the impact of delegation of control in Active Directory Users and Computer. Security setting here will have an impact on more than just Exchange recipients.

Address Lists

Exchange 2000 recipients can include Active Directory objects such as users, groups, and contacts. When an Exchange user sends email to a recipient, she can use one of many address lists to find the recipient. Address lists are defined and managed using the Exchange System Manager. A proper Exchange 2000 design does not only include the address lists needed (if any), but also which users can see the address lists. An administration plan should include the user or group of users responsible for managing the lists. Address lists are located under the Recipients container in the Exchange System Manager. The Exchange System Manager does not allow for delegation of control to the Recipients container; however, you can delegate control to the containers under the Recipients container. You can also use ADSI Edit to assign permission to the cn=Address Lists container. This container does not appear in the Exchange System Manager, but contains all address lists located in the Recipients container (see Figure 4.13).

Filter Rules

An *address list* is a list of Exchange 2000 recipients who meet the defined criteria of a set of filter rules. These rules include:

➤ *Type of Object*—Includes Users, Computers, Groups, Computers, Printers, Exchange Recipients and more. You can also choose to enter an LDAP query directly.

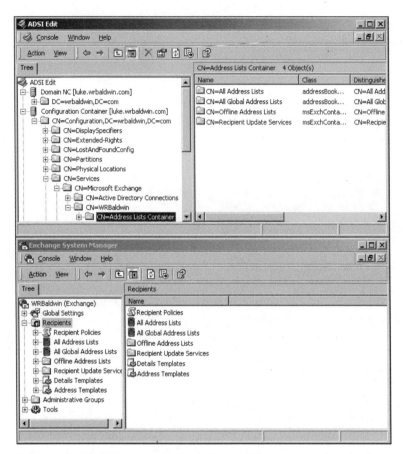

Figure 4.13 ADSI Edit address lists container versus Exchange System Manager Recipients container.

➤ *Type of Recipient*—Includes mailbox-enabled users, users, groups, contacts, and/or folders.

➤ *Storage*—Includes mailboxes on this server, any server, and/or mailboxes in a particular mailbox store.

➤ *Advanced*—Allows the user to define query type conditions on any recipient attribute. For example, ZIP code starts with 44 and county is equal to Lake.

Controlling Access to Address Lists

By default, members of the Authenticated Users group have permission to open All Address Lists. Using the Security tab, the Open Address List permission can be allowed or denied. Using security, you can control who has permission to see and use the address lists. Your administrative plan may include address lists and who can see them. More importantly, though, the plan should include who is responsible for creating and managing address lists.

All Address Lists

By default, the *All Address Lists* and the *Global Address Lists* containers are the only top-level address lists. The Exchange System Manager will only allow the creation of address lists below these lists. The Address List container cannot be renamed using the Exchange System Manager.

 Using ADSI Edit, you can rename and even delete the All Address Lists container. ADSI Edit can also create new top-level address lists.

Default Address Lists

Within the All Address Lists container, there are four default address lists. Although the filter lists of these address lists cannot be edited, you can delete or rename these lists. You can also nest lists within these lists:

➤ All Contacts

➤ All Groups

➤ All Users

➤ Public Folders

Custom Address Lists

Custom address lists can be created to meet more specific needs that may be present in the design. These lists are defined by the filter rules and are displayed to users just as default address lists are (see Figure 4.14)

Global Address Lists

Global Address Lists are similar to default and custom address lists. They are created using the same filter rules and can be created using the Exchange System Manager or ADSI Edit. Unlike default and custom lists, each Exchange user only sees one Global Address List. If users have access to multiple Global Address Lists, the users see the Global Address List of which they are members. If they have access and are a member of multiple Global Address Lists, they will see the largest Global Address List.

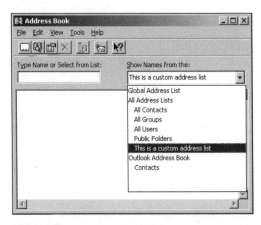

Figure 4.14 Custom address list.

Offline Address Lists

Users who need to send email while not connected to the Exchange server use Offline Address Lists. By default, the Default *Offline Address Lists* is created. This Offline Address Lists is the offline version of the Default Global Address Lists. The Default Offline Address Lists can be modified, renamed, or deleted. Additional Offline Address Lists can be created. An Offline Address Lists can contain one or more address lists (including default, custom, and/or Global Address Lists). Using security, access to individual Offline Address Lists can be controlled.

Recipient Update Service

In a large organization with many recipients, updating address lists can be time-consuming. The *Recipient Update Service* is responsible for creating and maintaining address lists. Settings for this service can be configured using the Exchange System Manager.

Note: The Recipient Update Service is a child of the cn=All Address Lists container in ADSI Edit. If users are delegated control to the cn=All Address Lists container using ADSI Edit, they will also have control over the Recipient Update Service.

Policies

Exchange 2000 uses policies to configure settings on mailbox stores, public stores, servers, and recipients. These policies can be defined once, then applied to many objects.

Recipient Policies

Recipient policies are applied to recipients to generate email addresses. These policies can be defined with filter rules similar to address lists. Using these policies, administrators can have different email addresses generated for different groups of recipients without having to modify each recipient.

System Policies

System policies are much more extensive than recipient policies. System policies can be configured with the settings of the Property pages of the object they apply to. These settings will override settings configured directly on the object. A system policy can be defined to apply settings for one or more tab in the Property page of that object. Table 4.1 show the tabs for the different objects.

 Whereas multiple policies can apply to the same object, an object can have only one policy tab apply to it at a time. This is an important consideration in case studies referring to policies.

The System Policy container belongs to an administrative group and therefore is managed by the administrator of that group. The policy applies to objects that are members of it (the policy itself is a container). You can add like objects from any administrative group to a policy. For example, an administrative group called PolicyAG could contain a server system policy name, MyServerPol. MyServerPol can contain only servers, and could contain LUKE, a server from the First Administrative Group administrative group (see Figure 4.15). Also notice that the System Policy container in the First Administrative Group has been deleted.

Table 4.1 System policies.	
Policy Type	**Tabs**
Server	General
Mailbox Store	General
	Database
	Limits
	Full-Text Indexing
Public Store	General
	Database
	Replication
	Limits
	Full-Text Indexing

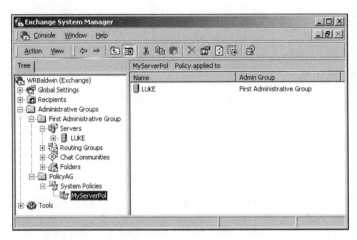

Figure 4.15   Server system policy.

Practice Questions

Case Study

New Windows for All has installed a new Exchange 2000 system and has asked you to assist with the design of an administrative plan. You will also be consulting a subsidiary, who is upgrading a pre-Exchange 2000 system.

Company Profile

New Windows for All is a manufacturer of replacement windows and doors. Their corporate headquarters is in Dunwoody, GA.

Business Plan

New Windows for All is in the process of automating several of their business practices. Until recently, very few of the two thousand employees had computers; most used dumb terminals connected to an aging minicomputer system.

Company Commentary

CEO: We have three manufacturing plants; two of these also house our Eest Coast and East Coast sales offices. While we've giving everyone an email account, not everyone has his or her own computer. Many employees on the manufacturing floors share computers and use Outlook Web Access for email.

Director of IT: We keep the windows and door sections separate and have different IT staff for each. This stems from the merger of the window company and the door company five years ago.

Other Businesses

Doorknobs for All is a subsidiary of New Windows for All. They have their own Windows 2000 forest and Exchange 5.5. They will be upgrading to Exchange 2000 soon. They have three locations—Cleveland, Chicago, and Detroit. Each location has its own Active Directory and pre-Exchange 2000 site. Their IS department consists of two people (one in Chicago and one in Detroit). Both are responsible for all aspects of the network.

Active Directory

An Active Directory domain **newwindowsforall.to** was recently created. All locations have two domain controllers and both domain controllers are also DNS and Global Catalog servers.

Exchange 2000

New Windows for All has two administrative groups, WindowsAG and DoorsAG.

Question 1

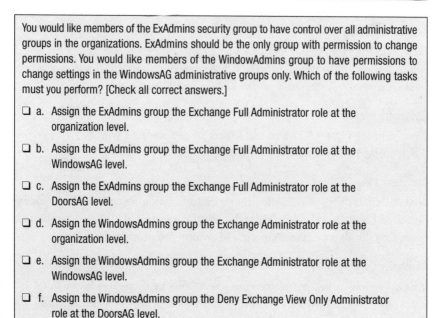

You would like members of the ExAdmins security group to have control over all administrative groups in the organizations. ExAdmins should be the only group with permission to change permissions. You would like members of the WindowAdmins group to have permissions to change settings in the WindowsAG administrative groups only. Which of the following tasks must you perform? [Check all correct answers.]

❑ a. Assign the ExAdmins group the Exchange Full Administrator role at the organization level.

❑ b. Assign the ExAdmins group the Exchange Full Administrator role at the WindowsAG level.

❑ c. Assign the ExAdmins group the Exchange Full Administrator role at the DoorsAG level.

❑ d. Assign the WindowsAdmins group the Exchange Administrator role at the organization level.

❑ e. Assign the WindowsAdmins group the Exchange Administrator role at the WindowsAG level.

❑ f. Assign the WindowsAdmins group the Deny Exchange View Only Administrator role at the DoorsAG level.

❑ g. Assign the WindowsAdmins group the Exchange View Only Administrator role at the organization level.

Answers a, e, and g are correct. The Exchange Full Administrator role will give ExAdmins full control over the entire organization. The WindowsAdmins will need at least Exchange View Only Administrator on the organization and Exchange Administrator on the WindowsAG administrative group. Answers b and c are incorrect because the ExAdmins role from the organization will be inherited from the organization to all administrative groups. Answer d is incorrect because the WindowsAdmins only need read access on the organization. Answer f is incorrect because there is no deny role. It would be wise to deny the WindowsAdmins group the read permission for the DoorsAG administrative group, but this was not an option.

Question 2

> You are creating a design for Doorknobs for All. How many administrative groups would you create in this design?
>
> ○ a. 0
>
> ○ b. 1
>
> ○ c. 2
>
> ○ d. 3
>
> ○ e. 6

The correct answer is b. Answers a, c, d, and e are incorrect. Because the same group of people will be responsible for all aspects of administration, there is no need for additional administrative groups.

Question 3

> If Doorknobs for All wanted to install the first Exchange 2000 in the Cleveland site, what must they do before installing the server?
>
> ○ a. Run ForestPrep and create a Cleveland administrative group.
>
> ○ b. Run DomainPrep and create a Cleveland administrative group.
>
> ○ c. Upgrade a server in the LA site to Exchange 2000.
>
> ○ d. Nothing.
>
> ○ e. None of the above.

The correct answer is d. When an Exchange 2000 server joins an existing pre-Exchange 2000 organization, it will see the pre-Exchange 2000 site as administrative groups. Answers a and b are incorrect, because ForestPrep and DomainPrep can be run during the Exchange 2000 installation. Answer c is incorrect, because it is not necessary for a pre-Exchange 2000 server to upgrade to Exchange 2000. Answer e is incorrect, because answer d is correct.

Question 4

Windows for All is considering delegating Exchange 2000 control to certain senior HelpDesk users. Which of the following are valid Exchange delegation roles?

○ a. Exchange Enterprise Administrator

○ b. Exchange Domain Administrator

○ c. Exchange Read Only Administrator

○ d. Exchange Administrator

○ e. Full Administrator

The correct answer is d. Assigning the Exchange Administrator to a user or group allows them to fully administrator Exchange system information. Exchange Administrators cannot change permissions. Answers a and b are incorrect, because Exchange Enterprise Administrator and Exchange Domain Administrator are not valid roles. Answer c is incorrect, because Exchange View Only Administrator is the valid role. Answer e is incorrect, because Exchange Full Administrator is the valid role.

Question 5

When designing an administrative plan for New Windows for All, which of the following factors is most important?

○ a. Size of organization

○ b. Number of locations

○ c. Administrative model

○ d. Current messaging system

○ e. Size of support staff

The correct answer is c. An administrative plan is going to be based on a company's administrative model. Answers a, b, and e are incorrect, because size and span of an organization have little impact on an administrative plan. Answer d is incorrect, because regardless of what messaging system they are using now, the plan is based on what will be.

Question 6

> While designing your administrative plan for Doorknobs for All, you interview the email administrator. She is very unhappy with the current site organization. The current site plan is based on geographical locations and not administration. In your administrative plan, when should administrative groups be created?
>
> ○ a. Before ForestPrep and before the first Exchange 2000 server is installed.
>
> ○ b. After ForestPrep, but before the first Exchange 2000 server is installed.
>
> ○ c. After the Last Exchange 5.5 server is upgraded.
>
> ○ d. After the first Exchange 2000 server is installed.
>
> ○ e. During the installation of the first Exchange 2000 server.

The correct answer is b. If you do not want the first Exchange 2000 server to join an existing pre-Exchange 2000 site, you will need to create an administrative group before the first Exchange 2000 server is installed. Answer a is incorrect, because you will have to run ForestPrep before you can create administrative groups. You could create pre-Exchange 2000 sites with the same names as the administrative groups in your plan, but the question specifically asks about administrative groups. Answers c and d are incorrect, because you do not need to install Exchange 2000 or remove Exchange 5.5 to create administrative groups. Answer e is incorrect, because you cannot create an administrative group during the installation.

Question 7

> You would like to change the names of some of New Windows for All's administrative groups. Which tool or tools should you use? [Check all correct answers.]
>
> ❑ a. Active Directory Users and Computers
>
> ❑ b. Exchange System Manager
>
> ❑ c. Active Directory Schema
>
> ❑ d. ADSI Edit
>
> ❑ e. Active Directory Tool.

The correct answers are d and e. ADSI Edit and the Active Directory Tool allow you to directly modify the Active Directory. Answer a is incorrect, because Active

Directory Users and Computers is used for managing Active Directory objects, including Exchange-enabled ones. Active Directory Users and Computers, however, cannot manage administrative groups. Answer b is incorrect, because the Exchange System Manager cannot rename administrative groups. Answer c is incorrect, because Active Directory Schema is used to modify the structure of the Active Directory, not the content.

Need to Know More?

 Konkle, Joshua, Scott Schnoll, Michael Cooper, and David McAmis Schnoll. *Exchange 2000 Server: The Complete Reference.* McGraw-Hill Professional Publishing, 2000. ISBN 0072127392. This is a very good, very thick, everything-you-ever-wanted-to-know book. Great reference.

 Shannon, Michael. *MCSE Exchange 2000 Design Exam Prep.* The Coriolis Group, Scottsdale, AZ, 2001. ISBN 1-58880-026-1. This book is good as both a study guide and reference.

 Read Chapters 3 and 6 of the *Microsoft Exchange 2000 Server Planning and Installation* located in the \Docs folder of the Exchange 2000 CD-ROM.

 Search **www.mcpmag.com** for Exam 70-225 or Exchange 2000. *MCP Magazine* will have good information to help prepare for the exam.

 Search **www.Win2000mag.com** using the term "Exchange 2000" and the terms at the beginning of the chapter.

 Search **www.microsoft.com/technet** and the "Exchange 2000" Server Help file using the terms at the beginning of the chapter.

5

Designing a Fault Tolerant Data Storage Topology

Terms you'll need to understand:

✓ Store
✓ Mailbox store
✓ Public folder store
✓ Rich text database file
✓ Streaming database file
✓ Storage groups
✓ Transaction logs
✓ Checkpoint files
✓ Reserved logs
✓ Circular logging

✓ Extensible Storage Engine (ESE)
✓ Operation
✓ ACID transaction
✓ Single Instance Storage (SIS)
✓ Spindle
✓ RAID
✓ Full-text indexing
✓ Backup
✓ Verify
✓ Restore

Techniques you'll need to master:

✓ Designing a storage group topology
✓ Planning for placement of databases and logs
✓ Developing a disaster recovery plan

One of the fundamental services provided by Exchange 2000 is data storage. When planning for an Exchange 2000 deployment, it is important to design a fault tolerant data storage topology that will maintain data even in the event of hardware or software failure. This chapter will focus on how and where Exchange 2000 stores data, as well as how clients access data. A thorough understanding of these topics will help you to design a fault tolerant data storage topology.

Stores

Exchange 2000 data is maintained in *stores*, databases that can contain many different types of data. An Exchange 2000 server can have many stores. There are two types of stores: *mailbox stores* and *public folder stores*.

Mailbox Store

A mailbox store is used to store user data. Each user's data is stored in a mailbox on one and only one store. This mailbox will contain the folders a user would see in Outlook (see Figure 5.1). Mailbox stores exist on a single Exchange 2000 server and cannot be replicated.

Note: Exchange 2000 Server can only have a single mailbox store and this mailbox store is limited to 16GB. Exchange 2000 Enterprise Server supports multiple mailbox stores, and their sizes are limited only by hardware.

Public Folder Store

A public folder store is used to store public data. This data is saved in the store in public folders. Exchange 2000 Server and Enterprise Server support multiple public folder stores. Each public folder can be replicated to multiple public stores.

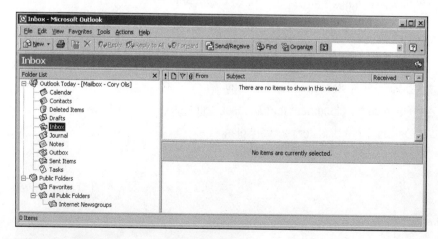

Figure 5.1 Mailbox, viewed with Microsoft Outlook.

By replicating public folders to multiple stores, fault tolerance and performance can be increased. Public folders are discussed in detail in Chapter 9.

Note: Each pre-Exchange 2000 server contains a single mailbox store. This store is called the private information store. Each pre-Exchange 2000 server contains a single public folder store. This store is called the public information store.

Database Files

Pre-Exchange 2000 servers have two stores each with a database file. The Priv.edb database file contains the private information store. The Pub.edb database file contains the public information store. Exchange 2000 stores have two database files each.

The *rich text database file* (.edb) contains the headers of all messages saved in the store. This database will store all data from messages stored using Microsoft Outlook and *Messaging Application Programming Interface (MAPI)*. MAPI is a standardized set of functions placed into a code library. MAPI is slowly being phased out in favor of standard messaging protocols like HTTP and IMAP4.

The *streaming database file* (.stm) contains the headers and data of all non-MAPI messages. This would include, but is not limited to, HTTP, NNTP, IMAP4, and POP3 messages. These messages are often formatted using *Messaging Internet Mail Extensions (MIME).*

 Don't be fooled on the test by thinking that all messages stored using Outlook use MAPI. Outlook uses MAPI to store data when the Microsoft Exchange Server service is used. Outlook can also be set up to use SMTP and POP3 or IMAP4 to access an Exchange Server. This function is similar to using Outlook Express. Outlook as a MAPI client stores messages in the rich text database. Outlook as a POP3 or IMAP4 client stores messages in the streaming database file.

Data in the Stores

MAPI and non-MAPI clients can access data in both database files. When a MAPI client needs to read email stored in the streaming database file, Exchange 2000 will convert the data in memory and pass the data to the MAPI client (see Figure 5.2). As long as the MAPI client does not change the data, the data will remain in the streaming database file. However, if the MAPI client changes and saves the data, the data is converted and stored in the rich text database file. A copy of the data will also remain in the streaming database so long as non-MAPI clients still have pointers to it.

Note: The process of converting, but not changing, data for clients in memory is referred to as on-demand, in-memory content conversion by Microsoft.

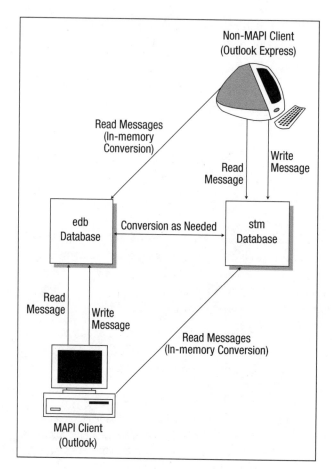

Figure 5.2 Data conversion process.

When a non-MAPI client needs to read email stored in the rich text database file, Exchange 2000 will convert the data in memory and pass the data to the non-MAPI client. As long as the non-MAPI client does not change the data, the data will remain in the rich text database file. However, if the non-MAPI client changes and saves the data, the data is converted and stored in the streaming database file. A copy of the data will also remain in the rich text database so long as MAPI clients still have pointers to it.

For the exam, it is important to remember that non-MAPI messages stored in the streaming database file always have their header information duplicated in the rich text database file. This information is provided to improve the performance when a MAPI client views the non-MAPI files in a list.

Designing a Store Topology

Because Exchange 2000 supports multiple stores, it is important to consider store design. For a design, you have to determine the number of stores each Exchange server will have; the number is affected by which users will reside in each store. Because stores can be backed up and restored individually, it may be wise to create many small stores. This way, in the event of a failure, the mailboxes from the most important store can be restored first. Also, the creation of multiple stores eases and often enables the separation of policies such as mailbox limit. Finally, using many stores increases load on the server. It is important to consider the effects of storage groups and transaction logs when determining how to design your store topology. The next section, "Storage Groups and Transaction Logs," will explain these topics.

Storage Groups and Transaction Logs

Exchange 2000 servers organize stores into storage groups. Each Exchange 2000 server can have a maximum of four storage groups. Each storage group can contain six stores. One store in each storage group is reserved for the system, so the maximum user-creatable store in a storage group is five. This gives a maximum of twenty stores per Exchange 2000 server.

For the exam, you may need to know the maximum number of stores per storage group and storage groups per server.

Transaction Logs

Exchange 2000 uses a transaction log-based database. Before data is written to the database, it is first written to transaction logs. After the data has been completely written to the transaction log, it is marked as committed. The data can then be written to the database when the database is idle. Transaction logs improve performance by preventing database writes from slowing database reads. Transaction logs also provide for a means of data recovery.

Exchange 2000 storage groups reduce the overhead of transaction logs. On pre-Exchange 2000 servers, each store contained its own set of transaction logs. With Exchange 2000, stores are grouped into storage groups. All stores in a storage group share a set of transaction logs. This can improve performance by allowing administrators to deploy multiple stores without the overhead of multiple transaction logs.

Log Files

All Exchange 2000 transaction logs are 5MB in size. The log for the first storage group is named E00.log. The log for the second storage group is named E01.log. This naming convention continues to increase by one with additional storage groups. After the Exx.log (where *xx* is 00, 01, 02, and so on) file becomes full, it is renamed and a new Exx.log file is created. The previous log files will add a sequential number to the log file name. For example, E02.log will be renamed to E0200001.log, and a new E02.log will be created. When the new E02.log is renamed, it will be called E0200002.log. See the example in Figure 5.3.

Note: Previous transaction logs will be deleted by the system and should not be manually deleted.

Log files can be used for automatic recovery of failed transactions during Exchange startup. When the Exchange service starts, any committed transaction in the logs, but not in the database, will be written to the database. This process is referred to as *rolling forward* transactions. Any uncommitted transaction in the logs will be deleted. This process is referred to as *rolling back* transactions. The Exchange service uses a *checkpoint file* (Exx.chk) to determine when committed

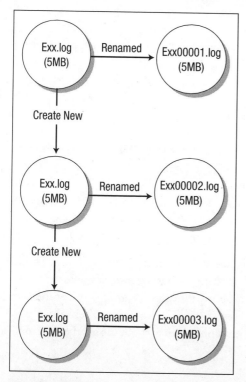

Figure 5.3 Example of a transaction log.

transactions in the logs have not been written to the database. The checkpoint file is a pointer to a position in a transaction log. If the checkpoint file is deleted, Exchange will check all committed transactions in all transaction logs to determine if they need to be written to the database. This process can be time-consuming.

A drive containing transaction logs running out of space would cause a serious problem for Exchange. To help prevent the loss of data, Exchange creates two empty 5MB *reserved logs* (res1.log and res2.log). If the drive containing the transaction logs for a storage group runs out of disk space, the reserved logs (starting with res2.log) are used to create a new transaction log. If these logs are needed, the Exchange service issues an event, writes all necessary transactions to the new log, and shuts down (see Figure 5.4).

Circular Logging

By default, previous transaction logs are deleted when a backup is performed. This is desirable for fault tolerance (see the section titled "Placement of Databases and Logs" later in this chapter for more information). Certain types of databases, however, do not require this level of fault tolerance. For example, a public folder used with the NNTP service could receive hundreds, even thousands, of messages per hour. The transaction logs for the storage group holding this store would grow at a tremendous rate. In a design where saving previous transaction logs is not a requirement, *circular logging* can be enabled for a storage group. With circular logging, Exchange will maintain a minimum number of transaction logs (at least four).

For the exam, you will need to know that circular logging is disabled by default and that Microsoft recommends enabling it only if recovery to the point of failure is not required in the design. It is also important to remember that this setting is performed on the storage group because the storage group not stores have transaction logs.

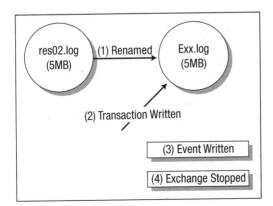

Figure 5.4   Drive containing transaction log runs out of space.

Designing a Storage Group Topology

Because Exchange 2000 supports multiple storage groups, it is important to consider storage group design. For a design, you have to determine the number of storage groups each Exchange server will have; this number is affected by which stores will reside in each storage group. Although stores can be backed up and restored individually, all stores in a storage group share the same transaction logs. To restore to the point of failure, the transaction logs will need to be restored.

In the example in Figure 5.5, there are two stores and one storage group. In this design, using a single set of transaction logs conserves resources. Although each store can be backed up and restored individually, the common logs will only be deleted after both stores are backed up.

In the example in Figure 5.6, there are two stores and two storage groups. In this design, additional resources will be needed to handle the second set of transaction logs. Each store and its own logs can be backed up and restored individually.

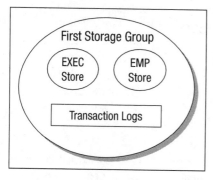

Figure 5.5   Single storage group with two stores.

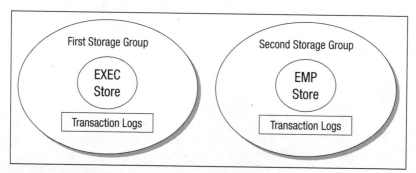

Figure 5.6   Two storage groups with one store in each.

Extensible Storage Engine

The *Extensible Storage Engine (ESE)* manages Microsoft Exchange 2000 stores. ESE is responsible for performing transactions on the databases. A transaction is a modification to the database. Each transaction is made up of several *operations*. An operation is a simple change to the database such as read, write, or delete.

Transactions performed by Exchange can be *atomic, consistent, isolated,* and *durable (ACID)*:

➤ *Atomic*—If one operation in the transaction fails, the entire transaction is scrapped. In other words, a transaction is not committed until all operations are complete. This prevents partial transactions from corrupting the database.

➤ *Consistent*—After each transaction, the database is left in a consistent state.

➤ *Isolated*—The transaction is not available until it is committed. Each operation in the transaction will not be visible in the database until the transaction is committed.

➤ *Durable*—Once a transaction has been committed, it cannot be lost with a system failure, because a committed transaction will exist in its entirety in the transaction log.

Single Instance Storage

In an effort to conserve database space, ESE uses *Single Instance Storage (SIS)* when storing messages in the same store. Duplicate messages in the same store are written to the database once. An example of this is a message sent to multiple recipients in the same store. Although the message appears in each recipient's mailbox, the unmodified message is stored once in the database. SIS works within a store, not a storage group. If a message is sent to recipients in multiple stores, the message is written to a database in each store once.

Note: If a recipient modifies and save a message, ESE creates a new copy of the message in the database.

Mounting and Dismounting Stores

When considering a store design, it is important to understand mounting and dismounting of stores. Each store, independent of its storage group, can be taken offline (dismounted). Offline maintenance can be performed on the offline store without affecting other stores on the server, or even stores in the same storage group. Once maintenance on the store has been completed, the store can be brought back online (mounted).

Placement of Databases and Logs

One of the most import design considerations when planning a fault tolerant data topology is the placement of database files and transaction logs. The design decisions made in this section will affect not only data recovery, but also system performance.

Performance

Transaction logs are only read during recovery. Transactions are processed in memory, written from memory to the logs, committed, and then written from memory to the database files when they are idle (see Figure 5.7).

Transaction logs are written sequentially to speed up performance. This means that each transaction is essentially added to the disk space just after the previous one. This sequential writing can be performed very quickly only if no other disk activity is occurring on the same physical disk *spindle*.

Note: A spindle refers to a physical disk, not a disk partition.

For example, placing transaction logs on their own partition of a spindle that also contains the system partition would have very little benefit over having the transaction logs on the system partition. Not only should the transaction logs be placed on their own spindle, but the transaction log for each storage group should be placed on the transaction log's own respective spindle. This will provide maximum performance for the transaction logs.

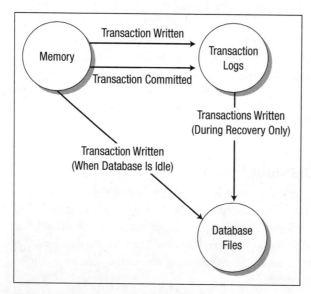

Figure 5.7   Data flow to logs and databases.

Microsoft recommends placing database files on their own spindle as well. Although placing each store's database files on its own spindle will increase performance, it is not as important as separating the transaction logs. Database files are both read and written to using random access.

Data Recovery

Data recovery is another important consideration when designing for placement of databases and logs. Because previous transaction logs are maintained until the storage group is backed up, they can be used to recover a database in the event of a failure. Figure 5.8 shows a single storage group with a single store.

Assume the storage group was last backed up on Friday. If the spindle holding the database fails on Tuesday, the database spindle can be replaced, and the database can be restored to its Friday state. Because the transaction logs are on a different spindle, they were not lost and can be used to roll the database forward to the point of failure. In the same example, if the transaction log spindle fails, no restoration would be needed. Transactions not yet written to the database will still be in memory. After all transactions in memory have been flushed, the transaction log spindle can be replaced, and Exchange will create a new transaction log.

 For the exam, you may be asked to create a design that will recover to the point of failure with any single spindle failure. As long as the database files and transaction logs are on different spindles and a full backup of the database exists, recovery to the point of failure is possible with any single spindle failure.

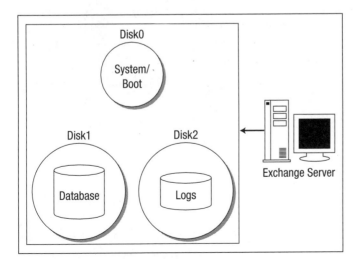

Figure 5.8   Single storage group and single store—database files and transaction logs on different spindles.

Hardware

When designing fault tolerance, the end of the line is the hardware. There are many different disk configurations that support fault tolerance. *Redundant array of inexpensive (or independent) disks (RAID)* is a series of fault tolerant disk specifications:

➤ *RAID 0*—Also known as *striping*, RAID 0 combines two or more disks into a single logical unit. RAID 0 provided great read and write performance but does not provide fault tolerance.

➤ *RAID 1*—Also known as *mirroring*, RAID 1 duplicates the entire contents of one drive to another. Because of this, the amount of usable disk space is half the total disk space. RAID 1 provides good read and write performance and provides fault tolerance in the event of any single spindle failure.

➤ *RAID 5*—Also known as *striping with parity*, RAID 5 combines three or more disks into a single logical unit. RAID 5 uses parity to provide redundancy, reducing usable disk space by the size of one of the drives. RAID 5 provides good read performance but writes are slowed by the overhead of writing parity. RAID 5 provides fault tolerance in the event of any single spindle failure.

➤ *RAID 10*—Also known as RAID 1 plus RAID 0, RAID 10 combines two or more disks into a single logical unit, then mirrors them to an equal number of disks. RAID 10 requires a minimum of four spindles and the amount of usable disk space is half the total disk space. RAID 10 provides excellent read and great write performance.

Because most designs are concerned with fault tolerance, using RAID 0 alone is rarely an option. Microsoft recommends using RAID 1 (mirroring) for system/ boot partitions and for transaction logs. They recommend using RAID 5 for databases. Figure 5.9 shows a typical example.

Note: Microsoft supports software RAID with Windows 2000, but whenever possible, hardware RAID should be used. Software RAID is much slower than hardware. When software RAID is used, the system and boot partitions can only be placed on a RAID 1 (mirror) array.

Full-Text Indexing

When databases get large, searching them for specific data can become time-consuming and resource-intensive. To help reduce search times on the database, Exchange supports full-text indexing. Exchange will index not only the messages and headers, but it will also index the text of certain attachments like Word documents and MIME messages. Although a full-text index will reduce the time it

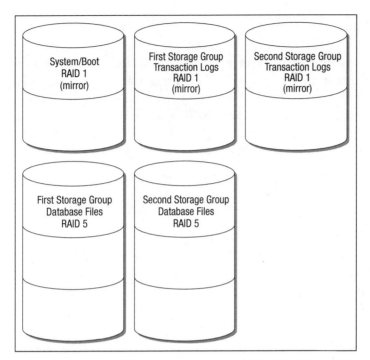

Figure 5.9   Example of disk configuration.

takes to search, there are some disadvantages. Creating and updating indexes can consume additional resources. Indexes will increase the disk space used by about 20 percent. Finally, if indexes are not updated, they can become out of date and user searches will be inaccurate.

Note: Full-text indexes are enabled on a per-store basis.

Backing Up and Restoring Data

Because much of the planning for fault tolerant data revolves around recovery, creating a backup plan is of the utmost importance. The tools used to back up are not as important as the procedures used to back up, verify, and restore.

Backup

As discussed earlier in this chapter in the section called "Data Recovery," placing databases and logs on separate spindles will enable recovery to the point of failure. An important part of this design is the backing up of the databases. Exchange 2000 stores can be backed up while online. This prevents disruption of email service during backup. Each store can be backed up individually or all stores in a storage group can be backed up.

Note: To back up the transaction logs for a storage group, the entire storage group must be backed up.

The amount of time needed to restore data may have an impact on the number and sizes of your stores. For example, assume the design calls for a minimum down time of 90 minutes after a single failure and restoration to the point of failure. If it takes one minute to restore 50MB of data, the maximum store size should be set at 4.5GB. The design should also separate logs and database files and not allow database files from different stores to share the same spindle.

Note: Some backup programs allow individual mailboxes to be backed up and restored. This is referred to as a brick-level backup. Brick-level backups can consume additional resources and take additional time. The Backup utility included with Windows 2000 does not support brick-level backups.

When designing a backup strategy, it is important to understand the different types of backups. When backing up a single store, the storage group transaction logs are never deleted (see Table 5.1).

An advantage of multiple stores in a storage group is the ability to back up and restore individual stores without backing up the entire storage group. Microsoft, however, recommends backing up the entire storage group as a single unit. Because the transaction logs will only be deleted when the storage group is backed up (see Table 5.2), having different backup routines for each store in a storage group may cause unexpected results.

Note: When transaction logs are deleted by Exchange, only logs where all transactions have been written to the databases are deleted.

Different backup types can be mixed to form a backup schedule or routine. Many organizations perform full backups daily. This can enable faster recovery times, because a single full backup will need to be restored in the event of a failure. A disadvantage of performing full backups is the time and space needed to perform a full backup. Assume a full backup of a server takes 12 hours. If a full backup

Table 5.1	Backup types (store backup).	
Type	**Description**	**Delete Transaction Logs?**
Full Backup	Backs up all the database files for the store and the transaction logs for the storage group	No
Copy Backup	Backs up all the database files for the store and the transaction logs for the storage group	No
Incremental	Backs up transaction logs that have changed since the last full or incremental backup	No
Differential	Backs up transaction logs that have changed since the last full backup	No

Table 5.2	Backup types (storage group backup).	
Type	Description	Delete Transaction Logs?
Full Backup	Backs up all the database files for all the stores in the storage group and the transaction logs for the storage group	Yes
Copy Backup	Backs up all the database files for all the stores in the storage group and the transaction logs for the storage group	No
Incremental	Backs up transaction logs that have changed since the last full or incremental backup	Yes
Differential	Backs up transaction logs that have changed since the last full backup	No

were performed every night, the system resources would be tasked for 50 percent of the time. This performance degradation is unacceptable for most organizations. The other end of the extreme is a full backup weekly and an incremental backup daily. This has the advantage of minimizing the time needed to perform daily backups. The disadvantage of an incremental backup is that it takes the last full backup and all incremental backups since the last full back to be restored in the event of a failure. A daily differential backup is a compromise between the two. Daily backups take longer than incremental backups, and as the time since the last full backup increases, the daily differential could approach the size of the full backup. The advantage of the differential over the incremental is in recovery. Only the last full backup and the last differential backup are needed to restore in the event of a failure. Table 5.3 illustrates the advantages and disadvantages of the three backup types.

Note: Depending on how much your data is changed, there could be little difference between the backup time of the different type of backups. For example, if you are performing a daily incremental backup and all your data is changed that day, the incremental backup would essentially be a full backup.

In addition to backing up the Exchange database, it is important to back up other components associated with Exchange. The Exchange 2000 configuration is stored in the Active Directory configuration partition. Because Active Directory configuration information is replicated to all domain controllers, it is usually not

Table 5.3	Advantages and disadvantages of backup types.	
Type	Advantage	Disadvantage
Full Daily Backup	Shortest restore time	Longest backup time
Incremental Daily Backup	Longest restore time	Shortest backup time
Differential Daily Backup	Average restore time	Average backup time

necessary to back up this information so long as multiple domain controllers exist. Exchange mailbox-enabled users are stored in the domain partition. Again, it is usually not necessary to back up this information so long as multiple domain controllers exist; however, for users, these must be multiple domain controllers in the same domain. Finally, Exchange uses Internet Information Services (IIS) for its protocols. It is important to make sure the IIS metabase is backed up as well. The IIS metabase is not part of Active Directory.

Note: When using the Backup utility included with Windows 2000, a Full backup is referred to as a Normal backup (see Figure 5.10).

Verify

After a backup program performs a backup, it may optionally verify the data. Depending on the data, verifying will occur in different ways. Exchange 2000 will verify that the data in the backup matches the data that was backed up. If the two do not match, an event will be logged. Although it is important for the backup program and Exchange to verify the data, this is not enough.

It is important to verify the backup logs on a regular basis. These logs will help ensure that no errors occurred during the backup and all data that was supposed to be backed up was. Many backup programs will alert an administrator in the event of failure. Even with an alert system in place, it is still important to manually check the backup logs regularly. If the alert system were to fail, this may be the only method of detection.

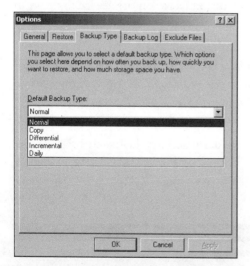

Figure 5.10   Windows 2000 Backup utility.

Your design should account for nontechnical failures. These include, but are not limited to, theft, natural disasters, and sabotage. It is important to maintain a certain number of backups offsite. Your design requirements will dictate how many backups you will need, and how often they should be rotated.

A final bit of verification is to perform a test restore. An administrator that realizes the backups don't work only after they need to be restored probably has lost his job. Although it may be impossible to perform a test restore on all backups, a sampling of the data restored to a test server can be enough to verify the backups are actually restorable.

Restore

A proper disaster recovery plan should be in place before it comes time to restore. A properly crafted plan can save valuable time when it comes time to restore. This plan should include everything needed to restore, such as location of backups and which backups are needed to be restored.

There are many different levels of restores, from a single message to an entire server. The procedures for each will vary greatly:

➤ *Restore a message*—Depending on how Exchange 2000 is configured, restoring a message can be either very easy or very difficult. If the *deleted item retention* has been enabled (it is disabled by default), messages are saved in Exchange for a period of time. The user can restore these messages. If the message was deleted and the deleted item retention has passed, the process is more difficult. A separate Exchange 2000 server will have to be set up off the network. If a brick-level backup is available, the user's mailbox should be restored; if not, the user's mailbox store must be restored. After the restoration, Outlook can be used to transfer the message to a personal store (.pst file).

➤ *Restore a mailbox*—This process is similar to restoring a message. If a brick-level backup is available, an individual mailbox can be restored to the live server. If a brick-level backup is not available, a separate Exchange 2000 server will have to be set up off the network, and the user's mailbox store must be restored. After the restoration, Outlook can be used to transfer the entire mailbox to a personal store (.pst file).

➤ *Restore a store*—If store exists on the server, it must first be taken offline (dismounted). After the restore, the store can be brought online (mounted). Other stores on the server should not be affected.

➤ *Restore a server*—In the event of a total server failure, Windows 2000 should be reinstalled. The server should join the domain and Exchange 2000 setup should be run. The setup program should be run in disaster recovery mode. A full restore of the server should be performed including Active Directory, IIS, and Exchange.

Note: When restoring a server, make sure the host system drive configuration is the same. Make sure not to join an existing site. After the full restore completes, perform Directory and Information store consistency adjustments and perform a full backup of the Exchange database to ensure the existence of a current archive.

Practice Questions

Case Study

Green Tractors, Inc., will be installing a new Exchange 2000 system.

Company Profile

Green Tractors, Inc., is a manufacturer of light-duty lawn and garden tractors. Their corporate headquarters is in Roswell, GA, 30 miles north of Atlanta. Green Tractors, Inc., has been in the tractor business for 80 years. Currently, business is neither shrinking nor growing; things have been pretty much the same for several years.

Business Plan

Green Tractors, Inc., is in the process of automating several of their business practices. Until recently, very few of the six thousand employees had computers; most used dumb terminals connected to an aging mainframe. There is still no corporate Internet access or email system in place. Green Tractors, Inc., is on a mission to modernize not only their office systems, but also their five manufacturing plants.

Existing Network Diagram

Figure 5.11 shows the network diagram for Green Tractors, Inc.

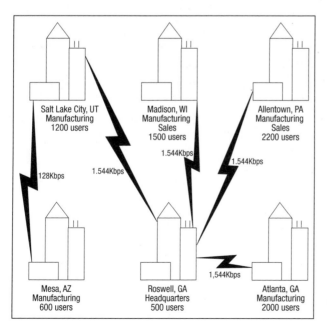

Figure 5.11   Network diagram.

Company Commentary

CIO: We have five manufacturing plants; two of these also house our West Coast and East Coast sales offices. Although we'll be giving everyone email accounts, not everyone will have his or her own computer. Many employees on the manufacturing floors will share computers and use Outlook Web Access for email.

Director of IT: The CIO has been on me about restore times. She would like me to provide the senior executives in Roswell and the managers at the other locations with the quickest restore time. All mailboxes should be backed up every night except those for the floor personnel; their mailboxes will be backed up only on the weekends.

Email Manager: I'll be in charge of assigning policies to groups of users. Users on the manufacturing floors will be restricted a maximum of 10MB for their mailboxes. Managers will need to be warned after their mailboxes reach 50MB and there are certain users at each location that should never be limited or warned. The five board members at Roswell will need to have their email as separate and secure at possible. Excessive usage by other users should never hamper their use.

Active Directory

A new Active Directory domain **greentractors.com** was recently created. All locations have two domain controllers and both domain controllers are also DNS and Global Catalog servers. A child domain, **rd.greentractors.com**, was created for the research and development department.

Hardware

There are two new servers per location, except Roswell, which will have only one. These servers will be used as Exchange servers. There are two server sizes: small and large. Large servers are quad processor machines with 4GB of RAM and ten 18GB hard drives. Small servers are dual processor machines with 2GB of RAM and ten 9GB hard drives. Table 5.4 show which locations have which servers. Both servers have hardware RAID controllers.

Table 5.4	Exchange servers at each location.	
Location	**Name**	**Server Size**
Roswell	ROSEX01	Small
Atlanta	ATLEX01	Large
Atlanta	ATLEX02	Large
Allentown	ALLEX01	Large
Allentown	ALLEX02	Large
Madison	MADEX01	Large
Madison	MADEX02	Small
Mesa	MESEX01	Small
Mesa	MESEX02	Small
Salt Lake City	SALEX01	Large
Salt Lake City	SALEX02	Small

Exchange 2000 Requirements and Goals

Green Tractors, Inc., would like to have a functional and efficient Exchange 2000 system. All systems should be able to recover to the point of failure from any single point of failure. Recovery time should be minimized whenever possible.

Question 1

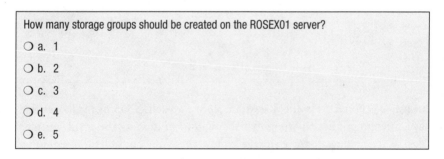

How many storage groups should be created on the ROSEX01 server?

○ a. 1

○ b. 2

○ c. 3

○ d. 4

○ e. 5

Answer b is correct. Because the executives should not have their performance limited by other users, they should have their own storage group. Answers a, c, d, and e are thus incorrect.

Question 2

How many storage groups should be created at the manufacturing sites that do not have sales offices?

○ a. 1

○ b. 2

○ c. 3

○ d. 4

○ e. 5

Answer c is correct. Because the managers should not have their performance limited by other users, they should have their own storage group. Also, because floor personnel will have their own backup routine, they should also have their own storage group. The third storage group will contain all other users. Answers a, b, d, and e are thus incorrect.

Question 3

How many stores should be created at the manufacturing sites that *do* have sales offices?

○ a. 1

○ b. 2

○ c. 3

○ d. 4

○ e. 5

Answer c is correct. Having a separate store for each group of mailboxes that have different policies will simplify policy administration for the email manager. Also, because there are three storage groups, there must be at least three stores. Answers a, b, d, and e are thus incorrect.

Question 4

You are designing the hard disk configuration for ALLEX01. This server will contain two storage groups, each with two stores. The servers disk have been configured as followed:

Drive C: (mirrored drive)

Drive D: (mirrored drive)

Drive E: (mirrored drive)

Drive F: (RAID-5 array)

Match the following files with the disks above:

First storage group transaction logs

Second storage group transaction logs

Mailbox store one

Mailbox store two

Mailbox store three

Mailbox store four

System/Boot partition

Answer:

Drive C: (mirrored drive)

System/Boot partition

Drive D: (mirrored drive)

First storage group transaction logs

Drive E: (mirrored drive)

Second storage group transaction logs

Drive F: (RAID 5 array)

Mailbox store one

Mailbox store two

Mailbox store three

Mailbox store four

Because transaction logs are written sequentially, it is more important to put transaction logs on their own spindle than database files. Microsoft recommends using RAID 1 (mirroring) for System/Boot partitions and for transaction logs. They recommend using RAID 5 for databases.

Question 5

How should the disks on a small server be configured?

○ a. RAID 0 for the System/Boot partition and transaction logs, and RAID 1 for the database files

○ b. RAID 1 for the System/Boot partition and transaction logs, and RAID 5 for the database files

○ c. RAID 0 for the System/Boot partition and transaction logs, and RAID 5 for the database files

○ d. RAID 1 for the System/Boot partition and the database files, and RAID 5 for transaction logs

○ e. RAID 5 for the System/Boot partition and the database files, and RAID 1 for transaction logs

Answer e is correct. This is a bit tricky. Because these systems are using hardware RAID, the System/Boot partition can be on a RAID 5 array. This design will provide the greatest performance by having the transaction logs on their own spindle. Answers a and c are incorrect, because they don't provide fault tolerance. Answers b is incorrect, because it is more important to have the transaction logs on their own spindle. Answer d is incorrect, because the transaction logs should have stores on a RAID 1 (mirror) array whenever possible.

Question 6

How should the disks on a large server containing one storage group and two stores be configured?

○ a. One RAID 1 array for the System/Boot partition and transaction logs and one RAID 5 array for the database files

○ b. One RAID 1 array for the System/Boot partition, one RAID 1 array for the transaction logs, and one RAID 5 array for the database files

○ c. One RAID 1 array for the System/Boot partition, one RAID 1 array for the transaction logs, and two RAID 5 arrays for the database files

○ d. One RAID 1 array for the System/Boot partition, two RAID 1 arrays for the transaction logs, and one RAID 5 array for the database files

○ e. One RAID 5 array for all files

Answer c is correct. The System/Boot partition and transaction logs should have their own RAID 1 (mirror) array. The database files should be on a RAID 5 array, because there are enough disks for two arrays and putting each store on its own array will increase performance. Answer a is incorrect, because the transaction logs need to be on their own spindle. Answer b is incorrect, because there are enough disks for two arrays and putting each store on its own array will increase performance. Answer d is incorrect, because this is only one set of transaction logs. Answer e is incorrect, because the System/Boot partition, transaction logs, and database files should be separated.

Question 7

A floor user in Mesa sends an email to two managers in each manufacturing location. How many copies of the email exist?

○ a. 1

○ b. 2

○ c. 5

○ d. 10

○ e. 20

Answer c is correct. Because all managers at each location are in the same store, a single copy of the message will be stored in each store. Answers a, b, d, and e are thus incorrect.

Question 8

A floor user in Mesa sends an email to each manager in each manufacturing location. After a manager reads the email in the Madison, what is the extension of the database file containing this message?

○ a. .edb

○ b. .stm

○ c. .log

○ d. .pst

○ e. .map

Answer b is correct. Because the message was sent from a non-MAPI client, it will be stored in the streaming database file (.stm). Answer a is incorrect, because only messages sent by MAPI clients are stored in the rich text database file. If the manager had made changes and saved the file, the new message would be stored in the rich text database file. Answers c, d, and e are incorrect, because .log, .pst, and .map are not valid database extensions.

Need to Know More?

 Konkle, Joshua, Scott Schnoll, Michael Cooper, and David McAmis Schnoll. *Exchange 2000 Server: The Complete Reference.* McGraw-Hill Professional Publishing, 2000. ISBN 0072127392. This is a very good, very thick, everything-you-ever-wanted-to-know book. Great reference.

 Shannon, Michael. *MCSE Exchange 2000 Design Exam Prep.* The Coriolis Group, Scottsdale, AZ, 2001. ISBN 1-58880-026-1. This book is good as both a study guide and reference.

 Read Chapters 7 and 14 of the *Microsoft Exchange 2000 Server Planning and Installation* located in the \Docs folder of the Exchange 2000 CD-ROM.

 Search **www.Win2000mag.com** using the term "Exchange 2000" and the terms at the beginning of the chapter.

 Search **www.microsoft.com/technet** and the Exchange 2000 Server Help file using the terms at the beginning of the chapter.

 Search **www.mcpmag.com** for Exam 70-225 or Exchange 2000. *MCP Magazine* will have good information to help prepare for the exam.

Designing a Routing Group Topology

Terms you'll need to understand:

✓ Routing group

✓ First Routing Group

✓ Routing group connector

✓ Bridgehead server

✓ Transport Layer Security (TLS)

✓ IP Security (IPSec)

✓ SMTP connector

✓ X.400 connector

✓ Connector cost

✓ Link state table

✓ Hub-and-spoke topology

✓ Chain topology

✓ Full-mesh topology

Techniques you'll need to master:

✓ Designing a routing group topology for Exchange 2000 and pre-Exchange 2000 servers

✓ Designing a routing group topology for an Exchange 2000 organization in native mode

✓ Analyzing an existing network environment

Efficient message flow within an organization is critical to the success of a design. When designing a routing group topology, you need to analyze a company's network infrastructure, including bandwidth and geographical locations. Using this information, you can determine how to best design a routing group deployment to fit the company's needs. Routing groups will then be connected to provide the best possible message flow solution.

Routing Groups

Exchange 2000 *routing groups* are used to control the flow of messages between servers. Routing groups should contain well-connected servers. Within a single routing group, message routing occurs point-to-point, and their connections form a *mesh topology* (see Figure 6.1).

 The exam may contain questions regarding communications within a routing group. You should know that Exchange 2000 servers within the same routing group use *Simple Mail Transfer Protocol (SMTP)* for communications.

First Routing Group

By default, all Exchange servers are members of the *First Routing Group*. A routing group called First Routing Group is created when the first Exchange 2000 server is installed. In many small and even large organizations, this single routing group is sufficient. Using the Exchange System Manager, additional routing groups can be created.

Note: By default, the Exchange System Manager does not display routing groups. The Properties page of the organization contains a checkbox for displaying routing groups (see Figures 6.2 and 6.3)

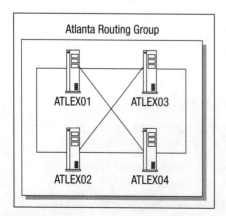

Figure 6.1   Mesh topology within a single routing group.

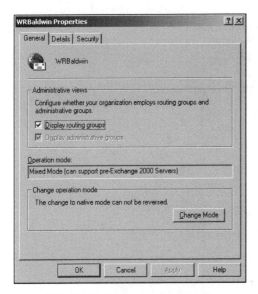

Figure 6.2   The Display Routing Groups option.

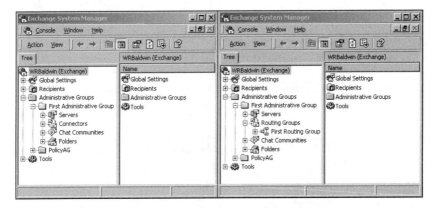

Figure 6.3   Effect of selecting the Display Routing Groups option (this example contains multiple administrative groups; each administrative group contains a First Routing Group).

Multiple Routing Groups

To control the flow of message traffic between Exchange servers, multiple routing groups and connectors need to be created. Connectors are discussed in the section called "Connectors" later in this chapter. Message routing between routing groups can be controlled in many ways. For example, large messages can be routed only during off-peak hours. This does not mean large messages cannot be sent during peak hours, simply that the Exchange server in one routing group stores the message in a queue during peak hours. During off-peak hours, the message is transferred to the appropriate routing group. In very large organizations, many

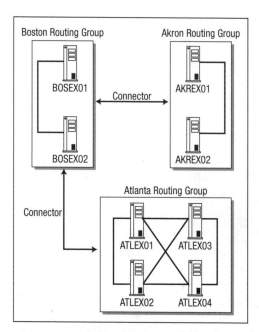

Figure 6.4   Example of a multiple routing group.

routing groups can be created. A message may be routed through several routing groups before reaching its final destination. In the example in Figure 6.4, a message sent from a mailbox on the AKREX01 server to a mailbox on the ATLEX03 server should be routed through the Boston routing group.

Mixed Mode versus Native Mode

In mixed mode, Exchange 2000 and pre-Exchange 2000 servers exist in the same organization. Pre-Exchange 2000 message routing was controlled by sites. Unlike Exchange 2000, pre-Exchange 2000 sites controlled both routing and administration. To maintain downward compatibility with pre-Exchange 2000 servers, an Exchange 2000 organization in mixed mode ties administrative groups to routing groups. For example, if a server is a member of the First Administrative Group, it can only be a member of a routing group that is also a member of the First Administrative Group. Because pre-Exchange 2000 servers do not understand routing groups, they will communicate with all Exchange 2000 servers in an administrative group as if they were in the same site. This does not prevent the creation of multiple routing groups in mixed mode; the pre-Exchange 2000 server will just not be aware of them. In the example in Figure 6.5, the DUNEX01 server is the only pre-Exchange 2000 server. Because all servers are in the same administrative group, DUNEX01 sees all the servers as if they were in the site (pre-Exchange 2000 equivalent to routing groups). Messages sent from a mailbox

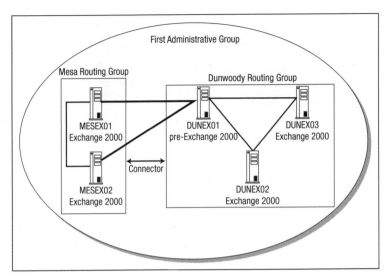

Figure 6.5   Routing groups in mixed mode.

on the DUNEX01 server to mailboxes on the Mesa server do not use the connector between the two routing groups. The Exchange 2000 servers, however, route messages between the routing groups through the connector. Connectors are discussed in detail in the "Connectors" section later in this chapter.

 The exam may contain questions about communications within a pre-Exchange 2000 site. Pre-Exchange 2000 servers use Remote Procedure Call to communicate with other servers in the same site. This will include communications with both pre-Exchange 2000 computers and Exchange 2000 computers.

Once an organization's servers have been changed to native mode servers, members in one administrative group can be members of routing groups in other administrative groups (see Figure 6.6).

It is important to remember that each Exchange 2000 server can be a member of a single administrative group and a single routing group. A server will join an administrative group when it is first installed and cannot be moved. Servers can be moved between routing groups using the Exchange System Manager, but only to routing groups in another administrative group when the organization is in native mode.

Connectors

Exchange 2000 uses connectors to route messages between routing groups, pre-Exchange 2000 sites, and other message systems. The three types of connectors used to connect Exchange 2000 routing groups are routing group connectors,

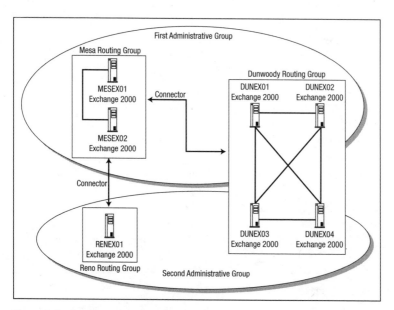

Figure 6.6 Routing groups in native mode.

SMTP connectors, and X.400 connectors. Routing group connectors are the preferred connectors and should be used whenever possible.

Routing Group Connectors

Routing group connectors are similar to pre-Exchange 2000 site connectors. Routing group connectors are easier to configure than other connectors and offer more flexibility. Routing group connectors provide a one-way routing group to routing group message routes. To connect two routing groups, a routing group connector must be created for each routing group. Figure 6.7 shows three routing groups: Mesa, Akron, and Boston, with connectors for Mesa/Akron and Akron/Boston. This scenario requires one connector in the Mesa routing group, two connectors in the Akron routing group, and one connector in the Boston routing group.

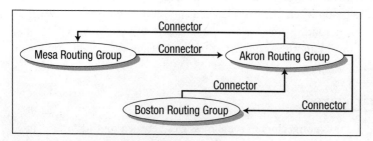

Figure 6.7 Example of routing group connectors.

The native protocol for routing group connectors is SMTP. Pre-Exchange 2000 site connectors, however, use Remote Procedure Calls (RPC). When an Exchange 2000 routing group connector is used to transfer messages to a pre-Exchange 2000 server, the Exchange 2000 will use RPC to communicate.

Bridgehead Servers

A routing group connector can specify zero or more remote and local *bridgehead servers*. A local bridgehead server is used to forward messages from the routing group members to a remote routing group. If no local bridgehead servers are defined, all available servers in the routing group will act as bridgehead servers. If multiple local bridgehead servers are configured, the connector will rotate messages to all available servers using a round-robin technique. The routing group connector must specify at least one remote bridgehead server. Local bridgehead servers will forward messages to remote bridgehead servers. If multiple remote bridgehead servers are configured, the routing will rotate messages to all available servers using a roundrobin technique. Figure 6.8 shows an example of local and remote bridgehead servers. This example shows a routing group connector as defined in the Boston routing group. This connector will enable messages from BOSEX02 to AKREX01 and from BOSEX02 to AKREX02. This could be configured as a single connector with multiple remote bridgehead (as in this example), or as two connectors each with the same local bridgehead.

Security

One major difference between using RPC with pre-Exchange 2000 site connectors and SMTP with Exchange 2000 routing group connectors is that by default Exchange 2000 routing group connectors are less secure. Pre-Exchange 2000 servers and Exchange 2000 servers encrypt data when using RPC to communicate. By default, SMTP traffic is not encrypted; it is encapsulated. Although encrypted data requires a key and can be very difficult to crack, encapsulated data is simply

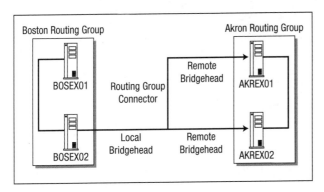

Figure 6.8   Example of a bridgehead server.

repackaged data within data. SMTP data packets are not clear text; however, they are not considered secure. This is not to say SMTP traffic cannot be encrypted, just that encryption must be enabled. SMTP can use either *Transport Layer Security (TLS)* or *IP Security (IPSec)* for data encryption.

Routing group connectors using SMTP will use Windows 2000 Kerberos to authenticate bridgehead server communication. Authentication does not protect the data; it just verifies the identity of the bridgehead servers before they communicate.

SMTP Connectors

Although SMTP connectors can be used as connectors between routing groups, their primary function is to provide message routing from one or more bridgehead servers to either another messaging system or the Internet. SMTP connectors replace the *Internet Mail Connector (IMC)* on pre-Exchange 2000 servers.

 When designing connections on the exam, don't confuse SMTP connectors with routing group connectors. Although both use the SMTP protocol, they have different capabilities.

Like routing group connectors, SMTP connectors can be configured with zero or more local bridgehead servers. Like routing group connectors, if no local bridgehead servers are defined, all available servers in the routing group will act as bridgehead servers. If multiple local bridgehead servers are configured, the connector will rotate messages to all available servers using a round-robin technique. A disadvantage of using SMTP connectors is they cannot have multiple remote bridgeheads. SMTP connectors can be configured with a single remote bridgehead called a *smart host*. This smart host is simply a server that relays the SMTP message. Instead of configuring a smart host, an SMTP connector can also be configured to use DNS to route SMTP messages. With this option, the SMTP connector will query a DNS server for a mail exchanger (MX) record that corresponds to each SMTP message's domain. Figure 6.9 shows an example of an SMTP connector configured for DNS lookup.

1. An Outlook client sends an email to **cory@examcram.com**.

2. The message is routed to the SMTP connector local bridgehead. This Exchange 2000 server will query the local DNS server for the MX record for **examcram.com**.

3. The local DNS server may query a DNS server on the Internet. Once the query has been resolved, the local DNS server will respond to the Exchange 2000 server.

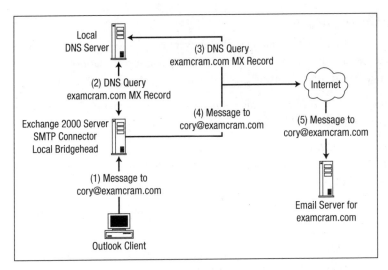

Figure 6.9   Example of an SMTP connector using DNS lookup.

4. The Exchange 2000 server will send the message using SMTP over the Internet to the email server defined in the MX record.

5. The email server for **examcram.com** will receive and process the message.

SMTP connectors and SMTP virtual servers are described in more detail in Chapter 10.

X.400 Connectors

The X.400 can be used for connecting to other routing groups, pre-Exchange 2000 sites, and other X.400 email systems. X.400 has two advantages over routing group and SMTP connector. X.400 connectors can be configured over TCP/IP or X.25 networks. Message attachments transferred over X.400 connectors have less overhead and are therefore smaller than SMTP messages. X.400 connectors, however, do not have the flexibility of routing group connectors and SMTP connectors. An X.400 connector can have only a single local bridgehead server and a single remote bridgehead server defined.

Public Folder Referrals

Connectors between routing groups can be used to control access to public folders for organizations. When a client attempts to open a public folder that is not on a server in its routing group, a connector can refer the request to a routing group containing a server with the public folder. Routing group connectors, SMTP connectors, and X.400 connectors have the option not to allow public folder referrals. This option is disabled by default, meaning that public folder referrals are enabled by default. Public folders are discussed in more detail later in Chapter 9.

Other Connectors

Exchange 2000 and pre-Exchange 2000 servers contain connectors for communicating with other messaging systems. These connectors cannot be used to communicate with other routing groups:

➤ *Connector for Lotus Notes*—This connector enables Exchange 2000 to communicate with Lotus/Domino 4.x and 5.x servers.

➤ *Connector for Lotus cc:Mail*—This connector communicates with the Lotus cc:Mail Import and Export programs. This will allow communication with Lotus cc:Mail post offices.

➤ *Connector for MS Mail*—This connector will route messages to and from MS Mail post offices.

➤ *Connector for Novell GroupWise*—This connector provides full integration with Exchange 2000 and Novell GroupWise. Messages, directory information, appointments, task, notes, and phone messages can be transferred with this connector.

➤ *Connector for MS SchedulePlus FreeBusy*—This connector will enable MS Mail post office users and Exchange mailbox users to share Free/Busy calendar information.

➤ *PROFS Connector*—The *Professional Office System (PROFS)* connector is not included with Exchange 2000. To enable communications with PROFS email systems, an Exchange 5.5 server must exist in the organization. This Exchange 5.5 server can be configured with a PROFS connector. PROFS email systems run on mainframe computers.

➤ *SNADS Connector*—The *SNA Distributed System (SNADS)* connector is not included with Exchange 2000. To enable communications with SNADS email systems, an Exchange 5.5 server must exist in the organization. This Exchange 5.5 server can be configured with a SNADS connector. SNADS email systems run on mainframe computers.

Costs and Link States

Large organizations with multiple routing groups will often have many connectors. When multiple paths to the destination server exist, Exchange must decide which path to take. An Exchange 2000 server uses two factors to determine which path to follow: connector costs and link states.

Connector Costs

Each connector has a cost value from 0 to 100. Exchange 2000 servers use the route with the lowest total cost. Figure 6.10 shows a simple example with three

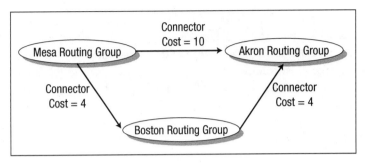

Figure 6.10   Example of connector costs.

routing groups. The connector from Mesa to Akron has a higher cost than the total cost of the connectors from Mesa to Boston and Boston to Akron. Messages sent from Mesa to Akron will be routed through bridgeheads in Boston.

Note: Connector costs will also be used for public folder referral. Public folders are discussed in more detail in Chapter 9.

Link States

There is a second factor Exchange 2000 uses to determine which path to follow to the destination server. A link state algorithm and a link state table replace pre-Exchange 2000 *Gateway Address Table (GWART)*. Unlike GWART, Exchange 2000's link state algorithm prevents endless looping of messages. In realtime, all Exchange 2000 servers propagate the status of the network. Because each server has a complete map of the network, the originating server can determine the best route for a message. There is a weak link (no pun intended) with link states in Exchange 2000. Each routing group has a *routing group master*. By default, the routing group master is the first Exchange 2000 server in the routing group. When bridgeheads in the routing group detect a link failure, they inform the routing group master; it is the routing group master's job to maintain the master link state table and propagate this information to other servers in the routing group and other routing group masters. It is possible to change the routing group master to another server, but this is a manual process.

 An effective plan should include procedures for recovering from a routing group master failure.

Routing Topology Designs

The most important routing design consideration is the routing topology. The topology has impact on the entire organization. An effective topology should always be a work in progress. Message traffic should be analyzed to determine the effectiveness of the plan. Also, as the organization's requirements change, the topology should have the flexibility to change with it. There are many topology designs; however, the most common are hub-and-spoke, chain, and full-mesh. Most designs do not fit these topologies perfectly; moreover, they are usually variations of these three.

Hub-and-Spoke Topology

The most elegant topology design is hub-and-spoke. The hub-and-spoke design relies on one centralized routing group, the hub. The hub routing group has connections to all other routing groups. All other routing groups have a connection only to the hub routing group. This design makes an administrator's job easier by centralizing all message routing. One main disadvantage of the design is that every message must cross at least two connectors; other major disadvantages include increased network traffic and excessive load on the hub routing group bridgehead servers. Figure 6.11 shows an example of a hub-and-spoke topology.

A variation on the hub-and-spoke design is the multiple hub-and-spoke design. This design has two or more hubs, each with multiple spokes. All hubs can either be directly connected to each other or be connected in a chain.

Chain Topology

There are many reasons *not* to use a chain topology and very little reason to use it. A chain topology links each routing group to two partner routing groups. Unless the chain forms a circle, the routing groups at the end of the chain only have single partners. Although chains and circles of chains work well for things like directory replication in Windows 2000, they are not recommended for message routing; the main disadvantage is that messages sent from one end of the chain may have to cross many connectors to be routed to a routing group on the opposite end.

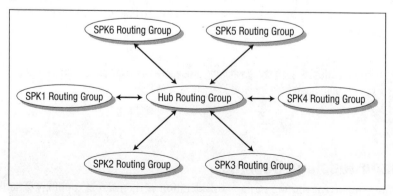

Figure 6.11   Example of a hub-and-spoke topology.

Full-Mesh Topology

A common topology for an organization with few routing groups is a full-mesh topology. A full-mesh design includes connectors to and from each routing group to each other routing group. The advantages come from the reduction in network bandwidth because all messages cross a single connector. This design also reduces the time it takes for messages to get routed. Again, because only one connector is crossed, fewer bridgehead servers have to process messages, and therefore this topology has the least effect on servers. The disadvantages come with many routing groups. As the number of routing groups increase, the number of connectors grow at a nonlinear rate. For example, four routing groups would have twelve connectors, five routing groups would have twenty connectors, and six routing groups would have thirty connectors. You can start to see the problem: ten routing groups in a hub-and-spoke with eighteen connectors is much easier to manage than a full-mesh with 90 connectors.

Routing Topology Design Considerations

Before embarking on a routing design, there are many important factors to consider, including the existing network infrastructure, existing messaging systems, and the potential of growth and change.

Existing Network Infrastructure

The existing network infrastructure has the greatest impact on a routing topology design. It is important to obtain a complete picture of both the existing network and the existing network operating system. Connections between physical locations and their bandwidth are crucial in determining routing groups and connectors. Because Exchange 2000 requires Windows 2000 Active Directory, an organization either already has an Active Directory in place, or often Exchange 2000 and Active Directory are in the same design. Active Directory sites don't always follow the same lines as routing groups, but they are still important to Exchange 2000. Exchange 2000 has to communicate with both domain controllers and Global Catalog servers; access to both is controlled by Windows 2000 sites.

Existing Messaging Systems

Very few organizations embark on an Exchange 2000 deployment without some messaging infrastructure in place. In the event that you are planning a fresh, clean deployment, lucky you. For the rest of world, an organization's existing messaging environment will play an important role in determining an effective routing group topology. If the organization has a pre-Exchange 2000 messaging system, a decision must be made about how to migrate. Most organizations will upgrade their existing organization, while others will create a new organization.

This decision will have an impact on design. For more information about migration, see Chapter 11.

Planning for Growth and Change

An often overlooked aspect of design is leaving room for growth and change. Exchange 2000 is much more flexible than pre-Exchange 2000 when it comes to change. In native mode, Exchange servers are easily moved between routing groups, but not administrative groups. Although this flexibility is nice, anticipating growth and change will reduce work later. Find out how many users the company plans to have in the coming years. Will they open new locations? Are there any mergers in their future?

Practice Questions

Case Study

You have been hired by PTO Furniture USA to help the company deploy Exchange 2000. You will be responsible for the routing group topology, including routing groups and connectors.

History

PTO Furniture USA was recently formed when three of the largest patio furniture manufacturers merged. The combined company has 30,000 employees in offices all over North America.

Company Profile

PTO is now the largest manufacturer of patio furniture in North America. The combined companies have built a reputation for building high-quality and affordable patio furniture. One of the merged companies had a problem with customer service; the combined companies hope to provide excellent customer service across the board.

The company headquarters is located in Scottsdale, AZ. The Scottsdale office also serves as the Southwest regional office. This office has 4,000 employees. The other two regional offices in Atlanta and Boston have 4,500 and 3,500 employees, respectively.

There are 5 manufacturing plants and 20 sales offices, see Tables 6.1 and 6.2.

Table 6.1 Manufacturing plants.	
Location	**Employees**
Mesa	5,000
Atlanta	1,000
Vancouver	4,000
Pittsburgh	2,200
Tampa	2,000

Table 6.2 Sales offices.	
Location	**Employees**
Mesa	50
San Francisco	250
Los Angeles	200
Chicago	85
Denver	75
Houston	45
Dallas	300
Detroit	150
Cleveland	100
New York City	200
Boston	600
Norfolk	400
Charlotte	30
Atlanta	100
Vancouver	400
Madison	100
Tampa	200
St. Louis	215
Kansas City	200
Rochester	100

Physical Network Diagram

This is PTO's current network diagram (see Figure 6.12).

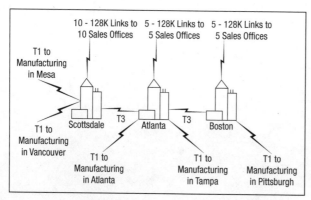

Figure 6.12   Network diagram.

Existing Messaging

All three companies were using different messaging systems, and one company actually had three messaging systems. All five messaging systems are operating, and communications between the systems occur via the Internet and SMTP. The messaging systems include Exchange 5.5, MS Mail, Lotus Notes, Novell Group Wise, and PROFS. Each company used a different domain for Internet email.

Directory Design

Two of the three merged companies were using Windows 2000 with Active Directory before the merger. The third company was using Novell Netware. Although a single Active Directory forest is now in place, several Novell Netware servers still exist. The Active Directory logical diagram is shown in Figure 6.13.

Active Directory Site Design

All locations contain a domain controller, so PTO decided to make each physical location an Active Directory site. IP site links have been created between all regional offices and all manufacturing plants are always available. IP site links also connect regional offices to sales offices. Due to limited bandwidth for these sites, site links are available only during off-peak hours.

Exchange 2000 Requirements and Goals

PTO would like to create a new Exchange 2000 organization. Although there will be no migration from Exchange 5.5, PTO would like to enable better connectivity to its existing messaging systems during the upgrade. PTO has decided to place Exchange servers in offices containing over 50 users. Users in offices with 50 users and fewer will use Outlook Web Access to access their mailbox. These users' mailboxes will be on the regional offices' Exchange servers. Offices containing over 50 users will have one Exchange 2000 server per 1,000 users.

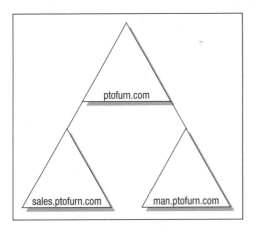

Figure 6.13   Active Directory design.

Question 1

> How many Exchange 2000 servers should PTO deploy?
>
> ○ a. 3
>
> ○ b. 8
>
> ○ c. 27
>
> ○ d. 41

Answer d is correct. This includes multiple servers for locations with over 1,000 users, and one server for those with more than 50 but fewer than 1,000 users. Answer a is incorrect, because this would be a single server at each location. Answer b is incorrect, because this would be a single server at each regional office and each manufacturing plant. Answer c is incorrect, because this would be a single server at each location. Locations with 50 or fewer users do not need a server, and those with more than 1,000 users need multiple servers.

Question 2

> If you were to design a hub-and-spoke routing group topology for PTO, how many hub routing groups would you have?
>
> ○ a. 1
>
> ○ b. 2
>
> ○ c. 3
>
> ○ d. 5
>
> ○ e. 8

Answer c is correct, and answers a and b are incorrect, because there is no single site with connections to all other sites. Because each regional office has multiple branches, three is the obvious choice. Answers d and e are incorrect because the manufacturing plants do not have spokes.

Question 3

What types of connector would you use to connect the manufacturing sites to the regional offices?

○ a. Routing group connector

○ b. SMTP connector

○ c. Site connector

○ d. RPC Connector

○ e. X.400 connector

Answer a is correct. Routing group connectors will provide the most flexibility when connecting routing groups. Answer b is incorrect because SMTP connectors are primarily used as connectors to the Internet. An SMTP connector does not have the flexibility of a routing group connector. Answer c is incorrect because site connectors are used on pre-Exchange 2000 servers. Answer d is incorrect because there is no RPC connector in Exchange 2000. Answer e is incorrect because the X.400 connector does not have the flexibility of the routing group connector.

Question 4

PTO is concerned about confidential messages sent to and from the sales offices. PTO would like to encrypt all messages between the regional offices and the sales offices. Which of the following Exchange 2000 connectors can be encrypted using Transport Layer Security? [Check all correct answers]

❏ a. Routing group connector

❏ b. SMTP connector

❏ c. IPSec Connector

❏ d. Site connector

❏ e. Internet Mail Connector

Answers a and b are correct. Routing group connectors and SMTP connectors both use SMTP to transfer messages. SMTP can be encrypted using IPSec or TLS. Answer c is incorrect because IPSec is not a connector. Answers d and e are incorrect because they are pre-Exchange 2000 connectors.

Question 5

> When can PTO change their Exchange 2000 organization to native mode?
>
> ○ a. After the first Exchange 2000 server is installed
>
> ○ b. After the last Exchange 2000 server is installed
>
> ○ c. After the first Exchange 5.5 server is decommissioned
>
> ○ d. After the last Exchange 5.5 server is decommissioned
>
> ○ e. After all non-Exchange 2000 servers are decommissioned

Answer a is correct. Because PTO is not migrating from Exchange 5.5, there is no need ever to have the organization in mixed mode. Exchange 2000 can still interact with other messaging systems in native mode. Pre-Exchange 2000 servers cannot be members of a native mode Exchange 2000 organization. The pre-Exchange 2000 servers are members of their own organization. Answers b, c, d, and e are thus incorrect.

Question 6

> Which of the following most affects PTO's routing group design?
>
> ○ a. Existing messaging system
>
> ○ b. Network topology
>
> ○ c. Active Directory physical design
>
> ○ d. Active Directory logical design
>
> ○ e. Administrative model

Answer b is correct. As with many organizations, PTO message routing is dictated by network bandwidth. Answer a is incorrect because PTO is not upgrading an existing messaging system. Answers c and d are incorrect because Active Directory design does not directly affect this design. Answer e is incorrect because PTO's administrative model is unknown.

Question 7

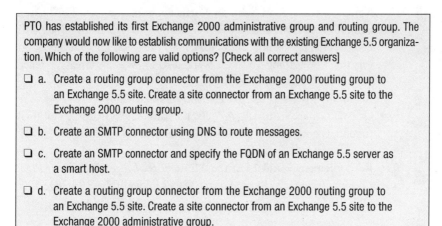

PTO has established its first Exchange 2000 administrative group and routing group. The company would now like to establish communications with the existing Exchange 5.5 organization. Which of the following are valid options? [Check all correct answers]

❏ a. Create a routing group connector from the Exchange 2000 routing group to an Exchange 5.5 site. Create a site connector from an Exchange 5.5 site to the Exchange 2000 routing group.

❏ b. Create an SMTP connector using DNS to route messages.

❏ c. Create an SMTP connector and specify the FQDN of an Exchange 5.5 server as a smart host.

❏ d. Create a routing group connector from the Exchange 2000 routing group to an Exchange 5.5 site. Create a site connector from an Exchange 5.5 site to the Exchange 2000 administrative group.

Answers b and c are correct. Only SMTP connectors can be used for communications between organizations. Because the Exchange 5.5 servers were already configured for Internet email, the SMTP connector can look up the domain's MX record using DNS. The smart host option will cause the SMTP connector to forward all mail to the specified Exchange 5.5 server. Answers a and d are incorrect because routing group connectors cannot connect to other organizations.

Need to Know More?

 Konkle, Joshua, Scott Schnoll, Michael Cooper, and David McAmis Schnoll. *Exchange 2000 Server: The Complete Reference.* McGraw-Hill Professional Publishing, 2000. ISBN 0072127392. This is a very good, very thick, everything-you-ever-wanted-to-know book. Great reference.

 Shannon, Michael. *MCSE Exchange 2000 Design Exam Prep.* The Coriolis Group, Scottsdale, AZ, 2001. ISBN 1-58880-026-1. This book is good as both a study guide and a reference.

 Read Chapters 7 and 14 of the *Microsoft Exchange 2000 Server Planning and Installation* located in the \Docs folder of the Exchange 2000 CD-ROM.

 Read Chapters 16, 21, and 22 of the *Exchange 2000 Server Resource Kit.*

 Search **www.Win2000mag.com** using the term "Exchange 2000" and the terms at the beginning of the chapter.

 Search **www.microsoft.com/technet** and the Exchange 2000 Server Help file using the terms at the beginning of the chapter.

 Search **www.mcpmag.com** using the terms "Exam 70-225" or "Exchange 2000". *MCP Magazine* will have good information to help prepare for the exam.

Planning for Server Roles and Placement

Terms you'll need to understand:

✓ Mailbox server

✓ Public folder server

✓ Front-end/back-end servers

✓ Outlook Web Access (OWA)

✓ Directory Service Access (DSAccess)

✓ Directory Service Proxy (DSProxy)

✓ Conferencing servers

✓ Instant Messaging servers

✓ Chat servers

✓ Perimeter networks

Techniques you'll need to master:

✓ Designing an Exchange 2000 server configuration

✓ Designing a firewall configuration for a
perimeter network

Exchange 2000 servers can fill many roles in an organization. Many organizations have one or a few Exchange 2000 servers, each performing many roles. Other organizations choose to have many Exchange 2000 servers, each performing few roles and often a single role. There are advantages and disadvantages to both models. By spreading Exchange 2000 roles over many servers, it is less likely that a single server failure will disable all Exchange 2000 functions. In general, a single large server would cost more than two smaller servers equipped to perform as well as the large server. Another advantage of separating server roles can be increased security. Clients may have access only to front-end servers; back-end servers can be protected behind firewalls. Separating server roles, however, can increase network traffic. Because many server roles require communication with each other, putting these roles on different servers creates additional network traffic. Many companies are choosing to build super-reliable super-servers. These servers are very expensive and often have 99.999 percent up time. In these instances, again in general, a single large server would cost less than two smaller servers equipped to perform as well as the large server. As you can see, there is no easy answer to this question. But Microsoft does have certain guidelines for separating server roles for better performance, increased reliability, and security.

Server Roles

An Exchange 2000 server can perform many services. Most of these services can be enabled and disabled. Enabling only certain services allows an Exchange 2000 server to perform a single role. It is also possible to combine some or all of these services such that a single server performs many or even all Exchange 2000 roles. Because an Exchange 2000 server requires certain Active Directory services, it is important to consider these services as well.

Mailbox Servers

An Exchange 2000 mailbox server is one that has one or more mailbox stores defined. By default, all Exchange 2000 servers have an empty mailbox store. If a server does not need to store mailboxes, such as a public folder server or a front-end server, then the mailbox store can be removed. A mailbox server's main function is to store user mailboxes and route messages to other Exchange 2000 servers. There are many factors that influence the design of a mailbox server:

> *Number of mailboxes*—The number of mailboxes has an effect on capacity and processor planning. It is important to factor in not only the number of current mailboxes, but also any mailboxes that will be created on or moved to this server. Microsoft recommends using two processors for Exchange 2000 servers with more than 500 mailboxes, and four processors for Exchange 2000 servers with more than 1,000 mailboxes. Microsoft also recommends 256MB of RAM

for every 500 mailboxes. These are general guidelines and can vary greatly depending on activity of clients, type of processors, speed of processors, and other roles being performed by this server.

➤ *Mailbox limit size*—Without knowing or having a limit on mailboxes, it can be difficult to properly plan for mailbox server capacity. Mailbox limits can be set on mailbox stores or individual mailboxes (see Figure 7.1). The mailbox limit and number of mailboxes can be used to quickly determine the upper capacity level. For example, 1,000 mailboxes with a 50MB mailbox limit could possibly consume 50GB of disk space. Although it is not likely that all 1,000 mailboxes would reach the limit, it is a good starting point when determining mailbox server capacity.

➤ *Deleted Item Retention*—Enabling Deleted Item Retention increases the size of a mailbox store, but not beyond the limit calculated using the number of mailboxes and mailbox limits. Messages stored in Deleted Item Retention count when the mailbox's size is calculated for mailbox limits.

➤ *Number of stores*—The separation of mailboxes into multiple mailbox stores does not increase the total necessary capacity of a server, but can affect the design of the storage system. Many designs call for each store to have its own separate RAID array, but often these databases are stored in separate folders on the same RAID array.

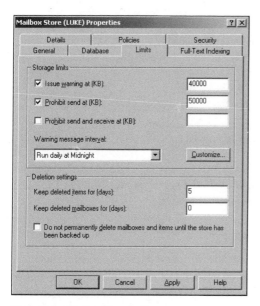

Figure 7.1 Mailbox store limits.

➤ *Number of storage groups*—The separation of mailbox stores into multiple storage groups has little effect on the storage needs of a server, but can affect the design of the storage system. Many designs call for each storage group's logs to have its own separate RAID array.

➤ *Protocols*—Clients can access mailboxes on a mailbox store using several different protocols, including MAPI, HTTP, HTTP-DAV, POP3, and IMAP4. It is possible to control access and increase security by only enabling protocols necessary for client connections. For more information on client protocols, see Chapter 12.

Public Folder Servers

Public folder servers behave in a similar way to mailbox servers. Both types of servers have storage groups and stores. Clients using a variety of protocols also access both types of servers. The differences lie in the types of data stored by public folder servers. In many designs, the data stored is less important than the data stored in mailboxes. However, other designs may put the data on the same level of importance, and others may even classify it as more important. It's not that any data is unimportant (some may argue this), but that the public folder data and mailbox data may require a different *service level agreement*. A service level agreement defines both the reliability of the service and the amount of time the service will be unavailable after a failure.

 When reading case studies on the exam, look for service level agreements that define both the reliability of the service and the amount of time the service will be unavailable after a failure.

Unlike mailbox servers, public folder servers can replicate data to other servers. The additional storage need for replicated folders must be accounted for. There can also be additional load on the server's replicating folders.

Public folder servers have the ability to support the NNTP protocol. Installing an NNTP virtual server enables a public folder server to host Internet and local newsgroups. NNTP is described in more detail in Chapter 9.

Front-End/Back-End Servers

In many situations, it may be advantageous to prevent clients from accessing mailbox and public folders directly. A front-end server is an Exchange 2000 server that does not contain any storage groups. The front-end server is responsible for processing client requests and passing them to a back-end mailbox and/or public folder servers. When a client connects to a front-end server, the front-end server checks Active Directory to find which back-end server the request needs to be passed to. It is important to understand that this is a proxy service, not a referral service. This means the front-end server passes data on the client's behalf, and does not refer the client. The client will never be in direct contact with the back-end server. A server can be converted to a front-end server using the Exchange System Manager (see Figure 7.2).

A back-end server can be any server in the organization with storage groups. There is no specific configuration setting enabling a server as a back-end server. There are many advantages to the front-end/back-end configuration:

➤ *Single namespace*—All clients can be configured to use the same Exchange 2000 server, even though their mailboxes may be spread across many mailbox servers. POP3 and IMAP4 clients would all have the same configuration, and Outlook Web Access clients could point to a single URL.

➤ *Increased scalability*—As demand increases, it is very easy to add additional back-end servers without having to reconfigure clients. Using multiple DNS entries and DNS round robin, multiple front-end servers can be configured as needed.

➤ *Increased security*—Although clients have access to front-end servers, back-end servers can be protected behind firewalls. Using filters on the firewall, only traffic from the front-end servers can be allowed through. Also, using IP

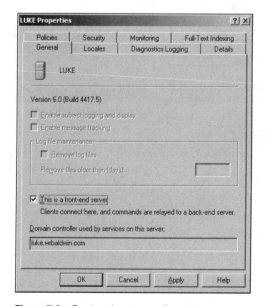

Figure 7.2   Front-end server configuration.

Security (IPSec), traffic between the front-end and back-end servers can be encrypted. This will enable encryption for traffic into the network, without having to set up complex encryption on the clients. For more information on placement or front-end and back-end servers, see the section called "Server Placement" later in this chapter.

➤ *Increased performance*—Front-end servers can handle encryption and decryption of client traffic as well as HTTP compression. Offloading these tasks from the back-end servers increases the performance of the back-end servers. This also enables each server to be configured for its given task. Front-end servers, for example, do not need large disk arrays for storing data.

Note: Front-end servers do not work with native Outlook access using MAPI. MAPI clients must connect directly to the mailbox and public folder servers.

Connector Servers

Also known as bridgehead servers, *connector servers* are responsible for routing messages between Exchange 2000 routing groups as well as other messaging systems. In many large organizations, connectors are so busy that it is advantageous to have dedicated connector servers. A connector server can run a single type of connector, or may be multitasked to run several connector types. If a server is to host multiple connector types, separating the folders used by the connectors onto separate spindles can increase performance. Similar to store databases, connector databases have transaction logs. These databases are primarily used as temporary storage; recovery from failure is not as important. Thus, there is no reason to separate the transaction logs from the databases, as is done with stores. Because these databases are written much more often than they are read, RAID 1 (mirror) is recommended. Table 7.1 shows Exchange 2000 connectors and their folders:

Tabel 7.1 Exchange 2000 connector database locations.		
Connector	**Folder**	**Setting Located**
Routing group connector	\exchsrvr\mailroot	IIS Metabase*
SMTP connector	\exchsrvr\mailroot	IIS Metabase*
X.400 connector	\exchsrvr\mtadata	Registry
Lotus Notes connector	\exchsrvr\conndata	Registry
Lotus cc:Mail connector	\exchsrvr\CCMCData	Registry
Novell GroupWise connector	\exchsrvr\conndata	Registry
MS Mail connector	\exchsrvr\connect\msmcon\maildata	Share

*The settings for the SMTP service used by routing groups and SMTP connectors are located in the IIS Metabase and can be edited using MetaEdit from the Windows 2000 Resource Kit.

Note: The routing group connector will use Remote Procedure Calls (RPC) to communicate with pre-Exchange 2000 servers. When using RPC to communicate, the routing group connector uses the MTA service. The MTA service stores its database in the \exchsrvr\mtadata.

Outlook Web Access (OWA) Server

An *Outlook Web Access (OWA)* server allows users to access the mailbox and many features of their mailbox through a Web browser (see Figure 7.3). OWA allows users access regardless of the platform they are using. A compatible Web browser is the only software needed.

OWA is installed by default on all Exchange 2000 servers. On servers that do not use OWA, it is a good idea to remove OWA to increase security. For increased security and performance, Microsoft recommends deploying OWA in a front-end/back-end server configuration. OWA is described in more detail in Chapter 12.

Active Directory Servers

Exchange 2000 servers require access to Active Directory data. While it is possible to install Exchange 2000 on a domain controller, thereby ensuring access to Active Directory, Microsoft does not recommend it. *Directory Service Access (DSAccess)* is an Exchange 2000 service that is used to retrieve data from Active Directory servers. DSAccess retrieves information from both domain controllers and Global Catalog servers. When DSAccess needs to query a domain controller, it uses DNS to obtain a list of up to 10 domain controllers. DSAccess attempts to contact a domain controller within the same Active Directory site as the Exchange 2000 server. If it cannot find a server in the same site, it will look outside the site.

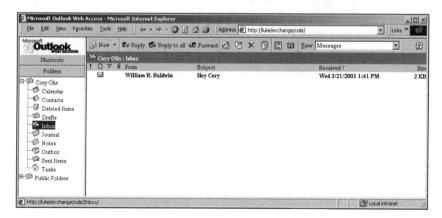

Figure 7.3   Outlook Web Access.

When DSAccess needs to query a Global Catalog server, it uses a *Lightweight Directory Access Protocol (LDAP)* query to a domain controller to find a Global Catalog server within the same Active Directory site as the Exchange 2000 server. If it cannot find a server in the same site, it will look outside the site. If the Exchange 2000 server is a domain controller and/or a Global Catalog server, it may have the information needed. If this is the case, it will not need to query another Active Directory server. By modifying the registry, it is possible to define static entries for domain controllers and Global Catalog servers.

Note: If static entries for domain controllers exist, DSAccess will not attempt to contact any other domain controllers. This means that if the domain controllers that have been statically defined are down, DSAccess will fail. If static entries for Global Catalog servers exist, DSAccess will not attempt to contact any other Global Catalog servers. This means that if the Global Catalog servers that have been statically defined are down, DSAccess will fail.

Outlook 2000 MAPI clients access Active Directory servers through a referral process. These clients contact an Exchange 2000 server and that server refers them to an Active Directory server. Pre-Outlook 2000 and legacy Exchange clients do not access Active Directory servers directly. Pre-Outlook 2000 and legacy Exchange clients query an Exchange 2000 server. Exchange 2000 sends the request to an Active Directory server on the behalf (proxy) of the client. The *Directory Service Proxy (DSProxy)* service on the Exchange 2000 server performs this action. DSProxy also proxies LDAP queries made by IMAP4 and POP3 clients.

Note: By modifying the registry, Outlook 2000 clients can be forced to use the DSProxy for Active Directory queries instead of being referred.

A *Global Catalog server* contains a partial copy of all Active Directory information. Each Global Catalog server contains every Active Directory object and a subset of their attributes. Because Exchange 2000 will most likely query these attributes, most Exchange 2000 Active Directory queries are made to Global Catalog servers. When considering a design, it is important to calculate the number and placement of Global Catalog servers. The number of Global Catalog servers can be computed as a factor of Exchange 2000 servers, or as a factor of users. Depending on the size and configuration of the servers and underlying network, this factor can vary.

 Look for metrics to calculate the number of Global Catalog servers in case studies on the exam. Examples include the following: Each Global Catalog server can handle five Exchange 2000 servers, or Global Catalog servers have been rated at one per 8,000 mailbox users.

Other Exchange Server Roles

Other less common roles for Exchange 2000 servers include conferencing servers, Instant Messaging, and chat.

➤ *Conferencing servers*—Conferencing servers provide both data and video-conferencing. These servers do not use a tremendous amount of disk space; however, they do contain mailboxes for the conferencing calendar and resources. These mailbox databases should be treated similarly to standard mailboxes, by splitting the databases and transaction logs. Microsoft recommends using 256MB of RAM for every 500 conferencing server users.

➤ *Instant Messaging servers*—Instant Messaging servers also do not use a tremendous amount of disk space. The Instant Messaging database is similar to a mailbox database, and it can be moved using the Exchange System Manager. This database should be treated similarly to standard mailbox database, by splitting the databases and transaction logs. Microsoft recommends using 256MB of RAM for every 5,000 Instant Messaging users.

➤ *Chat servers*—Chat servers use an insignificant amount of disk space, so storage planning is not necessary. Microsoft recommends using 256MB of RAM for every 10,000 chat users.

Server Placement

Deciding where Exchange and Windows servers will be placed is a crucial part of an Exchange 2000 design. Network traffic and client performance will be greatly affected by Exchange 2000 server placement.

Mailbox Servers

Outlook MAPI clients need direct access to their mailbox server. Having clients access these servers over slow *Wide Area Network (WAN)* links is not advisable. Unless clients are using non-MAPI clients—POP3, IMAP4, or HTTP—Exchange mailbox servers should be placed on the same *Local Area Network* (LAN) as the clients whenever possible.

Public Folder Servers

Accessing public folders across slow WAN links is similar to accessing a mailbox server. Because users tend to use public folders less frequently than their mailboxes, it is usually less important to place public folder servers on the same LAN; however, it is still recommended. Placing public folders on the same LAN as clients introduces a problem. Clients in different locations may need access to the same public folder or folders. If this is the case, there are three options. The first is to locate all the public folders in one location and have the other location access the folders over the WAN. The second option is to locate half the public folders in each location. Clients in each location would have to cross the WAN for half the folders. The third option is more common. Each location can contain all public folders, and the public folders can be configured to replicate with each other. For more information on public folder replication, see Chapter 9.

Front-End/Back-End Servers

For the exam, you will want to know the ins and outs of placing front-end/ back-end servers, perhaps more than anything else you learn in this chapter. The placement of these servers and the configurations of firewalls have a major impact on network security. Front-end/back-end servers are used with POP3, IMAP4, and HTTP protocols. Front-end servers can be placed inside or outside the firewall. They can also be placed in a *perimeter network*.

Perimeter Networks

A perimeter network, also known as a *demilitarized zone (DMZ)* or *screened subnet*, is a network isolated from the Internet by a firewall and isolated from the internal network by another firewall (see Figure 7.4). The perimeter network contains servers accessible from the Internet, like Web servers and Exchange 2000 front-end servers.

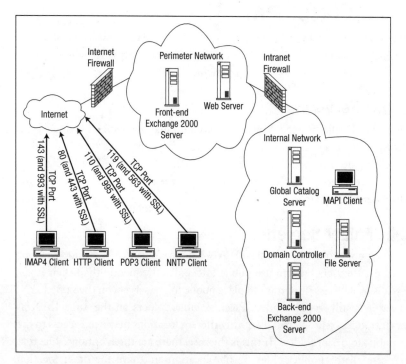

Figure 7.4 Example of a perimeter network.

Why two firewalls? The Internet firewall can be configured to allow access to the servers in the perimeter network only, and only for the necessary protocols. The Intranet firewall can be configured to allow only traffic from the perimeter network server to enter the internal network. In theory, this should block all traffic from the Internet from the internal network. When planning a perimeter network, it is important to understand how the firewalls must be configured—more specifically, what ports in the firewall must be opened. For the Internet firewall, the ports depend on the clients that will access the front-end server. Table 7.2 describes these ports. When using Secure Sockets Layer (SSL), both ports are used.

Communications from the perimeter network to the internal network are a bit more complicated. The front-end server is going to pass the client's request to the back-end server using the same protocol used by the client. This means any messaging protocols open on the Internet firewall should also be open on the Intranet firewall. The exception to this is SSL. The client can use SSL to communicate with the front-end server, but the front-end server does not use SSL to communicate with the back-end server. To enable encryption between a front-end and back-end server, use IPSec.

Note: Ports opened on the Intranet firewall should be opened for packets whose source IP address is one of the servers on the perimeter network.

The front-end servers use LDAP to communicate with Global Catalog servers and domain controllers on the internal network. To locate Active Directory servers, the front-end server needs to query a DNS server. This DNS server may be located on the internal network. These servers can also authenticate the front-end server using Kerberos. The front-end server uses certain RPC and netlogon ports for Active Directory discovery and client authentication. All these ports should be opened on the Intranet firewall and are listed in Table 7.3.

Note: When the front-end server is relaying HTTP traffic for OWA, it is not necessary to contact Active Directory servers.

Table 7.2 Messaging protocols.		
Protocol	**TCP Port**	**TCP Port with SSL**
Simple Mail Transfer Protocol (SMTP)	25	None
Hypertext Transfer Protocol (HTTP)	80	443
Post Office Protocol v3 (POP3)	110	995
Internet Message Access Protocol v4 (IMAP4)	143	993
Network News Transfer Protocol (NNTP)	119	563

Table 7.3 Other protocols.		
Protocol	TCP Port	UDP Port
LDAP (domain controller)	389	None
LDAP (Global Catalog server)	3268	
Kerberos	88	88
DNS	53	53
RPC ports	135 & 1024*	
Netlogon	445	

The first RPC service uses TCP port 1024; additional RPC services use 1025, then 1026, and so on.

Using a Single Firewall

Many companies cannot afford and do not need the security of two or more firewalls. With a single firewall, front-end servers can be placed on either side of the firewall. The placement of the front-end server affects how the firewall is configured.

➤ *Front-end server on the Intranet side (inside)*—This configuration protects the front-end server from Internet attacks. The firewall, however, must be configured to allow TCP traffic from any client for the necessary ports. The ports should be based on the messaging protocols (see Table 7.2). This is the most secure design because the firewall can be configured to allow access only to the front-end server.

➤ *Front-end server on the Internet side (outside)*—This configuration reduces the chance of someone breaking through the firewall from a client, but leaves the front-end server open to attacks. If the front-end server were compromised, a threat could gain access to the internal network via the front-end server. The front-end server is going to pass the client's request to the back-end using the same protocol used by the client. The front-end servers must communicate with Global Catalog servers and domain controllers on the internal network using LDAP. To locate Active Directory servers, the front-end server will need to query a DNS server. This DNS server may be located on the internal network. These servers will also authenticate the front-end server using Kerberos. The front-end server uses certain RPC and netlogon ports for Active Directory discovery and client authentication. All these ports should be opened on the firewall and are listed in Table 7.3.

Practice Questions

Case Study

You have been hired by PTO Furniture USA to help the company deploy Exchange 2000. You will be responsible for designing the configuration and placement of servers.

History

PTO Furniture USA was recently formed when three of the largest patio furniture companies merged. The combined company has 30,000 employees in offices all over North America.

Company Profile

PTO is now the largest manufacturer of patio furniture in North America. The combined companies have built a reputation for building high-quality and affordable patio furniture. One of the merged companies had a problem with customer service; the combined companies hope to provide excellent customer service across the board.

The company headquarters is located in Scottsdale, Arizona. The Scottsdale office also serves as the Southwest regional office. This office has 4,000 employees. The other two regional offices in Atlanta and Boston have 4,500 and 3,500 employees, respectively.

There are 5 manufacturing plants and 20 sales offices (see Tables 7.4 and 7.5).

Table 7.4 Manufacturing plants.	
Location	Employees
Mesa	5,000
Atlanta	1,000
Vancouver	4,000
Pittsburgh	2,200
Tampa	2,000

Table 7.5	Sales offices.
Location	**Employees**
Mesa	50
San Francisco	250
Los Angeles	200
Chicago	85
Denver	75
Houston	45
Dallas	300
Detroit	150
Cleveland	100
New York City	200
Boston	600
Norfolk	400
Charlotte	30
Atlanta	100
Vancouver	400
Madison	100
Tampa	200
St. Louis	215
Kansas City	200
Rochester	100

Physical Network Diagram

This is PTO's current network diagram (see Figure 7.5).

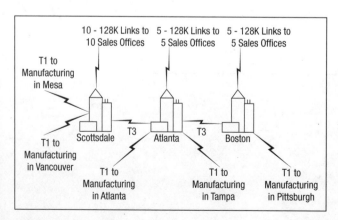

Figure 7.5 Network diagram.

Existing Messaging

All three companies were using different messaging systems, and one company actually had three messaging systems. All five messaging systems are operating and communications between the systems occur via the Internet and SMTP. The messaging systems include Exchange 5.5, MS Mail, Lotus Notes, Novell GroupWise, and PROFS. Each company used a different domain for Internet email.

Remote Client Access

The Scottsdale location will have a perimeter network (see Figure 7.6). Remote users will be able to access their mailboxes over the Internet using OWA. The traffic between the clients and the front-end server should be encrypted.

Directory Design

Two of the three merged companies were using Windows 2000 with Active Directory before the merger. The third company was using Novell NetWare. Although a single Active Directory forest is now in place, several Novell NetWare servers still exist. The Active Directory logical diagram is shown in Figure 7.7.

Active Directory Site Design

All locations contain a domain controller, so PTO decided to make each physical location an Active Directory site. IP site links have been created between all regional offices and all manufacturing plants are always available. IP site links

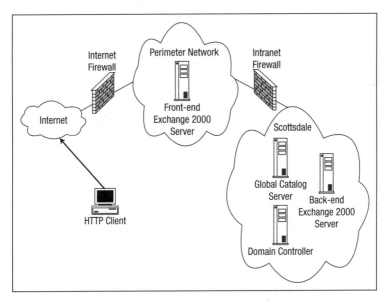

Figure 7.6   Scottsdale perimeter network configuration.

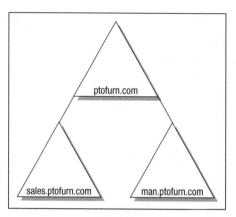

Figure 7.7 Active Directory design.

also connect regional offices to sales offices. Due to limited bandwidth for these sites, site links are available only during off-peak hours. Global Catalog servers are located on the regional offices only.

Exchange 2000 Requirements and Goals

PTO would like to create a new Exchange 2000 organization. Although there will be no migration from Exchange 5.5, PTO would like to enable better connectivity to its existing messaging systems during the upgrade. PTO has decided to place Exchange servers in offices containing over 50 users. Users in offices with 50 users and fewer will use OWA to access their mailbox. These users' mailboxes will be on the regional office exchange servers. Offices containing over 50 users will have one Exchange 2000 server per 1,000 users.

Question 1

Which two factors will most affect capacity planning of the mailbox servers in this design? [Choose all correct answers]

❏ a. Number of mailboxes

❏ b. Deleted Item Retention

❏ c. Mailbox limits

❏ d. Number of stores

❏ e. Number of storage groups

Answers a and c are correct. The number of mailboxes and the mailbox limits are a good starting point when planning for capacity. By multiplying the two, a maximum storage size can be determined. Answer b is incorrect, because the deleted items count toward a user's limit. This can have a small effect on capacity planning, but not as much as number of mailboxes and mailbox limits. Answers d and e are incorrect. The number of stores and storage groups will affect the configuration on drives, but they will not have as much effect on capacity as the number of mailboxes and mailbox limits.

Question 2

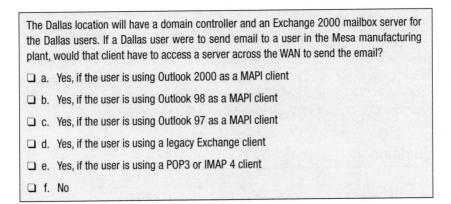

The Dallas location will have a domain controller and an Exchange 2000 mailbox server for the Dallas users. If a Dallas user were to send email to a user in the Mesa manufacturing plant, would that client have to access a server across the WAN to send the email?

❑ a. Yes, if the user is using Outlook 2000 as a MAPI client

❑ b. Yes, if the user is using Outlook 98 as a MAPI client

❑ c. Yes, if the user is using Outlook 97 as a MAPI client

❑ d. Yes, if the user is using a legacy Exchange client

❑ e. Yes, if the user is using a POP3 or IMAP 4 client

❑ f. No

Answer a is correct. Outlook 2000 will need to access a Global Catalog server to find the name of the Mesa user because that user is in a different Active Directory domain. Outlook 2000 uses a referral process to access a Global Catalog server. An Exchange 2000 server will give the Outlook 2000 MAPI client a list of servers, and the client will contact the server directly. Thus, answer f is incorrect. Answers b, c, d, and e are incorrect, because pre-Outlook 2000 and legacy Exchange clients will not access Active Directory servers directly. Pre-Outlook 2000 and legacy Exchange clients will query Exchange 2000 server. The Exchange 2000 will send the request to an Active Directory on behalf (proxy) of the client. The DSProxy service on the Exchange 2000 server will perform this action. DSProxy will also proxy LDAP queries made by IMAP4 and POP3 clients.

Question 3

> For the perimeter network at Scottsdale, what messaging port or ports should be opened on the Internet firewall? [Check all correct answers]
>
> ❑ a. 25
>
> ❑ b. 80
>
> ❑ c. 110
>
> ❑ d. 443
>
> ❑ e. 995

Answers b and d are correct. OWA uses the HTTP protocol that uses port 80. When using secure HTTP with SSL, port 443 is also used. Answer a is incorrect, because port 25 is used for SMTP. Answers c and e are incorrect, because POP3 uses port 110. When POP3 is secured with SSL, port 995 is also used.

Question 4

> For the perimeter network at Scottsdale, what port or ports should be opened on the Intranet firewall? [Check all correct answers]
>
> ❑ a. 25
>
> ❑ b. 80
>
> ❑ c. 110
>
> ❑ d. 443
>
> ❑ e. 995

Answer b is correct and answer d is incorrect. The front-end server will relay the HTTP (port 80) packet to the back-end server but it will not use SSL (port 443 when used with HTTP) to communicate with the back-end server. Answer a is incorrect, because port 25 is used for SMTP. Answers c and e are also incorrect, because POP3 uses port 110. When POP3 is secured with SSL, port 995 is also used.

Question 5

PTO has decided to have four dedicated bridgehead servers. Boston and Atlanta locations will each have a server configured with routing group connectors. Scottsdale will have a connector server with routing group connectors and another server with SMTP, Lotus Notes, MS Mail, and GroupWise connectors (see Figure 7.8).

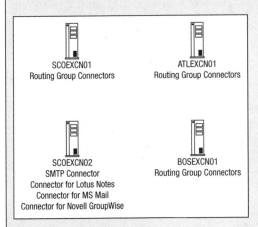

Figure 7.8   Connector servers.

The following are the different connectors used by the servers:

    Routing group connector

    SMTP connector

    Connector for Lotus Notes

    Connector for MS Mail

    Connector for Novell GroupWise

Before moving the folders to improve performance, match the folders below with the above connectors by which they are used. You may use items below more than once or not at all.

    \exchsrvr\mailroot

    \exchsrvr\mtadata

    \exchsrvr\smtpdata

    \exchsrvr\conndata

    \exchsrvr\connect\msmcon\maildata

    \exchsrvr\mailroot

    \exchsrvr\mailroot

    \exchsrvr\conndata

    \exchsrvr\conndata

    \exchsrvr\connect\msmcon\maildata

The \exchsrvr\mtadata folder is used by *Message Transfer Agent (MTA)*. The X.400 connector and the routing group connector use the MTA. The routing group connector will only use the MTA when it is communicating with pre-Exchange 2000 servers in the same organization. Because PTO is not going to have a pre-Exchange 2000 server in its Exchange 2000 organization (pre-Exchange 2000 servers will remain in the old organization), the routing group connectors on these servers will not use the MTA. The \exchsrvr\smtpdata folder is not a valid folder.

Question 6

To improve performance of the connector server used to route Internet email, you would like to place the Internet email logs on their own RAID 1 array. Where does this change need to be made?

❑ a. Registry

❑ b. Exchange System Manager

❑ c. IIS MetaBase

❑ d. Active Directory Sites and Services

❑ e. Internet Services Manager

Answer c is correct. The connector used to route Internet email is the SMTP connector. The SMTP connector uses the SMTP service. The SMTP service settings are stored in the IIS MetaBase and can be configured using MetaEdit from the Windows 2000 Resource Kit. Answer a, b, d, and e are incorrect, because the SMTP configuration information is not stored in these locations, nor can the settings be configured by these tools.

Question 7

> You have done some testing in a lab and determined that PTO's Global Catalog servers can handle 10,000 clients per server. If you assume clients will make no more than one WAN hop to reach a Global Catalog server, how many Global Catalog servers does PTO need?
>
> ❑ a. 3
>
> ❑ b. 4
>
> ❑ c. 5
>
> ❑ d. 6

Answer b is correct, and all others are incorrect. Because Scottsdale has 13,000+ users, it will need two Global Catalog servers. It will not need three, because there are not 7,000 sales users in the entire company. Because Boston and Atlanta have fewer than 10,000 users (even adding the maximum number of sales users), they will each need a single Global Catalog server.

Need to Know More?

 Shannon, Michael. *MCSE Exchange 2000 Design Exam Prep*. The Coriolis Group, Scottsdale, AZ, 2001. ISBN 1-58880-026-1. This book is both a good study guide and a reference.

 Read Chapter 15 of the *Microsoft Exchange 2000 Server Planning and Installation* located in the \Docs folder of the Exchange 2000 CD-ROM.

 Read Chapter 17 of the *Exchange 2000 Server Resource Kit*.

 Search **www.microsoft.com/technet** and the Exchange 2000 Server Help file using the terms at the beginning of the chapter.

 Search **www.Win2000mag.com** using the term "Exchange 2000" and the terms at the beginning of this chapter.

 Search **www.mcpmag.com** for "Exam 70-225" or "Exchange 2000". *MCP Magazine* will have good information to help prepare for the exam.

 Read the Exchange 2000 Front-End and Back-End Topology White Paper from **www.microsoft.com/exchange**, by Sean Lyndersay, Program Manager, Microsoft Exchange Server. This is a 26-page must-read before taking the exam.

Security Planning for Exchange 2000

Terms you'll need to understand:

✓ Internal threat
✓ External threat
✓ Virus
✓ TCP/IP filter
✓ IPSec
✓ Secure Sockets Layer (SSL)
✓ Public Key Infrastructure (PKI)
✓ Certificate Services
✓ Certificate Authority (CA)
✓ Key Management (KM) Server

Techniques you'll need to master:

✓ Configuring Outlook to display attachment warnings
✓ Identifying internal and external threats
✓ Designing a Public Key Infrastructure

As the use of messaging systems like Exchange 2000 increases, so does the need for increased security. The importance of securing these messaging systems is a number one priority for many organizations. Unlike other systems, securing messaging systems is much more complicated than simply securing the server. With the proliferation of email viruses, securing messages can be just as important. In this chapter, you will learn about the different types of security threats that can affect Exchange. You will then learn how to design a security plan using Exchange 2000, Windows 2000, and third-party services.

Why Do You Need Security?

Before learning about the services used to protect Exchange, it is important to understand why Exchange needs protecting. Security threats can come from all directions. Many companies make the mistake of only worrying about external attacks and never focusing on the internal threats.

Internal Threats

An internal attack typically comes from an employee of the company. Not all attacks on the system are deliberate. With an improperly secured system, it is easy for an uneducated user to cause harm. For example, many large companies prevent users from sending email to large distribution lists. This restriction prevents an uneducated user from sending a 5MB picture of his granddaughter to 10,000 users. Although the system should be able to handle this, it may not be the best use of resources. Restricted access to certain distribution groups is a good measure to secure against internal threats.

With the use of administrative groups, you can restrict administrator access. It is important to configure access correctly using Exchange roles and delegation of control. Administrative groups are discussed in detail in Chapter 4.

External Threats

Most Exchange 2000 systems are connected to the Internet. This connection to the Internet, as well as inbound email from the Internet, is where Exchange 2000 is most vulnerable. External threats are typically more dangerous and malicious than internal threats. External threats can come from many sources and may attack the servers or clients. In addition to protecting the clients and servers from network attacks, messaging attacks via email viruses are becoming more popular.

When reading a case study on the exam, look for possible internal and external threats. In the questions following the case study, you may need to address these threats.

Virus Protection

It is important for an organization to protect clients and servers from viruses. Before messaging viruses became so popular, most virus software was designed to scan the files on the system's hard drives, the system memory, and the network traffic. Although this is still important, scanning for email viruses has become a popular concern for most virus software companies.

Client-Side Protection

Detecting viruses on an email client can be easier and less expensive than a server-side solution for a small company. The first step in client-side protection is educating users. Most email viruses take the form of a script file attached to an email message (see Figure 8.1).

For an attached virus to infect the client, the attachment must be run. By default, Microsoft Outlook does not allow users to run certain files, such as Visual Basic and Java scripts, as well as Zip files. Outlook also warns users when other types of attachments are opened (see Figure 8.2). These warnings can be disabled, but it is not recommended.

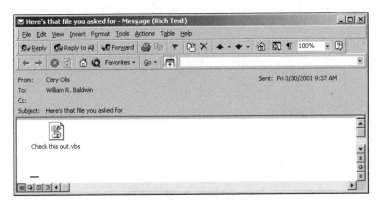

Figure 8.1   Attached virus in Outlook.

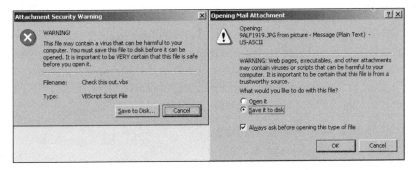

Figure 8.2   Outlook attachment warnings.

Client-side virus protection can also include virus protection software for the client. Virus software typically scans inbound email for a particular signature. The software contains many virus signatures to compare with. The virus signatures should be updated regularly to protect against new viruses. Once the software has found the virus, settings in the software determine the next course of action. These actions may include deleting the email or flagging the email for inspection later. There are many good programs that detect email viruses; Microsoft does not specifically recommend a particular brand.

Server-Side Protection

An email from the Internet passes through several systems before reaching the client. Detecting a virus with one of these systems is preferable to having the client detect the virus. By placing virus-scanning software on the server, the administrators have better control over the virus software. Administrators can also be alerted of viruses that clients may not inform them of.

Server-side virus protection includes virus protection software for the server. Virus software typically scans inbound and outbound email for a particular signature. The software contains many virus signatures to compare with. The virus signatures should be updated regularly to protect against new viruses. Once the software has found the virus, settings in the software determine the next course of action. These actions may include deleting the email or flagging the email for inspection later. There are many good programs that detect email viruses; Microsoft does not specifically recommend a particular brand.

TCP/IP Security

When protecting from both internal and external attacks, securing the *Transmission Control Protocol/Internet Protocol (TCP/IP)* packets is an efficient form of protection. From the external attacks, certain packets can be denied passage into the enterprise. Encrypting packets can help safeguard the data in the packets from both internal and external threats.

TCP/IP Filtering

TCP/IP filtering is most commonly associated with firewalls. A TCP/IP packet contains information in its header about the packet. This information can be used to either allow or disallow the packet entry into the enterprise. Filtering can also be used to prevent certain packets from exiting the enterprise. A TCP/IP packet is defined by the following fields in its header:

➤ Transmission protocol (TCP or UDP)

➤ Port

➤ Source IP address

➤ Destination IP address

Basic packet filtering either allows or disallows packets based on these fields. More advanced filtering can filter data based on other criteria, such as the type of data. When configuring a firewall between clients and an Exchange 2000 server, certain ports need to be enabled based on the type of messaging traffic. Table 8.1 shows some common Exchange 2000 ports.

For additional security, TCP/IP filtering can be enabled on individual network adapters on each Exchange 2000 server (see Figure 8.3). This basic filtering can help prevent attacks from inside the enterprise. Enabling filtering, however, on an Exchange 2000 server requires opening more than just its messaging ports; Exchange 2000 servers communicate with other Exchange 2000 servers, Active Directory servers, and MAPI clients. Chapter 7 discusses these ports in more detail.

Table 8.1 Exchange 2000 ports.	
Protocol	**Port**
Simple Mail Transfer Protocol (SMTP)	25
Hypertext Transfer Protocol (HTTP)	80
Kerberos	88
Message Transfer Agent (MTA)	102
Post Office Protocol v3 (POP3)	110
Network News Transfer Protocol (NNTP)	119
Mail Application Programing Interface (MAPI)	135
Remote Procedure Call (RPC)	135
Internet Message Access Protocol v4 (IMAP4)	143
Lightweight Directory Access Protocol (LDAP)	389
Hypertext Transfer Protocol (HTTP) with SSL	443
Network News Transfer Protocol (NNTP) with SSL	563
Internet Message Access Protocol v4 (IMAP4) with SSL	993
Post Office Protocol v3 (POP3) with SSL	995
Remote Procedure Call (RPC)	1024*
Instant Messaging (IM)	2980
LDAP (Global Catalog)	3268

*The first RPC service uses TCP port 1024; additional RPC services use 1025, then 1026, and so on.

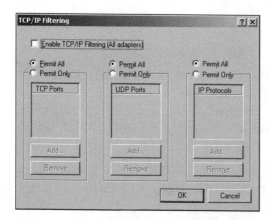

Figure 8.3   TCP/IP filtering in Windows 2000.

IPSec

TCP/IP communication was not designed to be a secure protocol. Fortunately, however, it was designed to be extensible, and this extensibility allows IP Security (IPSec) to secure TCP/IP traffic. When communicating using TCP/IP, it is important to maintain security by ensuring the identity of the computers communicating. IPSec authenticates computers using one of three methods:

➤ *Pre-shared string*—This is simply a test string shared by the computers. This string is passed using clear text and not very secure. The pre-shared string is primarily used for testing.

➤ *Certificate*—This is a private key certificate from a trusted Certificate Authority. This method is a good choice when all computers are not members of the same forest. Certificates have to be issued to each computer from a trusted Certificate Authority. Certificates work with non-Microsoft computers; however, currently IPSec only works with Windows 2000.

➤ *Kerberos*—This uses Windows 2000 Active Directory's Kerberos authentication. This method is very secure and does not require additional configuration or services.

IPSec authentication methods are defined by IPSec security rules. These rules also define encryption methods and levels. Each Windows 2000 computer can be assigned zero or one IPSec security rule. To simplify configuration of IPSec, Windows 2000 computers come with three unassigned pre-configured IPSec security rules (see Figure 8.4). Each rule is configured to use Kerberos authentication and strong encryption. These can be used as is or modified for custom configurations. You can also create new security rules:

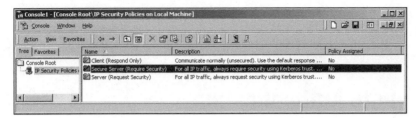

Figure 8.4   Default IP security policies.

➤ *Client (Respond Only)*—First, don't let the word *client* fool you; this can be configured on a server as well. This rule will only use IPSec if it is asked to by another computer.

➤ *Server (Request Security)*—Again, don't let the word *server* fool you; this can be configured on a client as well. This rule will request that traffic use IPSec, but will also communicate without using IPSec if need be.

➤ *Secure Server (Require Security)*—This rule will require all TCP/IP traffic to use IPSec and will not allow unsecured communications with this computer.

SSL

Secure Sockets Layer (SSL) version 3 is a protocol used to secure network traffic using a combination of public and secret key technology. SSL is Web-based and is therefore used in combination with Hypertext Transfer Protocol (HTTP). SSL requires certificates on both the client (Web browser) and the server (IIS server). SSL partners are authenticated using the private and secret keys. After authentication, data can be encrypted using different levels of encryption based on the level of security installed. Exchange 2000 virtual servers like HTTP and POP3 can be configured to use SSL (see Figure 8.5).

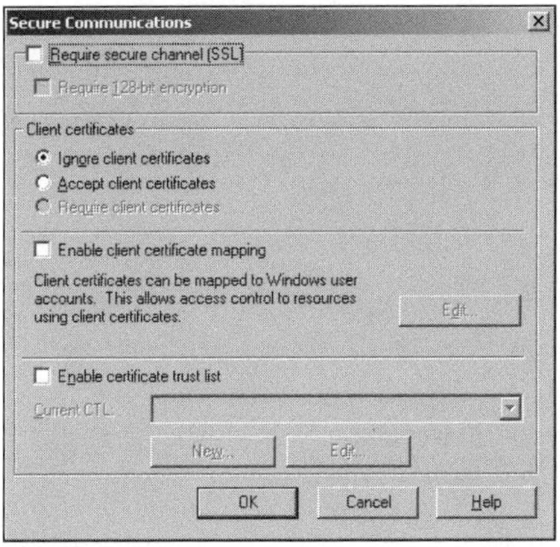

Figure 8.5   Secure Communications properties page.

It is important to know that HTTP virtual servers are configured using the Internet Services Manager, not the Exchange System Manager. IMAP4, NNTP, SMTP, and POP3 virtual servers are configured using the Exchange System Manager.

Remote Authentication

Remote clients accessing Exchange 2000 servers typically are required to authenticate via a remote access server. Requiring authentication helps prevent unauthorized access to Exchange 2000 and Windows 2000 services. Windows 2000 and Exchange 2000 support many authentication protocols, but not all protocols are supported by all clients. Windows 2000 supports the following authentication protocols:

➤ *CHAP*—Challenge Handshake Authentication Protocol is standard authentication protocol used with Microsoft and non-Microsoft clients. This is also referred to as Message Digest 5 Challenge Handshake Authentication Protocol, or MD5-CHAP.

➤ *MS-CHAP*—Microsoft Challenge Handshake Authentication Protocol is a standard authentication protocol used with Microsoft clients only.

➤ *MS-CHAPv2*—Microsoft Challenge Handshake Authentication Protocol version 2 is a standard authentication protocol used with Windows 2000 clients only. This is the preferred authentication protocol due to its mutual authentication and stronger encryption for data keys.

➤ *EAP*—Extensible Authentication Protocol contains application programming interfaces (APIs) that allow developers to write their own authentication protocols.

PKI

Public Key Infrastructure (PKI) is use to describe a system of digital certificates and Certificate Authorities (CA). Microsoft implements PKI with Windows 2000 Certificate Server and Exchange 2000 *Key Management (KM) Server*.

Certificate Server

The Windows 2000 Certificate Service is a trusted Certificate Authority providing PKI services for both Windows and non-Windows clients. Certificate Server can issue certificates to clients. Both users and computers can then use these certificates to verify identity on a network. For example, a Web user may use a certificate to verify her identity to her banking Web site.

KM Server

Microsoft Exchange Key Management (KM) Server provides Exchange servers and Outlook clients with a means for digital signatures and encryption. KM Server uses X.509v3 certificates to provide these services. KM Server must obtain these certificates from Windows 2000 Certificate Server and not other certificate services.

Secure Messaging

Exchange messages can be secured in a number of ways. This will include verification of users and clients and encryption of messages. KM Server is used for securing messages using *S/MIME (Secure Multipurpose Internet Mail Extensions)*.

Client-Side Security

Outlook 2000 and most email packages can be configured to secure messages using S/MIME and digital signatures. S/MIME is an industry standard for encrypting MIME content in an email. Encrypting using S/MIME on the client ensures the message is encrypted both during storage and transmission. Although the message is encrypted during transmission, the packet is not. To encrypt the packet, SSL or IPSec must be used. Using S/MIME will ensure the data stays encrypted, regardless of whether the data is stored on the server or the client.

Service-Side Security

Client-side security is good, but can require excessive time to configure. Exchange 2000 servers can be configured to encrypt messages. For email between Exchange 2000 servers, a setting in the SMTP virtual server will control encryption. For email sent to non-Exchange 2000 servers, encryption is more complicated. SMTP with *Transport Layer Security (TLS)* is used. TLS is similar to SSL and provides encryption and authentication.

Exchange 2000 supports SMTP for sending messages. Each Exchange 2000 server is configured with a virtual SMTP server. Any SMTP client can send email through the Exchange server using the virtual SMTP server. In most instances, you should not allow unauthorized clients to use your SMTP server to send email. SMTP virtual servers have settings to help prevent this:

➤ *Selecting which computer may access the virtual server*—You can configure the SMTP server to respond only to SMTP clients in a list, or to configure a list of clients not to communicate with.

➤ *Selecting which computer may relay through the virtual server*—Other SMTP servers can be configured to relay messages to another SMTP server. Although this can be desirable for other servers in your enterprise, you do not normally want to allow external SMTP servers to relay through your SMTP server.

➤ *Verifying Authentication*—By default, the SMTP virtual server allows anonymous access. Additional authentication can be required, including basic (clear text), basic (TLS), and/or Windows Kerberos.

➤ *Verifying Outbound Authentication*—This setting is used to configure how this server authenticates with another SMTP virtual server.

➤ *Providing Reverse DNS Lookup*—This option uses a DNS reverse lookup to verify the domain name of the SMTP client.

Practice Questions

Case Study

General Information

You have been hired by Cheap Food, Inc. (CFI), to assist the company with its deployment of Exchange 2000 Server. You are responsible for developing a security design to support Exchange 2000 Server while ensuring that your design meets the company's business and Information Technology goals.

CFI was created when five separate pre-packed food manufacturers in Ohio merged. The five companies had approximately 5,000 employees each. These employees have offices in several cities around Ohio. CFI has consolidated its offices so that it now has one office in each major city in Ohio. This includes headquarters, two regional offices, and two local offices.

The board required that the five former technology groups be consolidated, and that a single messaging system be deployed. They have asked management to merge the five companies while ensuring the company put out the same award-winning products it always has.

Figure 8.6 shows the physical locations of CFI's offices.

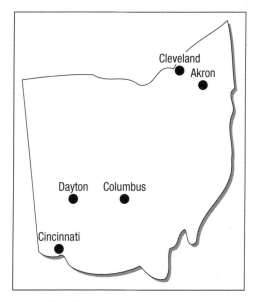

Figure 8.6   CFI's physical locations.

IT Environment

Each of the five companies that merged to create CFI used a third party to provide email services. CFI would like to bring that messaging inhouse with an Exchange 2000 deployment. CFI has already upgraded all servers to Windows 2000 Server and all clients to Windows 2000 Professional. They have deployed Active Directory and are running in native mode. All client computers have Office 2000 with Outlook 2000.

Active Directory has been deployed across CFI. The existing Active Directory design includes a single Active Directory tree and forest. There are four domains, one root domain and one for each of the Ohio regions, Northeast, Central, and Southwest. Each location has two domain controllers, each of which is a Global Catalog server. The groups are structured to keep replication traffic to a minimum. The administrators of each domain can create domain global and local groups, but they are not allowed to create a universal group. Only the Enterprise administrator can create universal groups. The physical structure of the Active Directory is shown in Figure 8.7, and the logical structure is shown in Figure 8.8.

The Cleveland office has a connection to the Internet. This connection is shared by all other locations.

Figure 8.7 Physical Active Directory design.

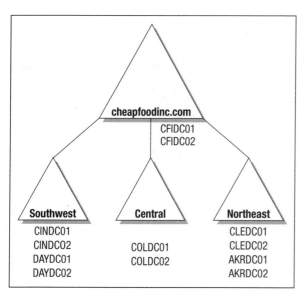

Figure 8.8   Logical Active Directory design.

Server Requirements and Goals

Front-end servers will be deployed in pairs to provide load balancing. Exchange 2000 servers should not have processor utilization that ever exceeds 70 percent. All clients and servers should be protected from viruses with anti-virus software. Clients will be informed not to open email attachments from unknown users.

CFI employs a large number of mobile users who travel throughout Ohio. CFI would like to deploy a remote email in every office.

Question 1

> Which two factors will most affect security planning for CFI? [Choose two correct answers]
> ❑ a. Internet connectivity
> ❑ b. Logical Active Directory design
> ❑ c. Physical Active Directory design
> ❑ d. Remote email

Answers a and d are correct. Enabling email for remote users requires certain ports in the firewall to be open and possibly a front-end server in a perimeter network. CFI's Internet connectivity affects how CFI is protected from external attacks. Answers b and c are incorrect, because the design of Active Directory will have less of an impact on the security design.

Question 2

If CFI wanted remote users to use POP3 to check email from home, what port or ports would they have to open in the firewall?

○ a. 25

○ b. 80

○ c. 110

○ d. 119

○ e. 993

○ f. 995

Answer c is correct. POP3 uses port 110 for retrieving messages. Answer a is incorrect, because port 25 is used by SMTP. SMTP can be used to send email; however, the question only wanted the users to check email. Answers b and d are incorrect, because port 80 is for HTTP and port 119 is for IMAP4. Answers e and f are incorrect, because ports 993 and 995 are used with SSL.

Question 3

If CFI wanted remote users to use IMAP4 clients to send and receive email from home and they wanted this connection to be secure, what port or ports would they have to open in the firewall? [Check all correct answers]

❑ a. 25

❑ b. 80

❑ c. 110

❑ d. 119

❑ e. 993

❑ f. 995

Answers a, d, and e are correct. IMAP4 uses port 119 and will use SSL with port 993 to secure traffic. IMAP4 clients use SMTP to send email and SMTP uses port 25. Answer b and c are incorrect, because port 80 is for HTTP and port 110 is for POP3. Answer f is incorrect, because port 995 is for SSL with POP3.

Question 4

> Which is the best way for CFI to prevent unauthorized external access to the SMTP virtual service?
>
> ○ a. Use reverse DNS lookup.
>
> ○ b. Require authentication.
>
> ○ c. Close inbound port 25 on the firewall.
>
> ○ d. Stop the SMTP virtual server.

Answer b is correct. By default, the SMTP virtual server accepts anonymous access. Requiring authentication is the best way to secure the service. Answer a is incorrect, because reverse DNS lookup will only ensure the SMTP client is not spoofing their domain name. Answers c and d are incorrect, because these would block all SMTP traffic.

Question 5

> CFI is planning on using a VPN for remote clients. They would like to use biometric scanners for authentication. Which of the following authentication protocols allow independent software vendors to supply new client and server authentication methods such as biometric scanners?
>
> ❑ a. CHAP
>
> ❑ b. MS-CHAP
>
> ❑ c. MS-CHAP v2
>
> ❑ d. MD5-CHAP
>
> ❑ e. EAP

Answer e is correct. Extensible Authentication Protocol (EAP) contains APIs that allow developers to write their own authentication protocols. Answer b is incorrect, because Microsoft Challenge Handshake Authentication Protocol (MS-CHAP) is a standard authentication protocol used with Microsoft clients only. Answer c is incorrect, because MS-CHAP v2 is a standard authentication protocol used with Windows 2000 clients only. Answers a and d are incorrect, because CHAP is standard authentication protocol used with Microsoft and non-Microsoft clients. This is also referred to as Message Digest 5 Challenge Handshake Authentication Protocol, or MD5-CHAP.

Question 6

> The CIO at CFI is concerned that servers at the Cleveland location might be vulnerable to external attacks because of the Internet connection at the Cleveland location. What are the best methods for securing the Cleveland servers from external attacks? [Check all correct answers]
>
> ❑ a. Setting up TCP/IP filtering on the servers
>
> ❑ b. Enabling IPSec on the servers
>
> ❑ c. Configuring a firewall between the Cleveland location and the Internet
>
> ❑ d. Configuring SSL on the servers

Answer b, c, and d are correct. A firewall properly configured at the Cleveland location is the best method to secure the servers from external attacks. IPSec and SSL will authenticate and encrypt TCP/IP traffic. This is a good way to protect servers. Answer a is incorrect, because configuring TCP/IP filters on the server could block traffic from internal clients and servers and are not recommended in this circumstance.

Question 7

> CFI would like to configure its clients and servers with IPSec. It wants the Windows 2000 servers always to use IPSec, and Exchange 2000 servers only to use IPSec when communicating with other IPSec clients. CFI wants to ensure internal Windows 2000 Professional computers running Outlook 2000 use IPSec when connecting to Exchange 2000 servers. If CFI configures Windows 2000 servers with the Secure Server and the Exchange 2000 servers with the client rule, what rule should it configure for the Windows 2000 Professional computers?
>
> ○ a. Server
>
> ○ b. Secure Server
>
> ○ c. Client
>
> ○ d. Secure Client

Answer a is correct. Because the Exchange 2000 servers are configured with client rule, they will only respond to IPSec when asked. The Server rule will request IPSec. Answer b is incorrect, because this would prevent Windows 2000 Professional computers from communicating with non-IPSec computers. Answer c is incorrect, because the client rule will only respond with IPSec and not request. If the Windows 2000 Professional computers were configured with the client rule, the traffic between the Windows 2000 Professional computers and the Exchange 2000 computers would not be encrypted. Answer d is incorrect, because Secure Client is not a valid rule.

Need to Know More?

 Shannon, Michael. *MCSE Exchange 2000 Design Exam Prep*. The Coriolis Group, Scottsdale, AZ, 2001. ISBN 1-58880-026-1. This book is good as both a study guide and reference.

 Read Chapter 13 of the *Microsoft Exchange 2000 Server Planning and Installation* located in the \Docs folder of the Exchange 2000 CD-ROM.

 Read Chapters 13 and 30 of the *Exchange 2000 Server Resource Kit*.

 Search **www.mcpmag.com** for "Exam 70-225" or "Exchange 2000". *MCP Magazine* will have good information to help prepare for the exam.

 Search **www.microsoft.com/technet** and the Exchange 2000 Server Help file using the terms at the beginning of the chapter.

 Search **www.Win2000mag.com** using the term "Exchange 2000" and the terms at the beginning of the chapter.

Designing Public Folder Usage and Implementation

Terms you'll need to understand:

✓ Public folder tree
✓ Default tree
✓ General-purpose tree
✓ Replication
✓ Replica
✓ Public Folder Instances container
✓ Public Folder container
✓ Replication Interval
✓ Replication Size Limit

✓ Message Priority
✓ Public folder referral
✓ Exchange Installable File System (EXIFS)
✓ Client permissions
✓ Directory rights
✓ Administrative rights
✓ Permission inheritance

Techniques you'll need to master:

✓ Creating a public folder design
✓ Designing public folder trees

✓ Adding public folder replicas
✓ Assigning permissions to public folders

Public folders are used to store information that can be shared by multiple users; they can contain information as simple as a text posting or as complicated as an inventory application. Public folder planning includes examining many aspects of public folders. Public folders can be replicated to multiple servers to provide improved access and fault tolerance. As with other functions of Exchange 2000, public folders integrate with Windows 2000 Active Directory. Accessing data in public folders can be accomplished using many different type of clients; different types of clients can affect your public folder design. To provide faster searches of public folders, full-text indexes can be implemented.

Public Folder Trees

A public folder tree represents a single hierarchy of folders. Public folder trees are similar to hard disk partitions in that all folders in the tree are children of the root. Unlike hard disk partitions, the root of a public folder tree can contain only folders. These top-level folders can contain additional folders and/or items. Each additional folder also can contain additional folders and/or items. Public folders can be created and managed using the Exchange System Manager (see Figure 9.1).

Note: In the Exchange System Manager, folders can be managed under either
<administrative group>\Servers\<server>\<storage group>\<store>\Public Folders
or the <administrative group>\Folders\<tree> containers. Folders can be added only
under the <administrative group>\Folders\<tree> container. Also, the <administrative
group>\Servers\<server>\<storage group>\<store>\Public Folders container contains
system folders. These system folders do not display under the <administrativegroup>
\Folders\ <tree> container (see Figure 9.1).

Figure 9.1 Public folders managed using the Exchange System Manager.

Figure 9.2   Public folders can be created using Microsoft Outlook.

MAPI clients, like Outlook 2000, can create public folders. Using client software, the contents of the folders can also be viewed and modified (see Figure 9.2).

Don't get confused on the exam. A public folder tree defines the structure of the folder hierarchy. The tree itself does not contain the items in the folders.

All Public Folders

When Exchange 2000 is installed, the All Public Folders tree is automatically created. This hierarchy is often referred to as the *MAPI tree* or *default tree*. MAPI and other clients can use this public folder tree. This is the only public folder tree available to MAPI clients. Every public folder server (a server with a public folder store) contains the default public folder tree. This is not to say that every public folder server contains every folder, just that every public folder server is *aware* of all public folders in the default public folder tree. Determining which of these servers contain which folders is discussed in the section called "Replication" later in this chapter.

General-Purpose Trees

Any additional public folder hierarchies are considered general-purpose trees. These trees are different from the default public folder trees in that MAPI clients, such as Outlook, cannot access these folders unless they are using non-MAPI methods such as HTTP. General-purpose trees are also not replicated

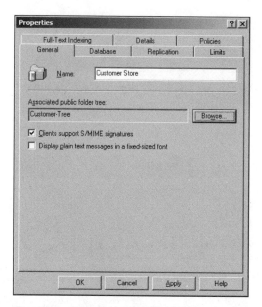

Figure 9.3   Public Folder Store Properties page.

to all public folder servers. General-purpose trees are only replicated to public folder servers with stores associated with the general-purpose tree. When creating a public folder store, a single public folder tree is associated with the store (see Figure 9.3). Each public folder tree can be associated with only one store per server.

Replication

It is important to distinguish the difference between public folder tree replication and public folder content replication. Remember, a public folder tree is the hierarchy of public folders. The tree contains only folder names and information, not the contents of the folders. The default public folder tree is replicated to all public folder servers. General-purpose trees are replicated only to public folder servers that contain a public folder store associated with that general-purpose tree.

The contents of public folders can be replicated to other public folder servers by creating public folder replicas. When a public folder is created, a single replica exists on the public folder server where it was created. Additional replicas can be created using the Exchange System Manager.

Note: Exchange uses multi-master replication to replicate public folders. Changes made on all replicas are replicated, and each folder replica is considered equal.

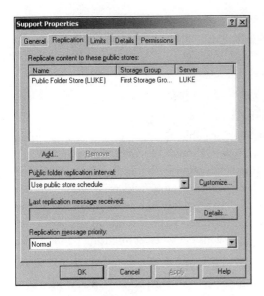

Figure 9.4   Public Folder Properties page example.

When adding replicas using the Exchange System Manager, you can replicate the folder to additional servers in the Properties page of the folder (see Figure 9.4). You also can add replicas to the Public Folder Instances container in the Exchange System Manager under the public folder store where the replica is to be added (see Figure 9.5). The Public Folder Instances container shows all public folder replicas in this store. The Public Folder container shows all public folders in the tree, regardless of the replicas in this store (see Figure 9.1).

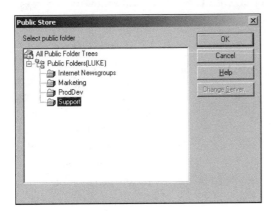

Figure 9.5   Adding a replica to the Public Folder Instances container.

Remember that all folders must contain at least one replica; to delete the last replica, the folder itself must be deleted using either the Exchange System Manager or Outlook.

Replication Configuration

When adding additional replicas to other public folder servers, proper planning must take place to determine which servers should contain replicas and how replication should be configured. In general, replicas should be placed such that users do not have to cross WAN links to access public folders. To accommodate this, replication of public folders will typically take place over WAN links. Using the Exchange System Manager, this replication can be configured, managed, and monitored. There are several settings to consider when configuring public folder replication:

➤ *Replication Interval*—Use this setting to configure how often new messages are transferred to other replicas. This setting can be configured on both the public folder store and on each public folder. Settings on a public folder override those on a public folder store.

➤ *Replication Size Limit*—When bandwidth is scarce, you can limit the size of messages that will be replicated. Messages beyond this limit will not replicate to other replicas. This setting can be configured on a public folder store only.

➤ *Message Priority*—Replication between replicas will use SMTP messages. By default, these message have a priority of Normal. These messages can also be configured as "urgent" or "not urgent." Connectors will route "urgent" messages first and "not urgent" messages last. This setting can be configured on a public folder only.

Connectors and Referrals

Exchange connectors are used to replicate folder contents between folder replicas. Routing groups, X.400, and SMTP connectors can be used to replicate public folder messages. Settings in the connectors can affect how data is replicated; in the same way, these settings affect email traffic. These connectors are also responsible for referring clients to public folder servers containing a replica of the folder they are requesting. For example, when a client tries to access a folder that does not have a replica in their public folder store, the store passes the request to an appropriate connector. The connector then uses standard routing techniques to determine which public folder store to refer the client to. These techniques include calculating connector costs and checking the link store table. (For more information on routing, see Chapter 6.) Connectors can also be configured to

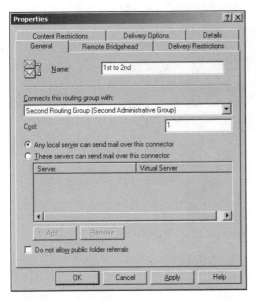

Figure 9.6   Do Not Allow Public Folder Referrals checkbox on a Connector Properties page.

not allow public folder referrals (see Figure 9.6). Preventing public folder referrals can be helpful when a design prohibits accessing public folders in different routing groups.

Active Directory

Public folders can have an SMTP email address and receive email like other recipients. Each public folder can be mail-enabled using the Exchange System Manager. Once a folder is mail-enabled, an object for that folder is added to Active Directory. This folder can now receive email and function as a normal Exchange recipient. Just because a folder is mail-enabled does not mean it will show up in the Exchange address lists. By default, mail-enabled folders are hidden from Exchange address lists, and email can be sent to them only using one of their email addresses (see Figure 9.7). All pre-Exchange 2000 public folders were mail-enabled and were hidden from Exchange address list. For backward compatibility, when Exchange 2000 is in mixed mode, new public folders created in the default public folder tree are mail-enabled and hidden from Exchange address lists. Public folders created in general-purpose folders are not mail-enabled by default. Once Exchange 2000 has been changed to native mode, all new public folders are not mail-enabled by default. Mail-enabling folders can be very useful for creating suggestion boxes or other repositories for gathering information from many users, that can be viewed and modified by many users.

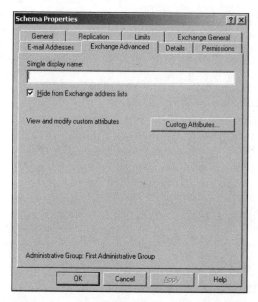

Figure 9.7 Hide from Exchange address lists setting on the Properties page of a mail-enabled public folder.

Accessing Data

Public folders can store many different types of data including messages and documents. This data can be accessed using different client software with different messaging protocols:

➤ *MAPI*—MAPI clients, such as Outlook 2000, can access only the default public folder tree. This tree and all its subfolders are displayed under All Public Folders in Outlook. MAPI clients cannot access general-purpose public folders.

➤ *EXIFS*—The *Exchange Installable File System (EXIFS)* maps Exchange data to a Windows 2000 drive letter (M: by default). The EXIFS can be accessed and searched in the same way as a standard Windows 2000 partition. Folders in the EXIFS can be shared and NTFS permissions can be assigned. The EXIFS volume accepts files in much the same way an NTFS volume does (see Figure 9.8).

➤ *NNTP access*—By default, each Exchange 2000 public folder server has the Network News Transfer Protocol (NNTP) installed. An NNTP virtual server is defined and can be used to make public folders accessible using NNTP clients, such as Outlook Express. Internet newsgroups can be created using the NNTP virtual server in the Exchange System Manager (see Figure 9.9). Internet newsgroups can be read-only or read/write. Messages in these public

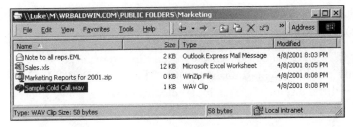

Figure 9.8   Exchange Installable File System (EXIFS).

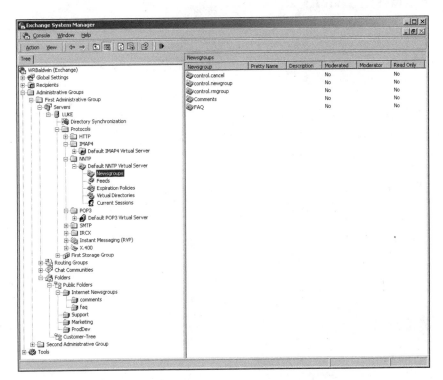

Figure 9.9   Internet newsgroups in the Exchange System Manager.

folders can be configured to expire, but cannot be deleted by posting users. Internet newsgroups can be configured with moderators who accept or reject messages before they are posted. These moderators can also delete unwanted messages. Internet newsgroups are useful when a design requires limited public folder access over the Internet.

➤ *HTTP access*—Outlook Web Access (OWA) is enabled by default on Exchange 2000. Public folders are accessible either though a user's OWA session at **http://<server name>/exchange** or by connecting to the folder directly at **http://<server name>/public/<folder name>**. Both the exchange and public Web sites are enabled by default and can be disabled using the Internet Services Manager or the Exchange System Manager.

➤ *IMAP4 access*—IMAP4 and POP3 clients are thin clients used to access email. These clients provide less functionality than MAPI. Unlike POP3, IMAP4 clients have the ability to access multiple folders, including public folders. Outlook Express supports both POP3 and IMAP4.

Permissions

One of the most important aspects of a public folder design is controlling access to public folders. Exchange 2000 has many different methods of assigning permissions. The way permissions behave and how they are assigned can have a dramatic impact on an Exchange 2000 design.

Types of Permissions

Public folders can be assigned three different types of permissions. These permissions can be assigned using four different tools.

Client Permissions

Client permissions for public folders in the default public folder tree can be assigned using the Exchange System Manager or Outlook. Client permissions control how clients access the folders, including the ability to manage the folders using client software. Client permissions can be assigned only to Exchange recipients. These permissions can be assigned by choosing a predefined role or by choosing custom permissions and creating a custom role (see Figure 9.10).

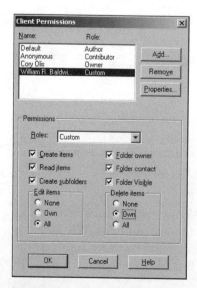

Figure 9.10   Client permissions for folder in the default public folder tree.

Only a user with the Folder Owner permission can change client permissions. Client permissions do not allow users to modify settings in the Exchange System Manager.

Directory Rights

Directory rights can be assigned only to mail-enabled public folders. These permissions control access to the Active Directory object associated with the mail-enabled public folder. An example of a directory right is Send As. Directory rights can be assigned to any Active Directory security principal. Directory rights do not allow users to modify settings in the Exchange System Manager.

Administrative Rights

Administrative rights are used to control access to public folder settings in the Exchange System Manager. Administrative rights include such permissions as modifying quotas and adding replicas. Administrative rights can be assigned to any Active Directory security principal.

Client Permissions in EXIFS

Windows Explorer can also be used to modify permissions when public folders are accessed using the EXIFS. These permissions function similarly as NTFS permissions and allow different control than client permissions. This includes assigning permissions to the individual items in a folder. Be careful when modifying these permissions; once the permissions are modified in this way on a public folder in the default public folder tree, the client permissions in Outlook and the Exchange System Manager will no longer work.

Client permissions for public folders in general-purpose public trees work in a similar way as Active Directory permissions. These permissions are assigned using the standard Access Control List (ACL) for Windows 2000. These permissions can be assigned to Windows 2000 security principals (see Figure 9.11).

Inheritance

Permissions for public folders work in a similar way as NTFS and Active Directory permissions. Permissions assigned to a parent folder can be configured to apply to the folder itself, subfolders, and/or items in that folder. You can also have permissions apply to any combination of the folder, its subfolders, and/or items in the folders. When creating a design, it is important to understand that some permissions propagate to subfolders and items by default, while others do not. It is always a good idea to verify inheritance when assigning permissions. To assign permissions to all public folders in a public folder tree, assign the permissions to the public folder tree itself. By default, permissions assigned to a tree are inherited by subfolder, but not inherited by items in those subfolders.

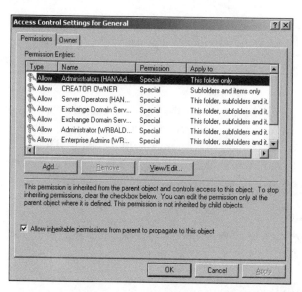

Figure 9.11 Client permissions for folders in general-purpose public folder trees.

Practice Questions

Case Study

General Information

You have been hired by Cheap Food, Inc. (CFI) to assist the company with its deployment of Exchange 2000 Server. You are responsible for developing a public folder design for Exchange 2000 Server while ensuring that your design meets the company's business and Information Technology goals.

CFI was created when five separate pre-packed food manufacturer in Ohio merged. The five companies had approximately 5,000 employees each. These employees have offices in several cities around Ohio. CFI has consolidated its offices so that it now has one office in each major city in Ohio. This includes headquarters, two regional offices, and two local offices.

The board required that the five former technology groups be consolidated, and that a single messaging system be deployed. They have asked management to merge the five companies while ensuring the company put out the same award-winning products it always has.

Figure 9.12 shows the physical locations of CFI's offices.

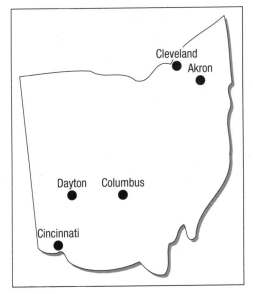

Figure 9.12   CFI's physical locations.

IT Environment

Each of the five companies that merged to create CFI used a third party to provide email services. CFI would like to bring that messaging inhouse with an Exchange 2000 deployment. CFI has already upgraded all servers to Windows 2000 Server and all clients to Windows 2000 Professional. It has deployed Active Directory and is running in native mode. All client computers have Office 2000 with Outlook 2000.

Active Directory has been deployed across CFI. The existing Active Directory design includes a single Active Directory tree and forest. There are four domains, including one root domain and one for each of the Ohio regions: Northeast, Central, and Southwest. Each location has two domain controllers, each of which is a Global Catalog server. The groups are structured to keep replication traffic to a minimum. The administrators of each domain can create domain global and local groups, but they are not allowed to create universal groups. Only the Enterprise administrator can create universal groups. The physical structure of the Active Directory is shown in Figure 9.13, and the logical structure is shown in Figure 9.14.

The Cleveland office has a connection to the Internet. This connection is shared by all other locations.

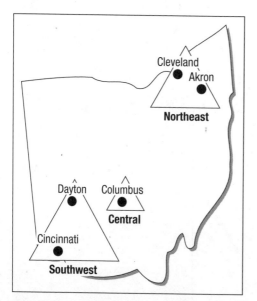

Figure 9.13   Physical Active Directory design.

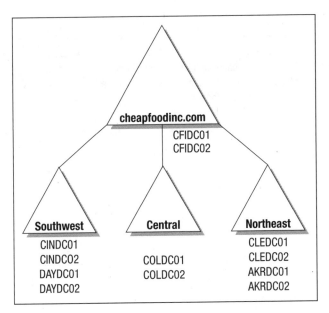

Figure 9.14   Logical Active Directory design.

Server Requirements and Goals

Front-end servers will be deployed in pairs to provide load balancing. Exchange 2000 servers should not have processor utilization that ever exceeds 70 percent. All clients and servers should be protected from viruses with anti-virus software. Client will be informed not to open email attachments from unknown users.

CFI employs a large number of mobile users who travel throughout Ohio. CFI would like to deploy a remote email in every office.

Question 1

CFI would like to provide remote clients with read access to public folders. Which of the following messaging protocols do *not* provide that functionality? [Choose all correct answers]

❑ a. IMAP4

❑ b. SMTP

❑ c. POP3

❑ d. NNTP

Answers b and c are correct. SMTP is used to send email and cannot be used to access public folders. POP3 can be used only to access a single folder and cannot be used to access public folders. Answers a and d are incorrect, because IMAP4 and NNTP can both be used to read Exchange public folders.

Question 2

CFI would like to create public folder hierarchies for each location. A manager at each location is responsible for managing his hierarchy. Each manager uses MAPI clients to manage his hierarchy. How many public folder trees need to be created?

○ a. None

○ b. One

○ c. Four

○ d. Five

Answer a is correct, and answers b, c, and d are incorrect. Outlook can access only the default public folder tree. This tree is created by default and does not have to be created. Instead of creating multiple trees, multiple top-level folders can be created, each representing it own hierarchy.

Question 3

After Exchange 2000 was deployed, a public folder was created on a public folder server in Cleveland (CLEEX01). This folder was created in the default public folder tree. A new Exchange 2000 server (DAYEX01) has just been deployed to Dayton. How would you move this folder to the Dayton server? Place the correct steps in the correct order.

Delete the replica on CLEEX01

Create a public folder tree on CLEEX01

Create a public folder tree on DAYEX01

Wait for replication

Create a public folder store on CLEEX01

Create a public folder store on DAYEX01

Add a replica to DAYEX01

The correct answer is:

Add a replica to DAYEX01

Wait for replication

Delete the replica on CLEEX01

Because the public folder is in the default public folder tree, there is no need to create an additional public folder tree or store. You should first add a replica, then wait for replication and delete the old replica.

Question 4

> After Exchange 2000 was deployed, three public folders were created on a public folder server in Cleveland (CLEEX02). These folders were created in a general-purpose public folder tree. A new Exchange 2000 server (COLEX03) has just been deployed to Columbus. How would you allow Cleveland and Columbus clients to access these folders without crossing WAN links?
>
> Delete the replicas on CLEEX02
>
> Create a public folder tree on CLEEX02
>
> Create a public folder tree on COLEX03
>
> Wait for replication
>
> Create a public folder store on CLEEX02
>
> Create a public folder store on COLEX03
>
> Add replicas to COLEX03

The correct answer is:

> Create a public folder store on COLEX03
>
> Add replicas to COLEX03

Because the public folder is in a general-purpose public folder tree, a new public folder store should be added in Columbus. This store will be associated with the general-purpose public folder tree. Once the store is created, replicas of the folders should be added to the Columbus store.

Question 5

Remote clients in Cincinnati will be accessing the top-level public folder CIN-TOP using a Web browser. They will gain access through a front-end server (CLEEX10) in Cleveland. The public folder replicas, however, will only exist on the CINEX02 server. If the administrators wanted to create a direct link to this folder on a Web page, what URL should they use?

○ a. **http://CLEEX02/public/cin-top**

○ b. **http://CINEX10/public/cin-top**

○ c. **http://CLEEX02/exchange/public/cin-top**

○ d. **http://CINEX10/exchange/public/cin-top**

○ e. **http://CLEEX02/exchange/cin-top**

○ f. **http://CINEX10/exchange/cin-top**

Answer a is correct. Outlook Web Access (OWA) is installed by default, and the public Web site is enabled for access to public folders in the default public folder tree. Answer b is incorrect, because the clients cannot gain access directly to the CINEX10 server; they will access the CLEEX02 server. The CLEEX02 server will redirect HTTP requests to the CINEX10 server. Answers c and d are incorrect, because "public" is an invalid folder under Exchange. Answers e and f are incorrect, because the Exchange Web site is used for accessing a user's mailbox.

Question 6

CFI would like to create public folder hierarchies for each location. A manager at each location will be responsible for managing her hierarchy. Each manager will use MAPI clients to manage her hierarchy. What type permissions should be assigned to grant these managers the rights they need?

○ a. Client permissions

○ b. Directory rights

○ c. Administrative rights

○ d. Exchange rights

○ e. Manager rights

Answer a is correct. Client permissions control how clients access the folders, including the ability to manage the folder using client software like Outlook. Answer b is incorrect, because directory rights can be assigned only to mail-enabled public folders. These permissions control access to the Active Directory object associated with the mail-enabled public folder. An example of a directory right is Send As. Answer c is incorrect, because administrative rights are used to control access to public folder settings in the Exchange System Manager. Answers d and e are incorrect, because Exchange rights and manager rights are not valid types of permissions.

Question 7

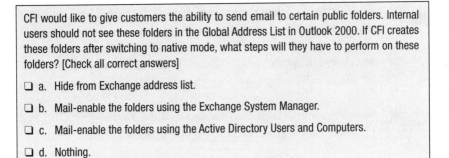

CFI would like to give customers the ability to send email to certain public folders. Internal users should not see these folders in the Global Address List in Outlook 2000. If CFI creates these folders after switching to native mode, what steps will they have to perform on these folders? [Check all correct answers]

❑ a. Hide from Exchange address list.

❑ b. Mail-enable the folders using the Exchange System Manager.

❑ c. Mail-enable the folders using the Active Directory Users and Computers.

❑ d. Nothing.

Answers b is correct. Once in native mode, all new public folders are not mail-enabled by default. Answer a is incorrect, because mail-enabled folders are hidden from Exchange address list by default. Answer c is incorrect, because Active Directory Users and Computers cannot be used to mail-enable public folders.

Need to Know More?

 Shannon, Michael. *MCSE Exchange 2000 Design Exam Prep.* The Coriolis Group, Scottsdale, AZ, 2001. ISBN 1-58880-026-1. This book is good as both a study guide and a reference.

 Read Chapter 4 of the *Microsoft Exchange 2000 Server Planning and Installation* located in the \Docs folder of the Exchange 2000 CD-ROM.

 Read the public folder sections of Chapters 9, 15, 16, 21, 22, and 31 of the *Exchange 2000 Server Resource Kit.*

 Search **www.mcpmag.com** for "Exam 70-225" or "Exchange 2000". *MCP Magazine* will have good information to help prepare for the exam.

 Search **www.microsoft.com/technet** and the Exchange 2000 Server Help file using the terms at the beginning of the chapter.

 Search **www.Win2000mag.com** using the term "Exchange 2000" and the terms at the beginning of the chapter.

10

Planning for Internet Connectivity

Terms you'll need to understand:

✓ Internet Information Services (IIS)

✓ Simple Mail Transfer Protocol (SMTP)

✓ Hypertext Transfer Protocol (HTTP)

✓ Network News Transfer Protocol (NNTP)

✓ Post Office Protocol version 3 (POP3)

✓ Internet Message Access Protocol version 4 (IMAP4)

✓ Virtual server

✓ Smart host

✓ SMTP connector

✓ Mail exchanger (MX) record

✓ Authentication

✓ Anonymous access

✓ Basic authentication

✓ Windows Integrated authentication

✓ Virtual Private Network (VPN)

✓ Layer 2 Tunneling Protocol (L2TP)

✓ Point-to-Point Tunneling Protocol (PPTP)

✓ Secure Sockets Layer (SSL)

✓ Certificates

Techniques you'll need to master:

✓ Creating an Internet email design

✓ Designing secure remote communications to virtual servers

It is rare to see an organization deploy a messaging system without connectivity to the Internet. Planning for Exchange 2000 Internet connectivity must include services, hardware, and software outside Exchange 2000. In this chapter, you will learn how Exchange 2000 uses Windows 2000's Internet Information Services (IIS) for connectivity to the Internet. Proper planning for Internet connectivity must also include understanding client connectivity and authentication. In addition to standard client access, Exchange 2000 also supports Network News Transfer Protocol (NNTP). You will learn how this protocol is used with Exchange 2000, and how to best plan for its deployment.

Internet Information Services (IIS)

Unlike pre-Exchange 2000 servers, Exchange 2000 servers do not provide Internet messaging transports. Exchange 2000 Internet messages are serviced by IIS. IIS is installed by default with Windows 2000. Before installing Exchange 2000, IIS must be installed and its three core protocols must be installed. These protocols are:

➤ *Simple Mail Transfer Protocol (SMTP)*—Used to send messages across a TCP/IP network. SMTP is the default messaging protocol for Exchange 2000 and is used by most Internet email systems. SMTP uses TCP port 25.

➤ *Hypertext Transfer Protocol (HTTP)*—Used by the World Wide Web to transfer Web pages. Exchange 2000 uses this protocol with its Outlook Web Access (OWA) service. OWA allows clients to view email and public folders through a Web browser. HTTP uses TCP port 80. When HTTP is secured using Secure Sockets Layer (SSL), HTTP also uses TCP port 443.

➤ *Network News Transfer Protocol (NNTP)*—Used to transfer bulk messages between servers and to retrieve those messages using client software that supports the NNTP protocol. Exchange 2000 can use NNTP to make public folders available to NNTP clients. Exchange 2000 also can use NNTP to pull NNTP messages (also known as newsfeeds) from other NNTP servers. NNTP uses TCP port 119. When NNTP is secured with SSL, NNTP also uses TCP port 563.

After Exchange 2000 is installed, IIS is modified to include additional messaging protocols. These protocols include:

➤ *Post Office Protocol version 3 (POP3)*—Used by clients to retrieve email messages from a server. POP3 cannot be used to send email; another protocol (typically SMTP) must be used to send messages. The POP3 protocol is very limited and provides no other functionality. POP3 uses TCP port 110. When secured with SSL, POP3 also uses TCP port 995.

➤ *Internet Message Access Protocol version 4 (IMAP4)*—Similar to POP3 in that it retrieves messages from a server, IMAP4 cannot be used to send email; another protocol (typically SMTP) must be used to send messages. IMAP4 has additional functionality over POP3. IMAP clients can check multiple mailboxes and access public folders.

Virtual Servers

When Exchange 2000 is installed, it creates a virtual server for each of the supported protocols. These virtual servers allow for each protocol to be configured with its own unique message formats, authentication methods, size limits, and other settings often specific to the protocol.

Note: With the exception of HTTP, all virtual servers should be maintained using the Exchange System Manager. The Exchange System Manager stores the settings directly into Active Directory. These settings are then written to the IIS metabase. When the Internet Services Manager is used to maintain these virtual servers, the Internet Services Manager writes directly to the IIS metabase. Settings from Active Directory update settings in the IIS metabase, and settings changed using the Internet Services Manager are lost.

It is also possible to create multiple virtual servers per protocol. Having multiple servers per protocol enables different settings for different sets of users. Each virtual server is defined by one or more IP addresses and TCP ports (see Figure 10.1).

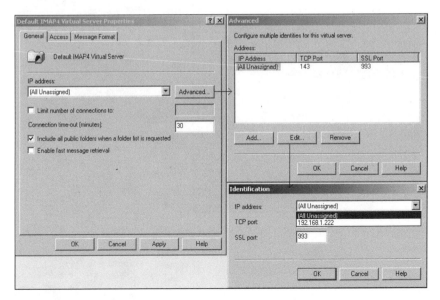

Figure 10.1 Configuring IP address and port information on a virtual server.

When multiple virtual servers are configured for the same protocol, they can share a common IP address and use different TCP ports. Configuring non-standard TCP ports for messaging protocol, however, is not recommended. Few clients have the ability to change the TCP port of a particular protocol. When multiple virtual servers are configured for the same protocol, they can share a common TCP port and have different IP addresses. This configuration is recommended. Creating virtual servers with different IP address requires Windows 2000 be configured with the same IP addresses. In Windows 2000 networking, a single network interface card (NIC) can be configured with multiple IP addresses by using the Advanced properties page of the TCP/IP protocol (see Figure 10.2).

When planning for Internet connectivity, virtual server design plays an important role. Internet connectivity design requirements may include encrypted messages, message size limits, message formats, and public folder access. Understanding what options are available for each virtual server is crucial to creating a proper plan. Table 10.1 highlights some of the options available for virtual server configuration. Each virtual server also has additional options specific to its protocol.

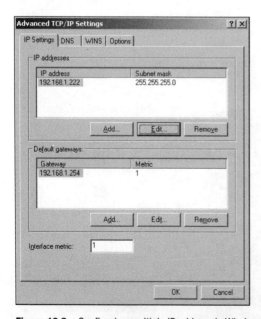

Figure 10.2   Configuring multiple IP address in Windows 2000 networking.

Table 10.1 Virtual server configuration.					
Setting	HTTP	IMAP4	NNTP	POP3	SMTP
Specific IP address	Yes	Yes	Yes	Yes	Yes
Specific port	Yes	Yes	Yes	Yes	Yes
Limit number of connections	Yes	Yes	Yes	Yes	Yes
Authentication method	Yes	Yes	Yes	Yes	Yes
Message size limits	No	No	Yes	No	Yes
Number of recipients limit	No	No	No	No	Yes
Fast message retrieval	No	Yes	No	No	No

Internet Email

Exchange 2000 servers use the SMTP virtual server for sending and receiving email across the Internet. The SMTP virtual server is installed by default on all Exchange 2000 servers and processes incoming and outgoing SMTP email.

Outgoing Mail

For outgoing email, the SMTP virtual server queries DNS for the *mail exchanger (MX) record* of the destination domain. This MX record contains the host name or names of the destination domain's incoming email server or servers. The host name is then resolved to an IP address and the outgoing mail is sent over the TCP/IP network using the SMTP protocol. To prevent the SMTP service from querying DNS for each destination domain, the SMTP virtual server can be configured to forward all outgoing email to another SMTP server. This external SMTP server is called *a smart host*. The smart host can forward the email, and more elaborate smart hosts can also convert and/or filter email.

If an organization has multiple Exchange 2000 servers, it is not typically desirable to have each server send email directly to the Internet. SMTP connectors can be created to send Internet email through one or more servers. When one or more SMTP connectors are present in an organization, Exchange 2000 Server forwards Internet email to these servers. An Exchange 2000 server attempts to find SMTP connectors in their own routing group first, and then looks outside the routing group. Like SMTP virtual servers, SMTP connectors can use DNS or a smart host for sending Internet email. SMTP connectors have additional configurations not found on SMTP virtual servers. The following settings can be configured:

➤ *Local bridgeheads*—This is one or more servers in the routing group responsible for routing SMTP for this connector. At least one local bridgehead must be configured.

➤ *Address space*—This is DNS domain or domains that this SMTP connector can be used to send email to. For an SMTP connector forwarding email to the Internet, a domain of asterisk (*) includes all domains.

➤ *Delivery restrictions*—SMTP connectors can accept or reject messages from Exchange recipients.

➤ *Content restrictions*—The type and size of messages can be restricted using these options.

➤ *Scheduled delivery*—Unlike the SMTP virtual server that is always running, the SMTP connector can be configured to run at specific intervals.

Incoming Mail

Any Exchange 2000 server configured with an SMTP virtual server can receive and process inbound SMTP email. It is good practice to specify only a few servers for inbound SMTP email. For Internet email to find an organization, at least one MX record for that domain must exist. The MX record is created in the organization's DNS domain. This MX record can point directly to one of the organization's Exchange 2000 servers, or multiple MX records can be created pointing to several Exchange 2000 servers. If multiple MX records are defined for a single domain, the MX record's priority (also know as cost) is used to determine which record to use. Lower priority takes precedence, and if two records have the same priority, Internet email is sent to each server using a round-robin technique. This DNS round-robin process provides load balancing to the servers and fault tolerance if a server should fail.

Due to bandwidth restrictions and for security reasons, many organizations do not want email sent directly to their Exchange 2000 servers. Many ISPs have SMTP servers that hold organizations' email for them. The organization then configures an Exchange 2000 server to pull the SMTP email at regular intervals. To configure an Exchange 2000 server to pull SMTP email, an SMTP connector must be created. The SMTP connector must send the SMTP server holding the email the **ETRN** command. The remote SMTP server then sends the SMTP email to the Exchange 2000 server. In the SMTP connector, you can specify to the **ETRN** command used when email is sent. If DNS is used instead of a smart host, this only pulls email from domains where email is sent. Under normal circumstances, you only want to select this option if a smart host is defined. If a smart host is not defined and the SMTP connector is using DNS to send email, the SMTP connector can be configured to send the **ETRN** command to a specific server. The **ETRN** request in the SMTP connector has its own schedule, which is independent of the SMTP connector's schedule.

Note: Exchange 2000 servers use MX records or smart hosts for sending Internet Email.

Remote Client Connectivity

Remote clients can connect to Exchange 2000 using the Internet. There are many different methods for connectivity. Each of these methods requires careful planning and unique configuratons for clients, servers, and firewalls. There are many different vendors supplying client email software. Microsoft exams, however, tend to focus on only two software applications: Outlook and Outlook Express. Other applications like Eudora and Pegasus Mail are widely used and function in a similar manner to Outlook Express.

Outlook 9X/2000

Outlook can be configured to send and receive email using MAPI and/or Internet Email. When configured to use Internet Email, Outlook must be configured with incoming and outgoing servers. The incoming server can be an email server with either the POP3 or the IMAP4 protocol running. Outlook does not allow you to specify the type of incoming server; it automatically uses the appropriate protocol for retrieving email. For sending email, an outgoing server must be specified. This email server must be a server using the SMTP protocol.

Outlook Express

Outlook Express can be configured to send and receive email using Internet Email only. Outlook Express cannot function as a MAPI client. Outlook Express must be configured with incoming and outgoing servers. The incoming server must be an email server with either POP3, HTTP, or IMAP4 running. Outlook Express does allow you to specifiy the type of incoming server (see Figure 10.3).

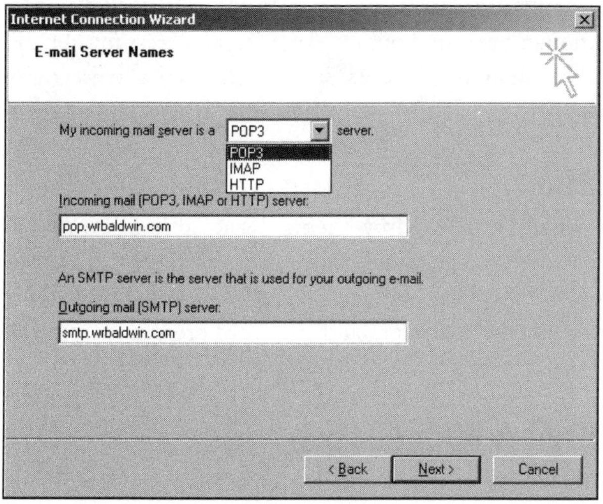

Figure 10.3   Internet Connection Wizard in Outlook Express.

For sending email, an outgoing server must be specified. This email server will be a server using the SMTP protocol. Outlook Express can also be configured as a news reader. Outlook Express uses NNTP to read and post messages to NNTP servers.

 Remember: Outlook Express can be used only with POP3 and IMAP4. Outlook Express does not support MAPI.

Outlook Web Access (OWA)

Using the HTTP protocol, Web browser clients can access email and public folders over the Internet or an intranet. OWA provides a limited version of Outlook through the Web browser interface. HTTP is used to transfer Web pages to and from the OWA server. OWA does not use POP3, IMAP4, or SMTP. For more information on OWA, see Chapter 12.

Authentication

Exchange 2000 virtual servers require a client to authenticate before using the server. Each virtual server has a different level of authentication. These levels of authentication determine how the client is authenticated, not which users are permitted access.

Anonymous Access

Anonymous access allows clients to access the virtual server without providing credentials such as usernames and passwords. The IMAP4 and POP3 virtual servers do not have the anonymous access option. Anonymous access for HTTP, SMTP, and NNTP may be desirable, if users outside the company use these services.

Basic Authentication

Basic authentication is widely supported by clients. Basic authentication re-quires a username and password be provided before access to the virtual server is provided. All protocols support basic authentication. Basic authentication is vulnerable to attacks because the username and password are sent across the network as clear-text.

Windows Integrated Authentication

Windows Integrated authentication is not widely supported by clients. Win-dows Integrated authentication requires a username and password be provided before access to the virtual server is provided. All protocols support Windows Integrated authentication. Windows Integrated authentication is less vulnerable to attacks because the username and password are encrypted as they are sent across the network.

Note: Windows Integrated authentication encrypts the username and password only. To encrypt the data, other methods must be used. See the "Secure Communications" section later in this chapter.

Secure Communications

When planning for remote client connectivity, securing communications is an important aspect of the plan. Remote clients can use Virtual Private Networks or certificates to secure communications.

Virtual Private Network

When clients need access to email over the Internet, a *Virtual Private Network (VPN)* is the best solution. A VPN is a secure connection between the client and the server. Windows 2000 clients support both *Point-to-Point Tunneling Protocol (PPTP)* and *Layer 2 Tunneling Protocol (L2TP)* for VPN communications. When MAPI access over the Internet is required, it is recommended that traffic be secured using a VPN.

Certificates and SSL

HTTP, POP3, IMAP4, and SMTP traffic can be secured using a VPN; however, encrypting the traffic using *Secure Sockets Layer (SSL)* can be as secure and can be easier to configure. Because SSL uses specific ports, most firewalls support SSL. Many firewalls do not support VPN protocols, and often the VPN server must be placed outside the firewall. To configure a virtual server for SSL, a certificate for the server must be obtained. After the certificate has been installed, each virtual server can be configured to force clients to use SSL (see Figure 10.4).

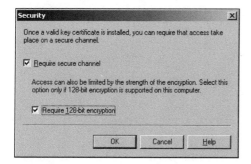

Figure 10.4   Forcing SSL communications.

Connection Control

It is often desirable to allow only certain computers or groups of computers to access a virtual server. For example, allowing only computers with IP addresses of the internal network helps to prevent unauthorized use by external computers. Each virtual server can be configured to allow all but certain computers, or to allow only certain computers (see Figure 10.5). When creating an Internet connection plan, it is often difficult to obtain a list of all IP addresses of the remote client computers. Connections can also be granted based on DNS domains; however, this requires that the clients be registered in DNS and a DNS reverse lookup must be performed.

Network News Transfer Protocol (NNTP)

IIS in Windows 2000 supports NNTP. Clients and servers used to support USENET newsgroups on the Internet use NNTP. With Exchange 2000 installed, a Windows 2000 server can use its NNTP virtual server to receive NNTP feeds from USENET servers. These newsgroups can be stored in public folders and accessed by Exchange clients.

Newsgroups can be set up in the default public folder tree or in a general public folder tree. There are many factors to consider when deciding which tree to use and what server and store to maintain the folders. USENET NNTP feeds can be very large and can contain thousands of folders with millions of messages. An Exchange 2000 server hosting newsgroups typically requires massive amounts of disk space. The server can be configured to pull NNTP feeds or have them pushed. Either way, the amount of network traffic associated with these feeds can also be massive. Proper bandwidth needs must be considered.

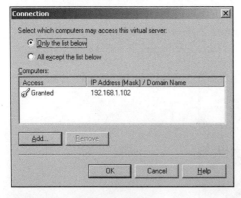

Figure 10.5   Connection control.

Note: Another way to reduce traffic is to only get certain newgroups from a newsfeed. When a feed is configured in an NNTP virtual server, you can get specific newsgroups or block specific newsgroups.

The news hierarchy includes many changes when updated. These changes include both new messages and changes to the folder structure. If this hierarchy is part of the default public folder tree, these folder changes are replicated to all public folder servers. It is a good idea to place newsgroup folders in their own general-purpose public folder tree. A downside to placing newsgroups in their own general-purpose public folder tree is that only non-MAPI clients can access general-purpose public folder trees.

Because the amount of changes to the newsgroup hierarchy can be massive, transaction logs and replication play a big part in a newsgroup plan. Transaction logs for newsgroups are dramatically larger than they would be for normal public folders and mailboxes. Newsgroup public folders should be placed in their own store in a separate storage group. The storage groups logs can then be configured for circular logging to prevent excessive transaction logs.

Replication from the other Exchange 2000 servers takes careful planning. The number of new messages in newsgroup folders can cause replication problems. The amount of data replicated because public folder servers are hosting newsgroups can again be massive. Maintaining many public folder newsgroup servers in remote locations can saturate wide area network (WAN) links. For newsgroups, it is typically recommended to have newsgroup servers connected by local area network (LAN) connections. Under most circumstances, the amount of traffic generated by clients accessing the newsgroup across the WAN is less than the replication traffic between newsgroup servers.

Another possibility for newsgroups access to remote locations is selective replication of newsgroup folders. If a remote location needs access to certain public folders, only those public folders can be replicated to the remote location. The remote client will see all the newsgroups, but will access certain newsgroups from the local server. When the non-replicated newsgroups are accessed, the client accesses the server at the central location. Figure 10.6 shows an example of selective replication.

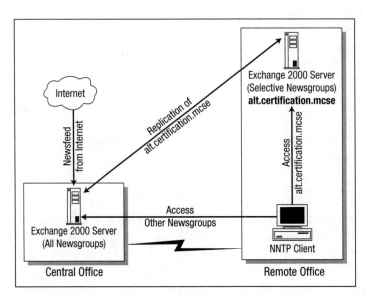

Figure 10.6   Example of selective newsgroup replication.

Practice Questions

Case Study

General Information

You have been hired by Cheap Food, Inc. (CFI) to assist the company with its deployment of Exchange 2000 Server. You are responsible for Internet connectivity for Exchange 2000 Server while ensuring that your design meets the company's business and Information Technology goals.

CFI was created when five separate pre-packaged food manufacturers in Ohio merged. The five companies had approximately 5,000 employees each. These employees have offices in several cities around Ohio. CFI has consolidated its offices so that it now has one office in each major city in Ohio. This includes headquarters, two regional offices, and two local offices.

The board required that the five former technology groups be consolidated, and that a single messaging system be deployed. They have asked management to merge the five companies while ensuring the company put out the same award-winning products it always has.

Figure 10.7 shows the physical locations of CFI's offices.

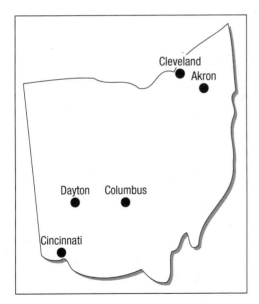

Figure 10.7   CFI's physical locations.

IT Environment

Each of the five companies that merged to create CFI used a third party to provide email services. CFI would like to bring that messaging inhouse with an Exchange 2000 deployment. CFI has already upgraded all servers to Windows 2000 Server and all clients to Windows 2000 Professional. They have deployed Active Directory and are running in native mode. All client computers have Office 2000 with Outlook 2000.

Active Directory has been deployed across CFI. The existing Active Directory design includes a single Active Directory tree and forest. There are four domains: one root domain and one for each of the Ohio regions—Northeast, Central, and Southwest. Each location has two domain controllers, each of which is a Global Catalog server. The groups are structured to keep replication traffic to a minimum. The administrators of each domain can create domain global and local groups, but they are not allowed to create universal groups. Only the Enterprise administrator can create universal groups. The physical structure of the Active Directory is shown in Figure 10.8 and the logical is shown in Figure 10.9.

The Cleveland office has a connection to the Internet. This connection is shared by all other locations. DNS is configured and all clients and servers have access to the Internet.

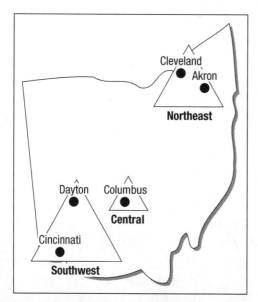

Figure 10.8   Physical Active Directory design.

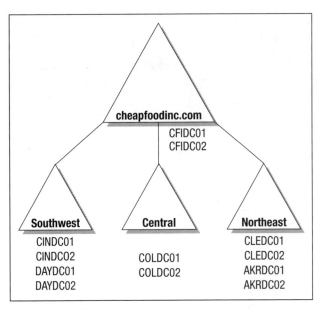

Figure 10.9 Logical Active Directory design.

Server Requirements and Goals

CFI would like to provide Internet email for all users. Email sent from the company should be passed to the Internet and email from the Internet should be sent into the company.

CFI would also like to provide users with access to USENET newsgroups from an Internet feed. CFI would like clients to use Outlook MAPI access to these newsgroups. The internal WAN traffic should be limited. Users will frequently use the alt.food and the alt.food.cheap newsgroup.

Question 1

> You are analyzing security on CFI servers. You need to determine what IIS protocols can be present on the different types of servers. You have classified CFI's server into the following:
>
> Windows 2000 domain controller (non-Exchange server)
>
> Windows 2000 member server (non-Exchange server)
>
> Windows 2000 domain controller (Exchange server)
>
> Windows 2000 member server (Exchange server)
>
> Match the IIS protocols with the servers they can exist on. You may not need to use all protocols.
>
> SMTP
>
> HTTP
>
> POP3
>
> NNTP
>
> IMAP4
>
> ETRN

The correct answer is:

Windows 2000 domain controller (non-Exchange server)

    SMTP

    HTTP

    NNTP

Windows 2000 member server (non-Exchange server)

    SMTP

    HTTP

    NNTP

Windows 2000 domain controller (Exchange server)

    SMTP

    HTTP

    POP3

    NNTP

    IMAP4

Windows 2000 member server (Exchange server)

SMTP

HTTP

POP3

NNTP

IMAP4

Windows 2000 Server has IIS installed by default. This default installation includes HTTP and SMTP. NNTP can be added to IIS. Once Exchange 2000 is installed, IMAP4 and POP3 are added to the IIS protocols. **ETRN** is an SMTP command used to request email from an SMTP server.

Question 2

> After Exchange 2000 is deployed, what additional steps must be taken to enable Exchange 2000 recipients to send email to Internet email addresses?
>
> ○ a. An SMTP connector should be configured in each routing group.
>
> ○ b. An SMTP connector should be configured in the Cleveland routing group.
>
> ○ c. An SMTP virtual server should be configured on a server at each location.
>
> ○ d. An SMTP virtual server should be configured at each location.
>
> ○ e. An MX should be created in the cheapfoodinc.com DNS domain.
>
> ○ f. None of the above.

Answer f is correct. For outgoing email, the SMTP virtual server queries DNS for the mail exchanger (MX) record of the destination domain. This MX record contains the host name or names of the destination domain's incoming email server or servers. The host name is then resolved to an IP address and the outgoing mail sent over the TCP/IP network using the SMTP protocol. Answers a and b are incorrect, because even though it is not typically desirable to have each server send email directly to the Internet, it is possible. SMTP connectors can be created to send Internet email through one or more servers. Answers c and d are incorrect, because every Exchange 2000 server is configured with an SMTP virtual server and every server in this organization has access to DNS and the Internet. Answer e is incorrect, because an MX record for the cheapfoodinc.com domain only needs to be created to receive incoming Internet email.

Question 3

> CFI would like its Exchange 2000 recipients to receive email from the Internet. CFI wants to load balance the incoming email between two Exchange 2000 servers at the Cleveland office. If one of these servers should fail, CFI would like the other server to handle all inbound email traffic. What is the best way to accomplish this?
>
> ○ a. Create two SMTP connectors, one for each server. Configure both connectors to point to the same smart host.
>
> ○ b. Create two SMTP connectors, one for each server. Configure both connectors to point to different smart hosts.
>
> ○ c. Create two SMTP connectors, one for each server. Configure both connectors to use DNS.
>
> ○ d. Create one SMTP connector and configure both servers as local bridgeheads. Configure the connector to use DNS MX records.
>
> ○ e. Create one MX record in the cheapfoodinc.com DNS domain. Configure the host name of both servers in the MX record.
>
> ○ f. Create two MX records in the cheapfoodinc.com DNS domain. Configure each MX record with the host name of one of the servers.

Answer f is correct. When email is sent from the Internet, an MX record is used to find the SMTP server. Configuring two MX records uses DNS for round-robin load balancing and to provide fault tolerance. Answers a, b, c, and d are incorrect, because SMTP connectors do not need to be created to receive email from the Internet. Answer e is incorrect, because MX records can have only a single host name.

Question 4

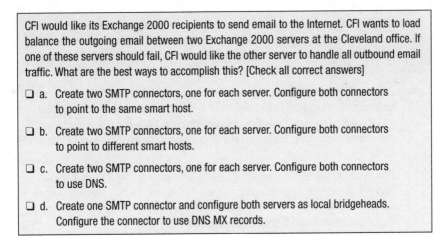

CFI would like its Exchange 2000 recipients to send email to the Internet. CFI wants to load balance the outgoing email between two Exchange 2000 servers at the Cleveland office. If one of these servers should fail, CFI would like the other server to handle all outbound email traffic. What are the best ways to accomplish this? [Check all correct answers]

❏ a. Create two SMTP connectors, one for each server. Configure both connectors to point to the same smart host.

❏ b. Create two SMTP connectors, one for each server. Configure both connectors to point to different smart hosts.

❏ c. Create two SMTP connectors, one for each server. Configure both connectors to use DNS.

❏ d. Create one SMTP connector and configure both servers as local bridgeheads. Configure the connector to use DNS MX records.

Answer a, b, c, and d are correct. An SMTP connector will enable users to send email to the Internet. The SMTP connector can be configured to either use DNS or a smart host. A single SMTP connector can be created with two local bridgehead servers, or two SMTP connectors can be created.

Question 5

Remote clients using Outlook Express in Cincinnati and Dayton will be able to check their email via an IMAP4 virtual server in Cleveland. The CLEEX05 server will host the virtual server. You would like to limit the number of concurrent users to five from each location. How would you best accomplish this task?

○ a.   Create one IMAP4 virtual server on CLEEX05. Configure CLEEX05 with two IP addresses. Configure the IMAP4 virtual server with two IP address, both using port 143. Configure the **Limit number of connections to** setting for each IP address port combination. Have clients from the different locations use different IP addresses for IMAP4.

○ b.   Create one IMAP4 virtual server on CLEEX05. Configure the IMAP4 virtual server with one IP address, and two ports, 143 and 144. Configure the **Limit number of connections to** setting for each IP address port combination to 5. Have clients from the different locations use different ports for IMAP4.

○ c.   Create two IMAP4 virtual servers on CLEEX05. Configure CLEEX05 with two IP addresses. Configure each IMAP4 virtual server one of the two IP address, both using port 143. Configure the **Limit number of connections to** setting for each virtual server to 5. Have clients from the different locations use different IP addresses for IMAP4.

○ d.   Create two IMAP4 virtual servers on CLEEX05. Configure each IMAP4 virtual server with the same IP address and have each use a different port, 143 and 144. Configure the **Limit number of connections to** setting for each virtual server to 5. Have clients from the different locations use different IP addresses for IMAP4.

○ e.   Create one IMAP4 virtual server on CLEEX05. Configure the **Limit number of connections to** setting to 10. Have clients from the different locations use same IP addresses for IMAP4.

Answer c is correct. A single server should be configured with multiple virtual servers. Each server will need its own IP address and can have its own settings. Answers a and b are incorrect, because the **Limit number of connections to** setting can be configured only once per virtual server. Answer d is incorrect, because Outlook Express cannot specify a different port for IMAP4. Answer e is incorrect, because it will not prevent 10 Cincinnati users and 10 Dayton users from using the IMAP4 virtual server.

Question 6

CFI would like to encrypt data when remote users check their email using Outlook Web Access. Which of the following will encrypt OWA traffic? [Check all correct answers]

❏ a. HTTP

❏ b. SSL

❏ c. Windows Integrated authentication

❏ d. Basic authentication

❏ e. PPTP

Answers b and e are correct. Clients could use a VPN with PPTP to connect to the CFI network. PPTP can be configured to encrypt traffic. SSL can be used to encrypt HTTP traffic, because the clients Web browser and the IIS server both support SSL. Answer a is incorrect, because HTTP is not encrypted. Answers c and d are incorrect, because authentication methods do not encrypt data. Windows Integrated authentication encrypts the username and password.

Question 7

How should CFI design a USENET solution? [Check all correct answers]

❏ a. Create a general-purpose public folder tree.

❏ b. Use the default public folder tree.

❏ c. Replicate all newsgroups to all locations.

❏ d. Replicate alt.food and alt.food.cheap to all locations.

❏ e. On the public folders servers at each location, create a separate storage group for the newsgroup folders and other public folders.

❏ f. On the public folders servers at each location, create a separate store for the newsgroup folders and other public folders.

Answers b and d are correct. Because clients will use MAPI, the default public folder store must be used. To reduce replication traffic, alt.food and alt.food.cheap should be replicated to each location. Answer a is incorrect, because MAPI clients cannot access general-purpose public folder trees. Answer c is incorrect, because replicating all newsgroups would cause more WAN traffic than the client access traffic. Answers e and f are incorrect, because the default public folder tree can exist in only a single store on each server. To separate newsgroups in the default public folder tree from other public folders, a separate public folder newsgroup server would have to be created at each location.

Need to Know More?

 Shannon, Michael. *MCSE Exchange 2000 Design Exam Prep*. The Coriolis Group, Scottsdale, AZ, 2001. ISBN 1-58880-026-1. This book is good as both a study guide and reference.

 Read Chapters 4 and 6 of the *Microsoft Exchange 2000 Server Planning and Installation* located in the \Docs folder of the Exchange 2000 CD-ROM.

 Read Chapters 21, 22, and 30 of the *Exchange 2000 Server Resource Kit.*

 Search **www.mcpmag.com** for "Exam 70-225" or "Exchange 2000". *MCP Magazine* will have good information to help prepare for the exam.

 Search **www.microsoft.com/technet** and the Exchange 2000 Server Help file using the terms at the beginning of the chapter.

 Search **www.Win2000mag.com** using the term "Exchange 2000" and the terms at the beginning of the chapter.

Migrating from and Coexisting with Exchange 5.5

Terms you'll need to understand:

- ✓ Coexistence
- ✓ In-place upgrade
- ✓ Active Directory Migration Tool (ADMT)
- ✓ SID history
- ✓ Access control list (ACL)
- ✓ Active Directory Connector (ADC)
- ✓ Connection agreement
- ✓ Resource mailbox
- ✓ Active Directory Cleanup Wizard
- ✓ Site Replication Service (SRS)
- ✓ Gateway Address Routing Table (GWART)
- ✓ Directory Access Programming Interface (DAPI)
- ✓ Intersite message routing
- ✓ Intrasite message routing

Techniques you'll need to master:

- ✓ Designing and applying deployment and migration strategies for Exchange 2000 based on an organization's needs
- ✓ Migrating a Windows NT domain to Windows 2000 Active Directory using an in-place upgrade
- ✓ Migrating data from an Exchange 5.5 organization to a Windows 2000 Active Directory domain using the Windows 2000 Active Directory Connector (ADC)
- ✓ Performing an in-place upgrade of an Exchange 5.5 organization to Exchange 2000
- ✓ Installing an Exchange 2000 server into an Exchange 5.5 organization
- ✓ Migrating an Exchange 5.5 organization to an Exchange 2000 organization using the Exchange Server Migration Wizard

When confronted with deployment, it is a rare occurrence that an existing messaging system is not already in place. Some sort of messaging system exists in most organizations. When migrating from an existing messaging system to Exchange 2000, in many scenarios the existing messaging system is a previous version of Exchange 2000. This chapter will focus on migrating Exchange 5.5 organizations to Exchange 2000. In the first section, you will gain a better understanding of which components will be migrated. You will then learn how to upgrade a pre-Windows 2000 environment to Windows 2000. You will also learn how to migrate and synchronize data between Exchange 5.5 and Windows 2000. Finally, you will learn to upgrade Exchange 5.5 using either an in-place upgrade or the Exchange Server Migration Wizard.

Overview

Messaging systems using pre-Exchange 2000 servers could be running Exchange Server 4.0, 5.0, or 5.5. Microsoft does not support nor recommend migrating from Exchange versions other than 5.5. Before planning a coexistence or a migration, all pre-Exchange 2000 servers should be running Exchange Server 5.5.

Migrating the Exchange Directory

Exchange 5.5 organizations maintain their own directory for Exchange recipients. These Exchange recipients are linked to Windows NT domain users. Because Exchange 2000 uses Windows 2000 Active Directory for storing its directory information, the Windows NT directory and the Exchange 5.5 directory should be migrated to Windows 2000 Active Directory. In Figure 11.1, Windows NT domain users are migrated to Active Directory users. Windows NT domain users linked to Exchange mailboxes are migrated to Active Directory mailbox-enabled users. In this chapter, you will see several methods for migrating this data, including migrating the data before Exchange 2000 is installed.

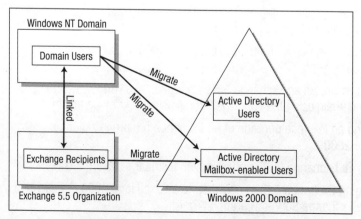

Figure 11.1 Migrating the Exchange 5.5 directory to Active Directory.

Migrating the Exchange Messaging System

The Exchange 5.5 messaging system includes two components: messages and system data. The messages contained in the public and private information stores must be migrated to Exchange 2000 systems. These messages can be upgraded by several methods, including upgrading the servers, moving mailboxes, and using the Exchange Server Migration Wizard. Exchange 5.5 system data includes Internet connections, sites, and site connectors. This data can be migrated by upgrading Exchange 5.5 servers to Exchange 2000. This data can also be documented and duplicated in a new Exchange 2000 organization. Many organizations also find that they need to reconfigure the system data due to the added capabilities of Exchange 2000.

Coexistence

Many organizations may wish to deploy Exchange 2000 and maintain pre-Exchange 2000 servers. Exchange 2000 servers can be deployed into existing pre-Exchange 2000 organizations. Exchange 2000 servers can also be deployed as a new Exchange 2000 organization and coexist with an existing pre-Exchange 2000 organization. Later in the "Coexistence with pre-Exchange 2000 Systems" section, you will learn how Exchange 2000 can share directory information and route messages with pre-Exchange 2000 servers and organizations.

Migrating Pre-Windows 2000 Domains to Active Directory

Before Exchange 5.5 can be migrated to Exchange 2000, pre-Windows 2000 domains must be migrated to Active Directory. Pre-Windows 2000 servers can be upgraded to Windows 2000, or the Active Directory Migration Tool can be used.

Performing an In-Place Upgrade

An in-place upgrade includes upgrading the pre-Windows 2000 *Primary Domain Controller (PDC)* to Windows 2000. Additional pre-Windows 2000 domain controllers, known as *Backup Domain Controllers (BDCs),* can then be upgraded. Before performing an in-place upgrade of a pre-Windows 2000 environment, many factors must be considered:

➤ All users in a domain are migrated at the same time. This may be an advantage or disadvantage, depending on the organization.

➤ Users' passwords are maintained and all enabled accounts remain enabled.

➤ Active Directory inherits the pre-Windows 2000 domain structure. Many organizations may want to change their domain structure to take advantage of new features in Active Directory.

➤ An in-place upgrade does not require additional servers.

➤ Existing servers must meet Windows 2000 system requirements.

➤ As long as Active Directory remains in mixed mode with at least one pre-Windows 2000 domain controller, the migration can be reversed.

➤ Existing trust relationships are maintained and do not have to be reconfigured.

➤ An in-place upgrade is typically less complicated and has a lower risk factor than using the Active Directory Migration Tool.

➤ Microsoft recommends that you take one BDC offline during the upgrade until the entire upgrade is complete and functional and then upgrade that BDC last for safety measures.

The Active Directory Migration Tool

The *Active Directory Migration Tool (ADMT)* is used to migrate pre-Windows 2000 domains to Windows 2000 Active Directory. ADMT can also be used to migrate from one Windows 2000 domain to another Windows 2000 domain. Migration between Windows 2000 domains can occur in the same forest or between different forests. ADMT copies security principals (users, computers, and groups) between domains. Many factors must be considered before using ADMT:

➤ Users can be migrated incrementally. ADMT allows you to migrate a small number of users at a time.

➤ Users' passwords are not maintained after the migration. ADMT can be configured to set the passwords to the username or to a complex random password. User accounts may be disabled in the destination domain to reduce security risks.

➤ Active Directory can have a different structure than the pre-Windows 2000 domain structure. Many organizations may want to change their domain structure to take advantage of new features in Active Directory.

➤ ADMT requires additional servers.

➤ Existing servers are not required to meet Windows 2000 system requirements. These servers can be decommissioned or redeployed after the migration.

➤ Parallel systems can be maintained for a period of time; however, rolling back to the old system may require additional steps. Changes made in the new system must be manually duplicated in the old system.

➤ Existing trust relationships are not maintained and have to be reconfigured.

➤ Using ADMT is typically more complicated and has a higher risk factor than an in-place upgrade.

➤ A user account with administrative rights in both source and destination domains must be used with ADMT.

➤ Before running ADMT, a two-way trust relationship must be manually created between the source and destination domains.

 If ADMT is installed on the PDC or PDC emulator in the source domain, ADMT changes the registry and reboots the server. If ADMT is run from another computer and not installed on the PDC, the following registry change must be made on the PDC in the source domain. Add the value TcpipClientSupport to the HKEY_LOCAL_MACHINE\SYSTEM\CurrentControlSet\LSA key. Set the data in TcpipClientSupport to 1. The PDC must be rebooted after this change is made.

SID History

Every security principal (users, computers, and groups) has a *security identifier (SID)*. This SID is used to validate access to resources. For example, giving a user permission to read a file places that user's SID in the access control list (ACL) of the file. When that user attempts to access the file, the user's SID is compared with the ACL, and the user is either granted or denied access. SIDs are guaranteed to be unique in a domain. When a security principal is moved from one domain to another, a new SID is created. ADMT accounts for these changing SIDs by saving the security principal's old SID in its SID history. When a Windows 2000 security principal attempts to access a resource, its SID and SID history is used to determine if it can access the resource (see Figure 11.2).

Note: SID history is supported only in Windows 2000 domains running in native mode.

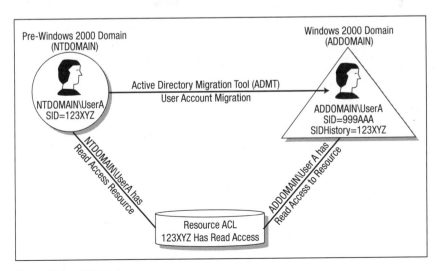

Figure 11.2 A SID history.

ADMT Wizards

ADMT can be used to migrate many different types of security principals from both pre-Windows 2000 domains and Windows 2000 domains. Migration from pre-Windows 2000 domains is considered *interforest migration*. ADMT also supports interforest and intraforest migration from Windows 2000 domains. ADMT includes different wizards to assist in performing these tasks:

➤ *User Account Migration Wizard*—This wizard copies user accounts from a pre-Windows 2000 or Windows 2000 domain. The wizard allows you to copy the user accounts into different containers or organizational units (OUs) in the destination domain (see Figure 11.3).

➤ *Group Migration Wizard*—This wizard copies groups from a pre-Windows 2000 or Windows 2000 domain. The wizard allows you to copy the groups into different containers or OUs in the destination domain.

➤ *Computer Migration Wizard*—This wizard copies computer accounts from a pre-Windows 2000 or Windows 2000 domain. The wizard allows you to copy the computer accounts into different containers or OUs in the destination domain.

➤ *Security Translation Wizard*—This wizard updates ACLs for resources in the destination domain.

➤ *Reporting Wizard*—This wizard creates reports to help the migration process. These reports include account conflicts and lists of accounts already migrated.

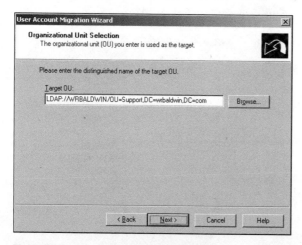

Figure 11.3   User Account Migration Wizard.

➤ *Service Account Migration Wizard*—This wizard copies service accounts from pre-Windows 2000 domains or Windows 2000 domains. These accounts are generally used with programs like Exchange for running various services.

➤ *Exchange Directory Migration Wizard*—This wizard copies the Exchange 5.5 directory to Active Directory. This wizard is similar to the Active Directory Connector (ADC); however, the Exchange Directory Migration Wizard is a one-way process and does not synchronize the directories.

➤ *Undo Wizard*—This wizard can be used to undo the last account migration.

➤ *Retry Task Wizard*—ADMT uses agents on individual computers to perform operations that must be performed locally. These agents run as services on the computers. The Retry Task Wizard is used to retry the tasks these agents might perform.

➤ *Trust Migration Wizard*—This wizard is used to duplicate trust relationships from the source domain to the destination domain.

➤ *Group Mapping and Merging Wizard*—This wizard can be used to map groups in the source domain with groups in the destination domain. When user accounts are not migrated all at once, it is important to maintain groups in both domains. When users are migrated, they need to be added to the appropriate groups in the destination domain.

Migrating and Synchronizing Data from Exchange 5.5 Organizations to Active Directory

To synchronize Exchange 5.5 directory information to and from Active Directory, the *Active Directory Connector (ADC)* is the proper tool (see Figure 11.4).

The Active Directory Connector

The ADC is used to copy and synchronize data between the Exchange 5.5 directory and Active Directory. The ADC can be used to copy data from Exchange 5.5 to Active Directory, from Active Directory to Exchange 5.5, or to synchronize data between both directories. Before synchronization using ADC is established, it is important to decide how the data will be maintained. It is recommended that you copy data from Exchange 5.5 to Active Directory, and then maintain the data using Active Directory. If the data is maintained using Active Directory, synchronization from Active Directory to Exchange 5.5 must

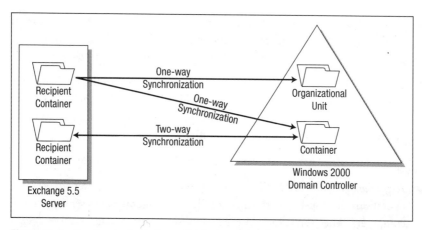

Figure 11.4 Synchronization between the Exchange 5.5 directory and Active Directory.

be established. Another option is to copy data to Active Directory and maintain the data using Exchange 5.5. For this option, synchronization from Exchange 5.5 to Active Directory must be established. It is also possible to establish two-way synchronization between Exchange 5.5 and Active Directory and maintain the database using both directories. This method is acceptable; however, careful planning must be taken to prevent loss of changes when administrators change the same data in different directories.

ADC Requirements

The ADC service must be installed on a computer running Windows 2000. Only members of the Enterprise Admins group can install the ADC. Although the ADC does not need to be installed on a domain controller, installing the ADC on a domain controller that is also a Global Catalog server can reduce network traffic. Because the ADC also needs to communicate with an Exchange 5.5 server, the ADC can be installed on an Exchange server; however, the server must be running Windows 2000 as well. The ADC has the following requirements:

➤ A service account for the ADC service must be assigned during installation. This service account must be a member of the administrators group in the domain where the service is installed.

Note: You should never use the administrator account or an account used to log on as a service account.

➤ The ADC needs access to an Active Directory domain controller in the domain where it is installed. The ADC may read from and write to the domain controller.

➤ The ADC needs access to an Active Directory Global Catalog server in the forest where it is installed. The ADC only reads from the Global Catalog.

➤ The ADC accesses all Exchange 5.5 servers it is configured to communicate with. The ADC may read from and write to the Exchange servers.

➤ The Exchange 5.5 server that communicates with the ADC must be running Exchange Server 5.5 with Service Pack 3 or later.

 For the exam, you should remember that to install the ADC, you must be a member of the Enterprise Admins group.

ADC Versions

There are two different versions of the ADC. The ADC that ships with Windows 2000 provides support for recipient objects only. Exchange 2000 includes an enhanced version of ADC. The ADC that ships with Exchange 2000 includes all the features of the Windows 2000 ADC, plus the ability to synchronize configuration and public folders information. Table 11.1 shows the features of both versions. When an Exchange 2000 server is installed into an Exchange 5.5 organization, the Exchange 2000 version of the ADC must be present in the organization. The Exchange 2000 version of the ADC allows the Exchange 2000 server to function in the Exchange 5.5 organization.

 For the exam, you should remember that the Exchange 2000 version of the ADC must be installed in an Exchange 5.5 organization before an Exchange 2000 server can join the Exchange 5.5 organization.

Synchronization of Objects

When objects are synchronized between Exchange 5.5 and Active Directory, the ADC maps the different object types. Because Exchange 5.5 and Active Directory use different names for the objects, it is important to understand how the objects are mapped. Table 11.2 shows how the ADC maps objects. When the ADC attempts to match objects between the two directories, it uses three attributes to

Table 11.1 Features in the different versions of the ADC.		
Objects	**Windows 2000**	**Exchange 2000**
Mailboxes	Yes	Yes
Custom Recipients	Yes	Yes
Distribution Lists	Yes	Yes
Configuration Information	No	Yes
Public Folder Information	No	Yes

Table 11.2 ADC object mapping.	
Exchange 5.5 Object	Active Directory Object
Mailbox	Mailbox-enabled User
Custom Recipient (with a Domain Account)	Mail-enabled User
Custom Recipient (without a Domain Account)	Mail-enabled Contact
Distribution List	Universal Security Group*

*When the destination Active Directory domain is in mixed mode, global security groups are used.

Table 11.3 ADC object matching.	
Active Directory Attribute	Description
LegacyExchangeDN	The ADC adds this attribute to the Active Directory object. The attribute should match the Exchange Distinguished Name (also known as the LDAP Name) in the Exchange 5.5 directory.
ObjectSID	This is the object Active Directory SID.
MSExchADCGlobalName	This attribute is created by the ADC and used to keep track of objects when they are moved to different domains in Active Directory.

match the objects (see Table 11.3). If the ADC does not find a corresponding object to synchronize with, the ADC can be configured to create a new object in the other directory. The creation of new objects is discussed in more detail in the "ADC Connection Agreements" section later in this chapter.

On pre-Exchange 2000, servers' distribution lists are used to secure access to public folders. In Exchange 2000, security groups are used to secure access to public folders. Because domains do not bind the scope of distribution lists, the Active Directory universal group is used. Active Directory only supports universal groups when it is in native mode. To ensure proper security for public folders, make sure the Active Directory domain is in native mode before synchronizing distribution lists using the ADC.

ADC Connection Agreements

After the ADC is installed, certain *connection agreements* are automatically created. Connection agreements are used to define synchronization between Exchange 5.5 and Active Directory. Each connection agreement represents one-way or two-way synchronization between an Exchange 5.5 recipient container and a container or organizational unit in Active Directory. When configuring a connection agreement, the following options are available:

➤ *Connection Agreement Type*—The Exchange 2000 version of the ADC allows the creation of recipient connection agreements, configuration connection agreements, and public folder connection agreements. Recipient connection agreements are used for synchronization of recipients. Public folder connection agreements are used for synchronization of public folder information. Configuration connection agreements are used to synchronize Exchange settings. Configuration connection agreements cannot be created manually. When the first Exchange 2000 server is installed in an Exchange 5.5 site, a configuration connection agreement is automatically created to replicate Exchange 5.5 configuration information to Active Directory.

➤ *Name*—Connection agreements defined for each installation of the ADC must have unique names. It is a good idea to give them a descriptive name such as *WRBaldwin Org —> WRBaldwin AD, WRBaldwin Org <— WRBaldwin AD,* or *WRBaldwin Org <—> to WRBaldwin AD.*

➤ *Replication Direction*—ADC connection agreements can be configure to replicate Two-Way, From Exchange To Windows, or From Windows To Exchange.

Note: Microsoft defines replication as updating multiple copies of data in the same directory in the same namespace. They define synchronization as updating multiple copies of data in different directories in different namespaces. The ADC synchronizes data between different directories; however, Microsoft uses the word "replication" instead of "synchronization" in much of the ADC user interface and documentation.

➤ *Active Directory Connector Server*—The ADC service on any computer running Windows 2000 Server or Advanced Server. The ADC management tools can be installed on any computer running Windows 2000 (including Professional). Each ADC connection agreement is associated with one server running the ADC service.

➤ *Windows Connections*—The ADC connection agreement needs to be configured to connect to one or more organizational units and/or containers in the Active Directory domain. The ADC connection agreement reads and/or writes via a single domain controller. This domain controller and the user account used to read and/or write must be defined. It is important to ensure the user account has the appropriate permission in Active Directory.

Note: When a connection agreement is defined to connect to a domain controller, that server must be available when the connection agreement is created.

➤ *Exchange Connections*—The ADC connection agreement needs to be configured to connect to one or more recipient containers in the Exchange organization. The ADC connection agreement reads and/or writes via a single Exchange server. This Exchange server and the user account used to read and/or write must be defined. It is important to ensure the user account has the appropriate permission in the Exchange organization.

Note: When a connection agreement is defined to connect to an Exchange server, that server must be available when the connection agreement is created.

➤ *Objects*—For both the Active Directory and the Exchange organization, the types of objects to replicate must be defined. From Windows, this includes users, contacts, and groups. From Exchange, this includes recipients, custom recipients, and distribution lists.

➤ *Deletion*—It is important to define how the ADC connection agreement will handle the deletion of objects in both directions. For an object deleted in Active Directory, the ADC can delete the matching object in Exchange or store a deletion list in a comma-separated values (CSV) file. For an object deleted in Exchange, the ADC can delete the matching object in Active Directory, or store a deletion list in a Lightweight Directory Information (LDF) file.

➤ *Schedule*—Each connection agreement can be configured to always run or only run during specific times. This setting can be useful if the ADC is causing excessive traffic on a slow wide area network (WAN) link. During the specified schedule, the ADC polls for changes every five minutes.

Note: The ADC polling interval can be changed by modifying the following registry value: HKEY_LOCAL_MACHINE\System\CurrentControlSet\Services\MSADC\ Parameters\SyncSleepDelay. This value is represented in seconds.

➤ *Primary Connection Agreements*—If a source container (Exchange recipient container, Active Directory organizational unit, or Active Directory container) has multiple connection agreements defined to synchronize objects to multiple destination containers, one of these connection agreements must be defined as the primary connection agreement for the destination system. Each connection agreement can be configured as the primary connection agreement for Windows, Exchange, or both. Figure 11.5 shows an example of how to configure primary connection agreements. In this example, Exchange 5.5 has three containers: East, West, and Central. In Active Directory, these containers have been consolidated into two containers: East and West. When new objects are created in West, ADC must know if these objects should be created in West or Central. Because the West<—>West connection agreement is the primary connection agreement for Exchange, new objects created in the West organizational unit must be created in the West recipients container. Because there is no Central organizational unit in Active Directory, ADC must be configured to create new objects in either the West or East organizational units. Because the Central<—>West connection agreement is the primary connection agreement for Windows, the new objects must be created in the West organizational unit.

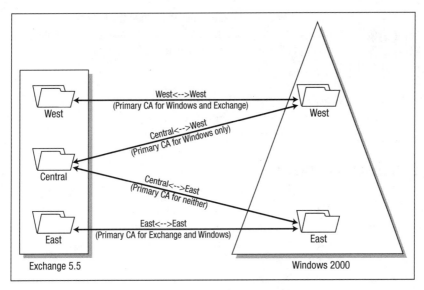

Figure 11.5   How to configure a primary connection agreement.

➤ *Windows Account Creation*—Under normal circumstances, objects created in Windows are not normally created in Exchange. When a user account in Active Directory is mail-enabled, the Exchange 5.5 mailbox is created and the ADC does not have to create the mailbox. When new mailboxes are created in Exchange, however, it is very important to configure how the ADC should handle creating accounts in Windows. If new accounts were automatically created in Active Directory, Exchange administrators would suddenly have permission to create Active Directory accounts. This may or may not be desirable. Each connection agreement allows for the creation of either enabled or disabled accounts in Active Directory. In addition, when new mailboxes are created by connection agreements, the connection agreement can be instructed to create Active Directory contacts instead of users.

➤ *LDAP Port*—The ADC uses LDAP to communicate with Exchange 5.5 and Active Directory. When communicating with Active Directory, the ADC uses port 389 when communicating with domain controllers, and port 3268 when communicating with Global Catalog servers. The port used by a connection agreement when the ADC is communicating with Exchange 5.5 is configured to port 389 by default. Unlike Active Directory communications, the port used for Exchange 5.5 communications is configurable. If the Exchange 5.5 server defined in the connection agreement is also an Active Directory domain controller, the default setting of port 389 does not work because Active Directory uses port 389. In this scenario, the setting must be reconfigured (port 390 is acceptable).

For the exam, you should remember that when the Exchange server defined in a connection agreement is also a domain controller, the LDAP port used must not be left at its default setting of 389.

➤ *Initial Replication Direction*—This option is used to determine which direction synchronization occurs first in a two-way connection agreement. By default, objects are replicated from Exchange first.

Resource Mailboxes

A *resource mailbox* is a mailbox used for the purpose of scheduling resources and rooms. Resource mailboxes are typically associated with a domain user that is also associated with other mailboxes, including their primary mailbox. Although associating a domain user with multiple mailboxes was okay in pre-Exchange 2000 system, with Active Directory and Exchange 2000, each user account can have a single mailbox. When the ADC tries to associate mailboxes with Active Directory users, it is possible it will associate one of the resource mailboxes with a user account. When the ADC attempts to associate that user's primary mailbox with a user's account, the ADC will not find one and will create a new disabled user account. To assist the ADC in determining which mailboxes are resource mailboxes, the text **NTDSNoMatch** can be added to the Custom Attribute 10 attribute for the resource mailboxes. This text can be added manually or by using the NTDSNoMatch tool.

Active Directory Cleanup Wizard

Under normal circumstances, an organization upgrades its pre-Windows 2000 domains to Windows 2000 before using the ADC to create and synchronize accounts. However, it is possible, and often desirable, for an organization to create a new Active Directory forest and establish synchronization using the ADC before upgrading their pre-Windows 2000 domains to Windows 2000. In this case, the organization has the same accounts in both the pre-Windows 2000 domains and the Windows 2000 domains. When the organization uses the ADMT to migrate accounts from the pre-Windows 2000 domains to the Windows 2000 domains, duplicate accounts are created in the Windows 2000 domains (see Figure 11.6).

There are different solutions for duplicate accounts. When ADMT is used to migrate accounts, it can be configured to merge the old accounts with the new accounts. This only works if the old domains and the new domains match; if not, ADMT is not able to match accounts. If ADMT is not used to merge accounts, the Active Directory Cleanup Wizard can be used to merge the duplicate

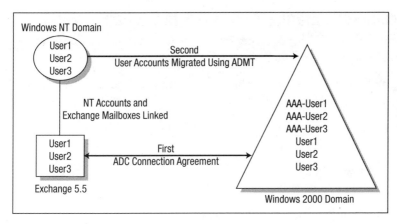

Figure 11.6   Duplicate accounts in Active Directory.

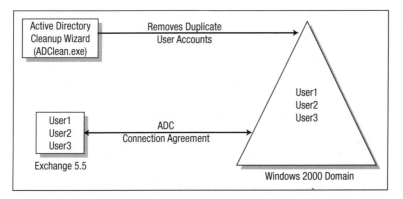

Figure 11.7   Using the Active Directory Cleanup Wizard to remove duplicate accounts.

accounts (see Figure 11.7). The Active Directory Cleanup Wizard ships with Exchange 2000.

Upgrading to Exchange 2000

For most organizations, the simplest path for migrating to Exchange 2000 is to upgrade their pre-Exchange 2000 organization. This section will describe upgrading pre-Exchange 2000 servers to Exchange 2000. It will also discuss adding Exchange 2000 servers to pre-Exchange 2000 sites, then moving mailboxes from the Exchange 5.5 servers to the Exchange 2000 servers.

Note: Microsoft does not support upgrading to Exchange 2000 from Exchange versions other than 5.5. Before upgrading a pre–Exchange 2000 server, it must be upgraded to Exchange Server 5.5 with Service Pack 3 or higher. Before installing an Exchange 2000 server into a pre–Exchange 2000 site, at least one Exchange server in the site must be running Exchange Server 5.5 with Service Pack 3 or higher.

Upgrading Exchange Server 5.5 to Exchange 2000

Upgrading existing Exchange 5.5 server to Exchange 2000 has many advantages and disadvantages. The characteristics of an in-place upgrade are as follows:

➤ Existing hardware can be used; however, existing hardware must support the requirements of both Windows 2000 and Exchange 2000.

➤ Exchange servers must be running Windows 2000 Server or Advanced Server with Service Pack 1 or later.

➤ The Windows NT domain associated with the Exchange server must be upgraded to Windows 2000 Active Directory.

➤ Single instance storage in the Exchange database is maintained.

➤ Clients using Microsoft Outlook do not need to reconfigure their Outlook profile.

➤ Mailbox messages read state are maintained.

➤ The Exchange 5.5 server must be taken offline prior to the upgrade. The upgrade could take a long time, depending on the size of the databases and speed of the hardware. Microsoft recommends allocating one hour per 8GB of database space that will be converted during the upgrade.

➤ Site connectors are converted to routing group connectors.

➤ The Internet Mail Services are converted to an SMTP connector and virtual server.

➤ X.400 connectors, MS Mail, Lotus cc:Mail, and Lotus Notes connectors are preserved; however, these connectors may function differently in Exchange 2000. The settings in these connectors should be checked and any function for which they were previously responsible should be verified.

➤ The Remote Access Service from Exchange 5.5 is not supported in Exchange 2000 and should be removed before the upgrade.

➤ The PROFS and SNADS connectors from Exchange 5.5 are not supported in Exchange 2000 and should be removed before the upgrade.

Outlook Web Access

Outlook Web Access (OWA) has been dramatically improved with Exchange 2000. When an Exchange 5.5 OWA server is upgraded to Exchange 2000, its OWA installation is also upgraded. Exchange 2000 does not support customized OWA deployments that used active server pages (.asp). The OWA server is upgraded and the pages saved; however, the customizations are no longer in effect.

Exchange 5.5 front-end/back-end deployments of OWA can be upgraded in stages. The back-end server must be upgraded first. An Exchange 2000 OWA front-end server does not communicate with Exchange 5.5 back-end servers. On the other hand, Exchange 5.5 OWA front-end servers communicate with Exchange 2000 back-end servers (see Figure 11.8).

 For the exam, you should remember that when upgrading Exchange 5.5 OWA servers, all Exchange 5.5 back-end servers should be upgraded first.

Backup

Before upgrading an Exchange 5.5 server, careful planning is required. An in-place upgrade is often simpler, but more risky, than other migration strategies. It is important to fully back up the Exchange 5.5 server before it is upgraded. Before backing up the server, Microsoft recommends running MTACheck utility as well as the *Knowledge Consistency Checker (KCC)*.

Verification

After the server is upgraded, the installation should be verified. This verification should include opening mailboxes and public folders on the upgraded server. If this server was the first Exchange 2000 server in the site or if the server had Exchange 5.5 site directory replication connectors, the ADC should be installed on the server. Within the ADC, a configuration connection agreement should have been created to provide Active Directory with Exchange 5.5 configuration information.

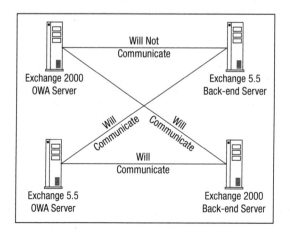

Figure 11.8 Exchange 5.5 and Exchange 2000 OWA front-end/back-end compatibility.

Moving Mailboxes from Pre-Exchange 2000 Servers to Exchange 2000 Servers

Installing one or more Exchange 2000 servers into an existing Exchange 5.5 site is a safer solution than an in-place upgrade. After the server or servers have been installed, mailboxes and public folders from the pre-Exchange 2000 servers can be moved to the Exchange 2000 server or servers. These mailboxes can be moved using a Windows 2000 computer running Active Directory Users and Computers. The computer running Active Directory Users and Computers must also have the Exchange 2000 management tools installed from the Exchange 2000 CD. The characteristics of moving mailboxes are as follows:

➤ Existing hardware does not need to support the requirements of Windows 2000 and Exchange 2000; however, additional servers are required.

➤ The Windows NT domain associated with the Exchange site must be upgraded to Windows 2000 Active Directory.

➤ Single instance storage in the Exchange database is not maintained when mailboxes are moved between servers in the same site. Additional storage space is required on the destination server.

➤ Clients using Microsoft Outlook do not need to reconfigure their Outlook profile. Even though their current profile is pointing to their old server, Outlook reconfigures itself for the new server so long as the mailbox is moved to a server in the same site.

➤ Mailbox messages read state is maintained.

➤ The pre-Exchange 2000 server does not have to be taken offline prior to the migration.

➤ Mailboxes can be moved from Exchange 4.0 and 5.0 servers without having to upgrade them to Exchange Server 5.5.

➤ The source and destination server are heavily tasked during the migration process. Network traffic and the amount of time to migrate will vary depending on the size of the database. Migration time, however, can actually be less than an in-place upgrade, depending on the hardware in the servers and the speed of the LAN.

➤ Site connectors have to be manually duplicated on the new server as routing group connectors.

➤ The Internet Mail Service has to be manually duplicated as an SMTP connector and virtual server.

➤ X.400 connectors, MS Mail, Lotus cc:Mail, and Lotus Notes connectors have to be manually duplicated on the new server. These connectors may function differently in Exchange 2000. The settings in these connectors should be checked and any function for which they were previously responsible should be verified.

➤ The Remote Access Service from Exchange 5.5 is not supported in Exchange 2000.

➤ The PROFS and SNADS connectors from Exchange 5.5 are not supported in Exchange 2000.

Many companies may want to upgrade their existing servers to Exchange 2000, but do not want to take servers offline to perform an in-place upgrade. By installing as little as one new server, organizations can accomplish this goal. There are many different ways to accomplish this task, including the Bulk method, the Swing method, and the Modified Swing method.

Bulk Method

A single server can be installed into a pre-Exchange 2000 site. The mailboxes and public folders from all pre-Exchange 2000 servers are then moved to the Exchange 2000 server. Exchange 2000 can then be installed on the pre-Exchange 2000 servers by either upgrading or reformatting and installing Windows 2000, then Exchange 2000. Finally, the mailboxes and public folders can be moved back to their original servers (see Figure 11.9). The main disadvantage to this method is that Exchange 2000 has to be large enough to handle all mailboxes in the site. Another disadvantage is that mailboxes are moved twice.

Swing Method

A single server can be installed into a pre-Exchange 2000 site. The mailboxes and public folders from one pre-Exchange 2000 server are then moved to the Exchange 2000 server. Exchange 2000 can then be installed on the pre-Exchange 2000 server by either upgrading or reformatting and installing Windows 2000

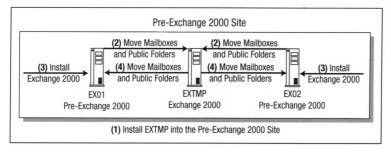

Figure 11.9   The Bulk method.

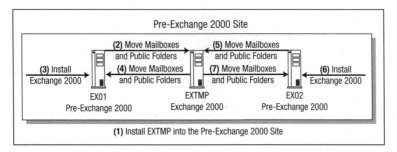

Figure 11.10 The Swing method.

then Exchange 2000. Finally, the mailboxes and public folders can be moved back to the original server. This process is repeated for all pre-Exchange 2000 servers in the organization (see Figure 11.10). The main disadvantage to this method is the process requires moving mailboxes twice.

Modified Swing Method

A single server can be installed into a pre-Exchange 2000 site. The mailboxes and public folders from one pre-Exchange 2000 server are then moved to the Exchange 2000 server. Exchange 2000 can then be installed on the pre-Exchange 2000 server by either upgrading or reformatting and installing Windows 2000, then Exchange 2000. Next, the mailboxes and public folders from another pre-Exchange 2000 server are moved to the newly created Exchange 2000 server. This process is repeated for all pre-Exchange 2000 servers in the organization (see Figure 11.11). The only real disadvantage to this method is that the server names all change. This can cause problems with connectors and requires proper planning.

Moving Public Folders

When public folders are moved from pre-Exchange 2000 servers to Exchange 2000 servers, certain steps must be taken first:

➤ The Windows 2000 domain must be in native mode. Windows 2000 uses universal groups to maintain the security settings on the public folders.

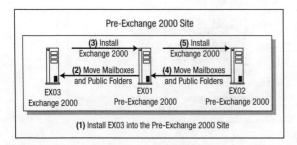

Figure 11.11 The Modified Swing method.

➤ A public folder connection agreement between Exchange 5.5 and Active Directory must be present.

➤ The account used to move the public folders must have administrative permissions on the public folders.

Coexistence with Pre-Exchange 2000 Systems

When an organization installs an Exchange 2000 server into a pre-Exchange 2000 environment, it is quite common for these different systems to coexist for some time. As you have seen, new Exchange 2000 servers can be added to pre-Exchange 2000 sites and servers running Exchange Server 5.5 can be upgraded to Exchange 2000. In either of these cases, it is important to understand how these systems communicate and coexist. Careful planning must take place to ensure Exchange directories are properly synchronized, messages are routed, and public folders replicated and accessible.

Directory Synchronization and Access

Pre-Exchange 2000 servers maintained their own directory in the dir.edb database. Exchange 2000 servers store their directory information in Active Directory. To maintain proper directory synchronization, Exchange 2000 uses the *Site Replication Service* (SRS) and the ADC.

SRS

The SRS is an Exchange 2000 service that emulates the Exchange 5.5 directory service. The SRS is used to synchronize directory information with the directory service on Exchange 5.5 servers and replicate directory with Exchange 5.5 servers in other sites. Within a site, SRS uses *Remote Procedure Calls (RPC)* to communicate with pre-Exchange 2000 servers. Between sites, the SRS can use standard messaging protocols to communicate with pre-Exchange 2000 servers (see Figure 11.12). When the SRS receives directory information from pre-Exchange 2000 servers, it passes this information to the ADC for synchronization with Active Directory. There is no need for Exchange 2000 servers in different sites to synchronize directory information directly; all Exchange 2000 servers synchronize directory information with each other through Active Directory using the ADC (see Figure 11.13).

ADC

When an Exchange 2000 server is installed into an existing pre-Exchange 2000 site, the Exchange 2000 version of the ADC is installed and a configuration connection agreement is automatically created. This connection agreement is used to synchronize directory information between the Exchange and Active Directory.

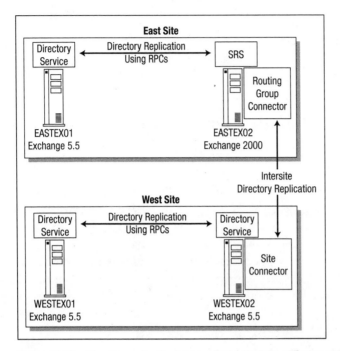

Figure 11.12 Directory replication between Exchange 5.5 and Exchange 2000.

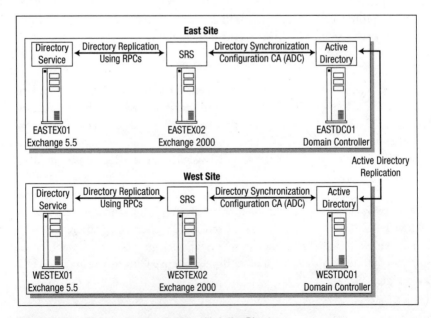

Figure 11.13 Directory synchronization with Active Directory.

GWART and Link State Table

Pre-Exchange 2000 servers use the Gateway Address Routing Table (GWART) for routing messages and replication over Exchange connectors. The Exchange 2000 link state table replaces the GWART. Exchange 2000 uses the SRS and ADC to gather connector information from pre-Exchange 2000 servers. This information is stored in the link state table. Because the pre-Exchange 2000 servers do not support the link state protocol, the state of the connections are not known and therefore not stored in the link state table.

Directory Access

Pre-Exchange 2000 servers use the *Directory Access Programming Interface (DAPI)* to perform directory lookups. Exchange 2000 servers use LDAP to query Active Directory for directory lookups.

Message Routing

Pre-Exchange 2000 servers use the *message transfer agent (MTA)* to route messages between servers. Exchange 2000 servers have a compatible MTA for routing messages with pre-Exchange 2000 servers. Exchange 2000 uses different methods and protocols when routing messages to pre-Exchange 2000 servers and Exchange 2000 servers. Exchange 2000 handles intrasite routing and intersite routing differently. Table 11.4 outlines Exchange 2000 intra- and intersite message routing with both pre-Exchange 2000 and Exchange 2000 servers.

Public Folder Replication and Access

Exchange 2000 supports two types of public folder trees. The default public folder tree is replicated to all public folder servers and is the only tree accessible by

Table 11.4   Exchange 2000 message routing.

Destination	Location	Method	Protocol
Exchange 2000 Server	Same Site	SMTP Virtual Server	SMTP
Exchange 2000 Server	Same Site	Routing Group Connector	SMTP
Exchange 2000 Server	Same Site	SMTP Connector	SMTP
Exchange 2000 Server	Same Site	X.400 Connector	X.400*
Pre-Exchange 2000 Server	Different Site	MTA	RPC
Pre-Exchange 2000 Server	Different Site	Routing Group Connector	X.400*
Pre-Exchange 2000 Server	Different Site	SMTP Connector	SMTP
Pre-Exchange 2000 Server	Different Site	X.400 connector	X.400*

*The X.400 protocol uses RPCs to transfer data over TCP/IP. Exchange 2000 does not support TP4 and X.25 with the X.400 protocol.

MAPI clients. General-purpose public folder trees are only replicated to specific servers and are only accessible by non-MAPI clients. Pre-Exchange 2000 servers have a single public folder hierarchy. In a mixed-mode organization, the Exchange 2000 default public folder tree and the pre-Exchange 2000 public folder hierarchy contain the same data. Replication of tree information and public folder messages function transparently between pre-Exchange 2000 servers and Exchange 2000 servers.

The directory handles replication of security information on public folders. Because pre-Exchange 2000 servers and Exchange 2000 servers use different directories, replication of this data is more complicated and requires proper planning. On pre-Exchange 2000 servers, distribution lists are used to secure access to public folders. In Exchange 2000, security groups are used to secure access to public folders. To ensure Exchange 2000 public folder are secured in the same way as their replicas in pre-Exchange 2000, it is important that distribution lists are synchronized with Active Directory universal security groups. Active Directory only supports universal groups when Active Directory is in native mode. Figure 11.14 shows an example of public folder security. EX01 and EX02 each have replicas of the SupData public folder. On EX01, SupData's ACL contains the Support and Sales distribution lists. On EX02, SupData's ACL contains the Support and Sales universal groups. Because these groups contain users from both domains and are assigned to resources in both domains, they must be universal groups. If these domains were not in native mode, these groups would have been created as global groups. Although global groups can contain users from other domains, they cannot be assigned to resources outside their domain. Figure 11.15 shows how security settings are lost when the domains are in mixed mode.

Exchange 2000 clients and pre-Exchange 2000 clients have access to public folders on both types of servers. The only change from pre-Exchange 2000 of which you need to be aware is that public folder referrals are transitive in Exchange 2000 and are *not* transitive in pre-Exchange 2000. For example, in Exchange 2000, connectors between sites 1 and 2 and sites 2 and 3 allow public folder referrals from sites 1 to 3 and site 3 to 1. To help control this, Exchange 2000 allows public folder referrals to be enabled or disabled on each connector.

Other Coexistence Scenarios

Installing Exchange 2000 servers into pre-Exchange 2000 sites is not the only scenario where Exchange 2000 must coexist with pre-Exchange 2000 servers. The following is a list of other possibilities for coexistence:

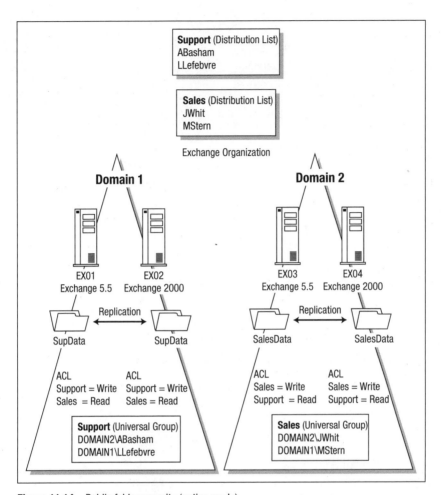

Figure 11.14   Public folder security (native mode).

➤ Exchange 5.5 servers can be installed into Exchange 2000 administrative groups and can coexist with Exchange 2000 as long as the Exchange 2000 organization is in mixed mode.

➤ Exchange 5.5 sites can be added to Exchange 2000 organizations as long as the Exchange 2000 organization is in mixed mode.

➤ An Exchange 2000 organization in mixed or native mode can route messages to a pre-Exchange 2000 organization using SMTP connectors for the Exchange 2000 organization and the Internet Mail Connector for the pre-Exchange 2000 organization.

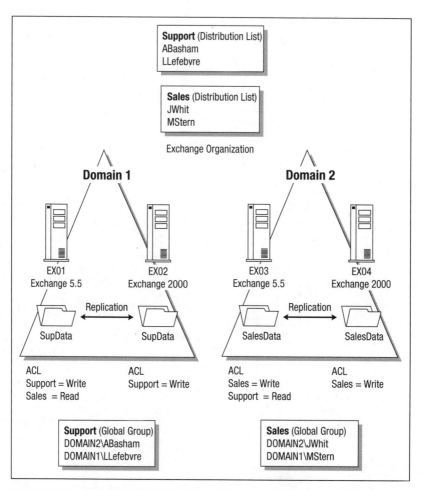

Figure 11.15 Public folder security (mixed mode).

The Exchange Server Migration Tool

The Exchange Server Migration Tool can be used to migrate mailboxes from other messaging systems to Exchange 2000. A newer version of the tool included with Exchange 2000 Service Pack 1 supports moving mailboxes from one Exchange organization to another. These organizations can be running pre-Exchange 2000 servers or Exchange 2000 servers. Pre-Exchange 2000 organizations may find using this tool to move data to a new organization beneficial. The features of the Exchange Server Migration Tool are:

➤ Both organizations can be maintained at the same time. There is no need to take any Exchange servers offline.

➤ Existing hardware does not need to support the requirements of Windows 2000 and Exchange 2000; however, additional servers are required.

➤ Single instance storage in the Exchange database is not maintained when mailboxes are moved to the new organization. Additional storage space is required on the destination server.

➤ Clients using Microsoft Outlook need to reconfigure their Outlook profile.

➤ Mailbox messages read state is maintained.

➤ The pre-Exchange 2000 server does not have to be taken offline prior to the migration.

➤ Public folders have to be moved using a different method, such as exporting public folders to personal stores (.pst).

➤ Mailboxes can be moved from Exchange 4.0 and 5.0 servers without having to upgrade them to Exchange Server 5.5.

➤ The source and destination server are heavily tasked during the migration process. Network traffic and the amount of time to migrate vary depending on the size of the database. Migration time, however, can actually be less than an in-place upgrade, depending on the hardware in the servers and the speed of the LAN.

➤ Site connectors have to be manually duplicated on the new server as routing group connectors.

➤ The Internet Mail Service has to be manually duplicated as an SMTP connector and virtual server.

➤ X.400 connectors, MS Mail, Lotus cc:Mail, and Lotus Notes connectors have to be manually duplicated on the new server. These connectors may function differently in Exchange 2000. The settings in these connectors should be checked and any function for which they were previously responsible should be verified.

➤ The Remote Access Service from Exchange 5.5 is not supported in Exchange 2000.

➤ The PROFS and SNADS connectors from Exchange 5.5 are not supported in Exchange 2000.

It is important to plan for connectivity between the organizations during the migration. Using this method requires that connectors be established between the organizations. An Internet Mail Connector (IMC) for the pre-Exchange

2000 organization and an SMTP connector for the Exchange 2000 organization can be configured to route messages between organizations. In the old organizations, custom recipients can be created to replace migrated users. The email addresses of the custom recipients should point to the new system. In the new organization, mail-enabled users can be created for users who have not been migrated yet. Once a user is migrated, the mail-enabled user can be converted to a mailbox-enabled user.

Practice Questions

Case Study

General Information

You have been hired by Cheap Food, Inc. (CFI), to assist the company with its deployment of Exchange 2000 Server. You are responsible for Internet connectivity for Exchange 2000 Server while ensuring that your design meets the company's business and Information Technology goals.

CFI was created when five separate pre-packaged food manufacturers in Ohio merged. The five companies had approximately 5,000 employees each. These employees have offices in several cities around Ohio. CFI has consolidated its offices so that it now has one office in each major city in Ohio. This includes headquarters, two regional offices, and two local offices.

The board required that the five former technology groups be consolidated, and that a single messaging system be deployed. They have asked management to merge the five companies while ensuring the company put out the same award-winning products it always has.

Figure 11.16 shows the physical locations of CFI's offices.

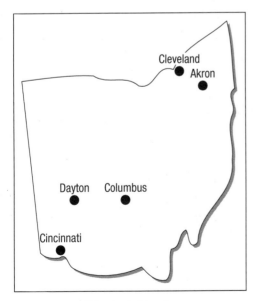

Figure 11.16   CFI's physical locations.

IT Environment

Each of the five companies that merged to create CFI used Exchange to provide email services. Each of the five companies still has its own Exchange organization. Four of the organizations are using Exchange 5.5, while one is using Exchange 5.0. CFI has already upgraded all servers to Windows 2000 Server and all clients to Windows 2000 Professional. They have deployed Active Directory and are running in mixed mode. All client computers have Outlook 2000.

Active Directory has been deployed across CFI. The existing Active Directory design includes a single Active Directory tree and forest. There are four domains: one root domain and one for each of the Ohio regions—Northeast, Central and Southwest. Each location has two domain controllers, each of which is a Global Catalog server. The groups are structured to keep replication traffic to a minimum. The administrators of each domain can create domain global and local groups, but they are not allowed to create universal groups. Only the Enterprise administrator can create universal groups. The physical structure of the Active Directory is shown in Figure 11.17 and the logical is shown in Figure 11.18.

Each Exchange 2000 organization is in its own Windows NT 4 domain. Users have accounts in both the Active Directory and in each domain. Two-way trust relationships have been established between these domains and each domain in Active Directory. Each Exchange organization has either one or two sites.

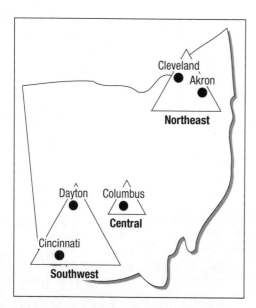

Figure 11.17 Physical Active Directory design.

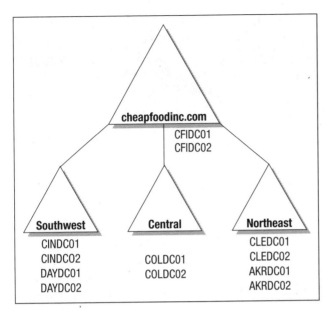

Figure 11.18   Logical Active Directory design.

Requirements and Goals

CFI would like to have a single Exchange 2000 organization for the entire company.

Question 1

Which of the following methods should CFI use to migrate to Exchange 2000?

○ a. Perform an in-place upgrade of all its pre-Exchange 2000 servers.

○ b. Install Exchange 2000 servers into the existing organizations. Move pre-Exchange 2000 mailboxes to Exchange 2000 servers.

○ c. Install Exchange 2000 servers into one of the existing organizations. Move pre-Exchange 2000 mailboxes to Exchange 2000 servers using the Active Directory Connector.

○ d. Create a new Exchange 2000 organization and move mailboxes using the Exchange Server Migration Wizard.

○ e. Create a new Exchange 2000 organization and move mailboxes using the Active Directory Connector.

○ f. Install Exchange 2000 servers into one of the existing organizations. Move pre-Exchange 2000 mailboxes to Exchange 2000 servers using the Exchange Server Migration Wizard.

Answer d is correct. Because CFI would like all Exchange servers to be in the organization, installing a new organization and migrating the mailboxes is the best solution. The Exchange Server Migration Wizard is the best tool to migrate the mailboxes between organizations. Answers a and b are incorrect, because CFI would like all servers in the same organization. Answers c and e are incorrect, because the Active Directory Connector does not move mailboxes. Answer f is incorrect, because none of the existing organizations are members of any Active Directory domains.

Question 2

Before the CFI companies merged, each had their own Windows NT domain. Before decommissioning those domains, CFI created the new Active Directory structure and populated it using the Active Directory Connector. Next, CFI used the Active Directory Migration Tool to migrate all users and groups from the various domains to Active Directory. Before deploying Exchange 2000, CFI will need to merge duplicate accounts created from this process. What tool or tools should they use?

○ a. Active Directory Connector

○ b. Active Directory Cleanup Wizard

○ c. Active Directory Migration Tool

○ d. Active Directory Merge Tool

○ e. None of the above

Answer b is correct. The Active Directory Cleanup Wizard can be used to merge the duplicate accounts. The Active Directory Cleanup Wizard ships with Exchange 2000. Answer a is incorrect, because the Active Directory Connector cannot merge accounts. Answer c is incorrect, because the Active Directory Migration Tool can only merge accounts during the migration. Answer d is incorrect, because there is no Active Directory Merge Tool.

Question 3

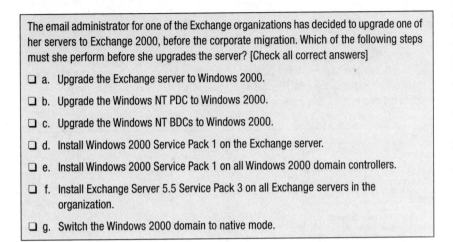

The email administrator for one of the Exchange organizations has decided to upgrade one of her servers to Exchange 2000, before the corporate migration. Which of the following steps must she perform before she upgrades the server? [Check all correct answers]

❑ a. Upgrade the Exchange server to Windows 2000.

❑ b. Upgrade the Windows NT PDC to Windows 2000.

❑ c. Upgrade the Windows NT BDCs to Windows 2000.

❑ d. Install Windows 2000 Service Pack 1 on the Exchange server.

❑ e. Install Windows 2000 Service Pack 1 on all Windows 2000 domain controllers.

❑ f. Install Exchange Server 5.5 Service Pack 3 on all Exchange servers in the organization.

❑ g. Switch the Windows 2000 domain to native mode.

Answers a, b, and d are correct. Exchange 2000 Server must be installed on a computer running Windows 2000 Server or Advanced Server with Service Pack 1 that is a member of an Active Directory domain. Answers c and g are incorrect, because Exchange 2000 does not have to be installed into a native mode domain. Answer e is incorrect, because only the server running Exchange 2000 has to be running Windows 2000 Service Pack 1. Answer f is incorrect, because only the Exchange server that is being upgraded to Exchange 2000 has to be upgraded to Exchange Server 5.5 Service Pack 3 or higher.

Question 4

CFI has established ADC two-way connection agreements between recipient containers in Exchange 5.5 and Active Directory organizational units. CFI will now need to configure which connection are to be the primary connection agreements for Exchange and Windows. If by chance a user is created in Active Directory that does not exist in Exchange, a new mailbox should be created in the ABC Foods organization. Match the appropriate settings to each connection agreement (see Figures 11.19 and 11.20).

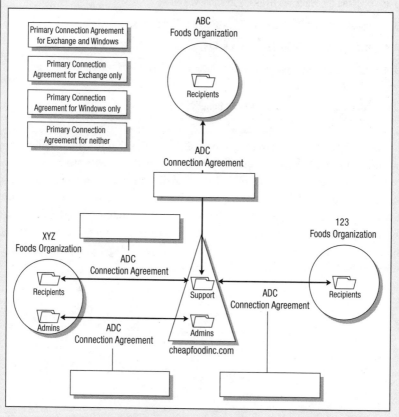

Figure 11.19 Drag-and-drop question.

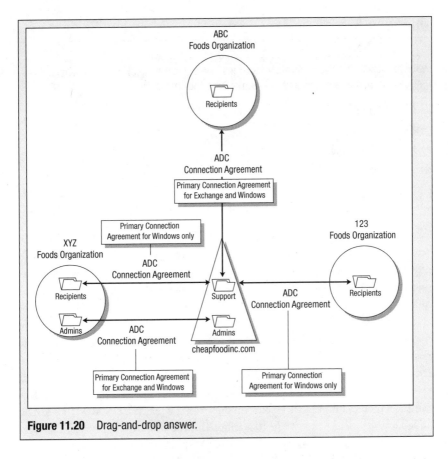

Figure 11.20   Drag-and-drop answer.

If a source container (Exchange recipient container, Active Directory organizational unit, or Active Directory container) has multiple connection agreements defined to synchronize objects to multiple destination containers, one of these connection agreements must be defined as the primary connection agreement for the destination system. Each connection agreement can be configured as the primary connection agreement for Windows, Exchange, or both. When a connection agreement is defined as the primary connection for Windows, the connection agreement will create new accounts in that Windows container. When a connection agreement is defined as the primary connection for Exchange, the connection agreement will create new accounts in that Exchange container.

Question 5

> Before establishing ADC connection agreements, what tool should CFI use to ensure that the ADC does not create disabled accounts in Active Directory for primary mailboxes?
>
> ○ a. NTDSNoMatch
>
> ○ b. NTDSCleanUp
>
> ○ c. NTDSNoAccount
>
> ○ d. ADMT
>
> ○ e. ADSIEdit

Answer a is correct. A resource mailbox is a mailbox used for the purpose of scheduling resources and rooms. Resource mailboxes are typically associated with a domain user that is also associated with other mailboxes, including their primary mailbox. Although associating a domain user with multiple mailboxes was okay in pre-Exchange 2000 system, with Active Directory and Exchange 2000 each user account can have a single mailbox. When the ADC tries to associate mailboxes with Active Directory users, it is possible it will associate one of the resource mailboxes with a user account. When the ADC attempts to associate that user's primary mailbox with a user's account, the ADC will not find a user account and will create a new disabled user account. To assist the ADC in determining which mailboxes are resource mailboxes, the text NTDSNoMatch can be added to the Custom Attribute 10 attribute for the resource mailboxes. This text can be added manually or by using the NTDSNoMatch tool. Answers b and c are incorrect, because NTDSCleanUp and NTDSNoAccount are not valid tools. Answers d and e are incorrect, because these tools will not help the ADC find the primary mailbox for a user with multiple mailboxes defined.

Question 6

A junior administrator shadowed you during the migration of user accounts from the old NT domains to Active Directory. You used the Active Directory Migration Tool. He wants to know how the users still have permissions to resources even after their accounts were moved. What feature of Windows 2000 enables moved users to maintain access to resources?

○ a. ADC

○ b. ACL

○ c. SID History

○ d. ACL Mapping

○ e. None of the above

Answer c is correct. Every security principal (users, computers, and groups) has a security identifier (SID). This SID is used to validate access to resources. For example, giving a user permission to read a file will place that user's SID in the access control list (ACL) of the file. When that user attempts to access the file, the user's SID is compared with the ACL and the user is either granted or denied access. SIDs are guaranteed to be unique in a domain. When a security principal is moved from one domain to another, a new SID is created. ADMT accounts for these changing SIDs by saving the security principal's old SID in its SID history. When a Windows 2000 security principal attempts to access a resource, its SID and SID history is used to determine if it can access the resource. Answer a is incorrect, because the ADC is used to synchronize directories. Answer b is incorrect, because the access control list (ACL) stores the SID; this applies to both pre-Windows 2000 and Windows 2000 domains. Answer d is incorrect, because there is no feature named ACL Mapping.

Question 7

CFI has decided to use the Exchange Server Migration Tool to migrate mailboxes from the old Exchange organizations to the new one. CFI plans to migrate 50 mailboxes from each organization at a time. To maintain messaging connectivity, what steps should CFI take before proceeding? [Check all correct answers]

❏ a. Add Internet Mail Connectors in each organization.

❏ b. Create SMTP connectors in the new organization for each old organization.

❏ c. Create custom recipients in the old organizations for the moved users.

❏ d. Mail-enable all users in Active Directory and assign the Exchange email address.

Answers a, b, c, and d are correct. An Internet Mail Connector (IMC) for the pre-Exchange 2000 organization and an SMTP connector for the Exchange 2000 organization can be configured to route messages between organizations. In the old organizations, custom recipients can be created to replace migrated users. The email address of the custom recipients should point to the new system. In the new organization, mail-enabled users can be created for users who have not be migrated yet. Once a user is migrated, the mail-enabled user can be converted to a mailbox-enabled user.

Need to Know More?

 Shannon, Michael. *MCSE Exchange 2000 Design Exam Prep*. The Coriolis Group, Scottsdale, AZ, 2001. ISBN 1-58880-026-1. This book is good as both a study guide and reference.

 Read Chapter 17 of the *Microsoft Exchange 2000 Server Planning and Installation* located in the \Docs folder of the Exchange 2000 CD-ROM.

 Download and read Chapters 3, 5, 6, and 7 of the Exchange 2000 Server Upgrade Series Deployment Guide from **http://www.microsoft.com/technet/exchange/guide/**.

 Download and read Chapter 4 of the Exchange 2000 Server Upgrade Series Planning Guide from **http://www.microsoft.com/technet/exchange/guide/**.

 Search **www.microsoft.com/technet** and the Exchange 2000 Server Help file using the terms at the beginning of the chapter.

 Search **www.Win2000mag.com** using the term "Exchange 2000" and the terms at the beginning of the chapter.

Planning for Clients

Terms you'll need to understand:

✓ Corporate Or Workgroup mail service

✓ Internet Only mail service

✓ Secure Multipurpose Internet Mail Extensions (S/MIME)

✓ WebDAV

✓ Reach browser

✓ Rich browser

✓ Internet Relay Chat (IRC)

✓ Extended Internet Relay Chat (IRCX)

✓ Instant Messaging (IM)

Techniques you'll need to master:

✓ Planning for MAPI client deployments

✓ Assessing client access needs and choosing the appropriate messaging client

✓ Accessing Exchange data using OWA

✓ Configuring Instant Messaging service records in DNS

So far in this book, you have learned about many Exchange clients and the protocols they use. The chapter is designed to summarize topics, such as messaging protocols, covered earlier in this book. This chapter also provides additional information about the types of Exchange clients and how they connect to Exchange 2000.

Outlook 2000

Outlook 2000 is the default messaging client for Exchange 2000. Of all the clients capable of communicating with Exchange 2000, Outlook 2000 provides the most functionality. Outlook 2000 can function as an Exchange client for all versions of Exchange.

Outlook 2000 can be configured in two different ways. When installed, the user has the option of Corporate Or Workgroup or Internet Only. The mail service chosen determines the protocols supported by Outlook. Table 12.1 summarizes these two mail services. After installation, Outlook's configuration can be changed by reconfiguring mail support through the Options settings (see Figure 12.1).

When configured with the Corporate Or Workgroup mail service, Outlook 2000 uses Messaging Application Programming Interface (MAPI) to connect to Exchange. MAPI currently provides more functionality than other messaging protocols. MAPI clients have full email, calendaring, tasks, journaling, multimedia messaging, and HTML support.

When configured with the Internet Only mail service, Outlook does not support connection using MAPI. Outlook 2000 in Internet Only mode must use IMAP4 or POP3 as well as SMTP to connect to Exchange 2000. Using these protocols limits functionality. When configured with Internet Only mail service, Outlook

Table 12.1 Protocols available with different Outlook configurations.		
Protocol	**Corporate Or Workgroup**	**Internet Only**
MAPI	Yes	No
MS Mail	Yes	No
Lotus cc:Mail server	Yes	No
NNTP	Yes	Yes
POP3	Yes	Yes
IMAP4	Yes	Yes
SMTP	Yes	Yes
LDAP	Yes	Yes
HTTP	Yes	Yes

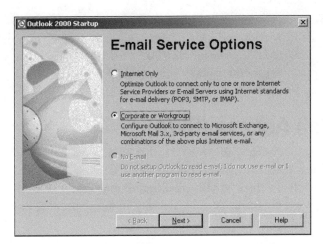

Figure 12.1   Outlook mail services.

2000 has increased performance and requires fewer resources. Clients connecting to Exchange over the Internet can use IMAP4, POP3, and SMTP for increased security and performance. Although MAPI can be used for remote mail across the Internet, configuration can be difficult, and there is more overhead than simpler protocols like IMAP4, POP3, and SMTP.

Pre-Outlook 2000 clients such as the Exchange client, Outlook 97, and Outlook 98 have similar functionality as Outlook 2000. Pre-Outlook 2000 MAPI clients were not configurable with the Internet Only option. These clients use MAPI and have less functionality than Outlook 2000. Also, because pre-Outlook 2000 MAPI clients expect the directory to be hosted by the Exchange server, Exchange 2000 servers pass pre-Outlook 2000 MAPI directory requests to a Global Catalog server. This passing of directory requests increases network traffic. Whenever possible, Outlook 2000 should be used over pre-Outlook 2000 MAPI clients.

Outlook Express

A common misconception is that Outlook Express is a stripped-down version of Outlook 2000. Outlook Express is actually an enhanced version of Microsoft's old Internet Mail and News client. Outlook Express provides email and news support. Outlook Express does not support MAPI.

Outlook Express's main advantages are that it's free, easy to use, and uses limited resources in comparison to Outlook 2000. Outlook Express supports IMAP4, HTTP, and POP3 for retrieving email and SMTP for sending email. Outlook Express can search directories using LDAP. News servers can be accessed using NNTP.

For secure communications, Outlook Express can use *Secure Sockets Layer (SSL)* to encrypt POP3, HTTP, IMAP4, and SMTP. Messages can be secured using *Secure Multipurpose Internet Mail Extensions (S/MIME)*. S/MIME uses digital ID to encrypt message content and/or digitally sign a message. Using digital ID, users can verify messages' origins.

Outlook Web Access (OWA)

One of the disadvantages of using Outlook 2000 is that it is not available on all operating systems. Most operating systems can use either Outlook Express or third-party email clients, but without MAPI access, limited functionality is available. Microsoft's solution to providing more functionality for more operating systems is Outlook Web Access (OWA).

Using the HTTP protocol, Web browsers can access many of the same features as Outlook 2000 over the Internet or/and intranet. OWA provides a limited version of Outlook through the Web browser interface. HTTP is used to transfer Web pages to and from the OWA server. OWA does not use POP3, IMAP4, or SMTP.

OWA provides benefits to remote and non-Windows clients. OWA has many disadvantages, however, including:

➤ *No offline access*—OWA does not support offline access of any kind. The Web browser must communicate with the Exchange 2000 server for OWA to function.

➤ *No tasks*—OWA does not currently support task management.

➤ *No journaling*—OWA does not currently support journaling.

➤ *No spellchecker*—OWA does not currently support spellchecking.

➤ *Limited calendaring*—Many of the viewing and scheduling features of calendaring are not available in OWA.

➤ *No rules*—OWA does not currently support inbox rules.

➤ *View limitations*—OWA does not support the three-pane view or viewing of certain flags.

➤ *No searching*—OWA does not allow folders to be searched.

➤ *Limited security*—OWA does not support S/MIME for digital encryption and digital signatures.

➤ *No recycling*—OWA does not support the deleted items folder.

Browser Support

OWA uses HTTP through IIS to access the Exchange server. An extended version of HTTP, called *WebDAV*, is used to access Exchange mailboxes and public folders. OWA supports many different browsers; however, certain features of OWA are available only when using Internet Explorer version 5 or higher.

Reach Browsers

OWA supports browsers that support Hypertext Markup Language (HTML) version 3.2 and higher. These browsers include Internet Explorer version 3.x and higher and Netscape Navigator version 3.x and higher. Microsoft calls these browsers *reach* browsers. OWA supports many functions with these browsers; however, the user experience is reduced. Reach browsers can:

➤ Send, receive, and forward email

➤ View and modify appointments (calendar)

➤ View and modify contacts

➤ Send messages formatted with Rich Text

Rich Browsers

Microsoft calls Internet Explorer version 5 or higher a *rich* browser. Internet Explorer 5 supports *Dynamic Hypertext Markup Language (DHTML)* and *Extended Markup Language (XML)*. Users of rich browsers have a more Outlook-like experience (see Figure 12.2). Rich browsers have all the same features of reach browsers, plus, using a rich browser, you can:

➤ Embed objects into messages

➤ Send messages formatted with HTML

➤ Drag and drop messages between folders

➤ Drag and drop text and objects while editing

➤ Right-click to access shortcut menus

Authentication

OWA requires a client to authenticate before accessing Exchange data. The Exchange HTTP virtual server is managed though the Internet Services Manager; OWA authentication and access control, however, must be configured using the Exchange System Manager (see Figure 12.3). Active Directory stores OWA authentication settings and updates these to the IIS metabase. If the settings are configured in the Internet Services Manager, those in Active Directory overwrite them. OWA can be configured to support one or more of the

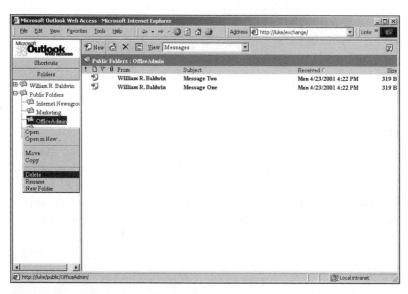

Figure 12.2   OWA using a rich browser.

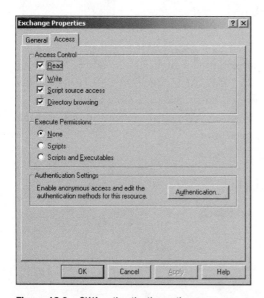

Figure 12.3   OWA authentication options.

three levels of authentication. These levels of authentication determine how the client is authenticated, not which users are permitted access. The three levels of authentication are:

➤ *Anonymous access*—This method allows clients to access the virtual server without providing credentials such as a user's name and password.

➤ *Basic authentication*—This method is widely supported by clients. Basic authentication requires a username and password be provided before access to the virtual server is provided. Basic authentication is vulnerable to attacks because the username and password are sent across the network as clear-text.

➤ *Windows Integrated authentication*—This method requires a username and password be provided before access is provided. Windows Integrated authentication is less vulnerable to attacks because the username and password are encrypted as they are sent across the network. This method is only available with Internet Explorer version 5 and higher.

Chat Clients

The Enterprise version of Exchange 2000 includes the Chat service. Chat allows multiple users to communicate to different chat communities using various chat clients. Exchange 2000 Chat services support the following clients:

➤ Microsoft Chat version 2.1 or later

➤ Internet Relay Chat (IRC) protocol clients

➤ Extended IRC (IRCX) protocol clients

Chat is an unsecured form of communication. Chat uses TCP port 6667, but cannot be secured using SSL. To secure chat communications, clients must use TCP/IP security such as PPTP, L2TP, or UPSec.

For the exam, remember that chat servers and clients use TCP port 6667. This port is configurable on both the clients and the servers.

Instant Messaging Clients

Exchange 2000 supports one-on-one user communication via Instant Messaging (IM). Exchange 2000 includes the MSN Messenger. This is currently the only client available for connecting to Exchange 2000 IM services. Before installing the MSN Messenger, Internet Explorer 5.0 or higher must be installed.

Note: For Windows 95 clients access to IM services from the Internet, Windows Sockets 2.0 or higher is required.

IM clients find IM services through the DNS service. IM uses service (SRV) records for storing the location of the *rendezvous protocol (RVP)*. The _rvp record must be manually created for each IM server. Figure 12.4 shows an example of an IM SRV record. For more information on IM, see Chapter 13.

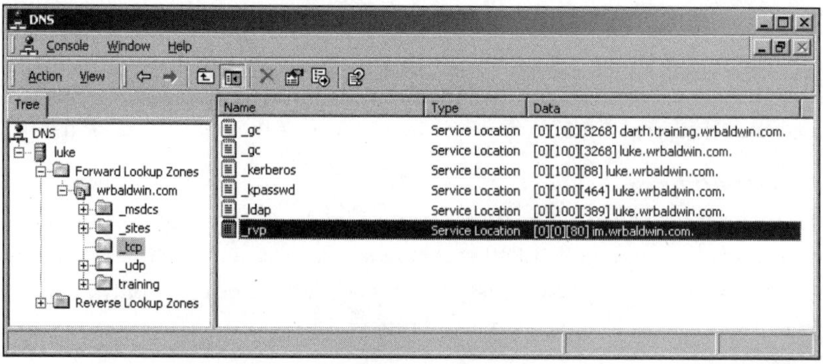

Figure 12.4 IM SRV record for im.wrbaldwin.com server in the wrbaldwin.com domain.

Practice Questions

Case Study

General Information

You have been hired by Cheap Food, Inc. (CFI), to assist the company with its deployment of Exchange 2000 Server. You are responsible for client access to Exchange 2000 Server.

CFI was created when five separate pre-packaged food manufacturers in Ohio merged. The five companies had approximately 5,000 employees each. These employees have offices in several cities around Ohio. CFI has consolidated its offices so that it now has one office in each major city in Ohio. This includes headquarters, two regional offices, and two local offices.

The board required that the five former technology groups be consolidated, and that a single messaging system be deployed. They have asked management to merge the five companies while ensuring the company put out the same award-winning products it always has.

Figure 12.5 shows the physical locations of CFI's offices.

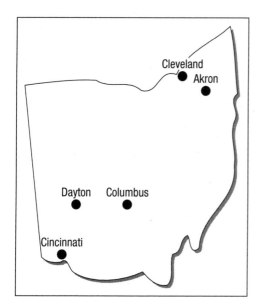

Figure 12.5 CFI's physical locations.

IT Environment

Each of the five companies that merged to create CFI used Exchange to provide email services. Each of the five companies still has its own Exchange organization. Four of the organizations are using Exchange 5.5, while one is using Exchange 5.0. CFI has already upgraded all servers to Windows 2000 Server and all clients to Windows 2000 Professional. They have deployed Active Directory and are running in mixed mode. All client computers have Outlook 2000.

Active Directory has been deployed across CFI. The existing Active Directory design includes a single Active Directory tree and forest. There are four domains: one root domain and one for each of the Ohio regions—Northeast, Central, and Southwest. Each location has two domain controllers, each of which is a Global Catalog server. The groups are structured to keep replication traffic to a minimum. The administrators of each domain can create domain global and local groups, but they are not allowed to create universal groups. Only the Enterprise administrator can create universal groups. The physical structure of the Active Directory is shown in Figure 12.6 and the logical is shown in Figure 12.7.

CFI has various email clients including Outlook Express, OWA, Outlook 98, and Exchange Client version 5.0.

Figure 12.6 Physical Active Directory design.

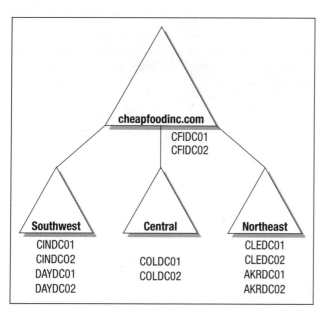

Figure 12.7   Logical Active Directory design.

Requirements and Goals

CFI would like to provide all clients with access to their mailboxes.

Question 1

Before deploying Exchange 2000, CFI may decide to upgrade all inhouse clients to the same messaging software. They want to make sure the new client will be able to access all current Exchange deployments using MAPI. What client software would you recommend they install?

○ a. Exchange Client version 5.0

○ b. Outlook 97 version 8.03

○ c. Outlook 98

○ d. Outlook 2000

○ e. Outlook Express

Answer d is correct. Outlook 2000 is backward-compatible with all versions of Exchange. Answers a, b, and c are incorrect, because they are older versions and not the best options. Answer e is incorrect, because Outlook Express is not a MAPI client.

Question 2

Dayton would like to provide remote users access to their mailboxes and public folders. They want these remote users to have the fastest access and the ability to work offline. They want to secure communications using SSL. What is the best solution?

○ a. Outlook Express using SMTP and POP3

○ b. Outlook 2000 using MAPI

○ c. OWA

○ d. None of these

Answer d is correct. Answer a is incorrect, because POP3 does not provide access to public folders. IMAP4 or NNTP must be used to access public folders. Answer b is incorrect, because SSL will not work with MAPI. Answer c is incorrect, because OWA does not support offline access.

Question 3

CFI is planning to deploy OWA for some remote clients. You would like to ensure OWA clients have access to view and modify appointments in their calendar. What Web browsers can they use? [Check all correct answers]

❑ a. Netscape Navigator 3.x

❑ b. Netscape Navigator 4.x

❑ c. Netscape Navigator 5.x

❑ d. Internet Explorer 3.x

❑ e. Internet Explorer 4.x

❑ f. Internet Explorer 5.x

All answers are correct. OWA supports viewing and modifying appointments from both reach and rich browsers. Reach browsers include those supporting HTML 3.2 and higher. These include Internet Explorer 3.x and higher and Netscape Navigator 3.x and higher.

Question 4

CFI would like to encrypt data when remote users check their email using Outlook Express. Which of the following will encrypt Outlook Express traffic? [Check all correct answers]

❑ a. POP3

❑ b. SSL

❑ c. Windows Integrated authentication

❑ d. IMAP4

❑ e. PPTP

Answers b and e are correct. SSL can be used to encrypt POP3, IMAP4, and SMTP traffic. Clients can use a VPN with PPTP to connect to the CFI network. PPTP can be configured to encrypt traffic. Answers a and d are incorrect, because POP3 and IMAP4 are not encrypted by default. Answer c is incorrect, because authentication methods cannot be used to encrypt data. Windows Integrated authentication encrypts the username and password.

Question 5

Internet Explorer 4.02 clients accessing CFI mailboxes via OWA can use which authentication methods? [Check all correct answers]

❑ a. Anonymous

❑ b. Basic

❑ c. Secure basic

❑ d. Windows Integrated

Answers a and b are correct. Internet Explorer versions before 5 supported only anonymous and basic authentication methods. Answer c is incorrect, because secure basic is not a valid authentication method. Answer d is incorrect, because Windows Integrated authentication is supported only by Internet Explorer version 5 and higher.

Question 6

CFI would like to set up an Instant Messaging solution. Which of the following records will have to be created for the IM01 server?

○ a. _rvp._tcp.cheapfoodsinc.com SRV 0 0 80 im01.cheapfoodinc.com

○ b. _tcp._rvp.cheapfoodsinc.com SRV 0 0 80 im01.cheapfoodinc.com

○ c. _rvp.cheapfoodsinc.com SRV 0 0 80 im01.cheapfoodinc.com

○ d. _rvp._msdcs.cheapfoodsinc.com SRV 0 0 80 im01.cheapfoodinc.com

○ e. None of the above

Answer a is correct. IM clients locating IM servers use RVP to access IM servers. They find IM servers using the DNS service (SRV) record _rvp in the _tcp subfolder of the domain.

Question 7

After configuring OWA, you decide to reconfigure the authentication to allow only Windows Integrated authentication. A day later you notice that users are still able to use basic authentication. What is the problem?

○ a. OWA authentication must be configured using the Internet Services Manager; the recent changes were probably made using the Exchange System Manager.

○ b. OWA does not support Windows Integrated authentication.

○ c. OWA authentication must be configured using the Exchange System Manager; the recent changes were probably made using the Internet Services Manager.

○ d. When a client accesses OWA using basic authentication, they can still use basic authentication if their browser does not support Windows Integrated authentication even if OWA is configured to not use basic authentication.

Answer c is correct, and answer a is incorrect. Active Directory stores OWA authentication settings and updates these to the IIS metabase. If the settings are configured in the Internet Services Manager, those in Active Directory settings configured using the Exchange System Manager will overwrite them. Answer b is incorrect, because OWA supports Windows Integrated authentication. Answer d is incorrect, because OWA does not accept basic authentication if basic authentication is disabled using the Exchange System Manager.

Need to Know More?

 Shannon, Michael. *MCSE Exchange 2000 Design Exam Prep.* The Coriolis Group, Scottsdale, AZ, 2001. ISBN 1-58880-026-1. This book is good as both a study guide and reference.

 Read Chapter 19 of the *Exchange 2000 Server Resource Kit.*

 Read Chapters 4, 10, 11, and 12 of the *Microsoft Exchange 2000 Server Planning and Installation* located in the \Docs folder of the Exchange 2000 CD-ROM.

 Download and read Chapter 8 of the Exchange 2000 Server Upgrade Series Planning Guide from **http://www.microsoft.com/technet/ exchange/guide/**.

 Search **www.microsoft.com/technet** and the Exchange 2000 Server Help file using the terms at the beginning of the chapter.

 Search **www.Win2000mag.com** using the term "Exchange 2000" and the terms at the beginning of the chapter.

Designing an Instant Messaging Solution

Terms you'll need to understand:

✓ Presence monitoring

✓ Internet Server Application Programming Interface (ISAPI)

✓ Instant Messaging home server

✓ Instant Messaging router

✓ Instant Messaging domain

✓ Fully Qualified Domain Name (FQDN)

✓ Separate namespace

✓ Unified namespace

✓ Service locator (SRV) records

✓ Rendezvous protocol (RVP)

✓ MSN Messenger

Techniques you'll need to master:

✓ Designing an Exchange 2000 Instant Messaging solution

✓ Configuring Instant Messaging service locator records to provide a unified email and Instant Messaging namespace

In recent years, the popularity of Instant Messaging has increased dramatically. Instant Messaging offers the low cost advantages of email, with the immediate response of telephone and video conferencing. Exchange 2000 includes the capability of hosting Instant Messaging sessions from MSN Messenger clients. The Exchange 2000 Instant Messaging virtual server provides such capabilities. This chapter will discuss the basics of Instant Messaging, the services provided by Exchange 2000, and the client software used to communicate.

Instant Messaging

Instant Messaging allows clients to collaborate realtime by typing messages to each other. These messages are routed through servers; however, the messages are not permanently stored on the servers. Instant Messaging services also provide presence information. When an Instant Messaging client is running, other clients can know its status on the network. This *presence monitoring* allows clients to keep track of contacts. Unlike email, messages can be sent only to clients who are online (see Figure 13.1).

Many Internet companies, such as Microsoft, Yahoo, and AOL, provide Instant Messaging services on the Internet. Using their proprietary software, clients of each service can communicate with clients of the same service only. Attempts have been made to bridge the competing services; however, each service provider has opposed access to their services from foreign clients. Exchange 2000's Instant Messaging service is only compatible with Microsoft's MSN Messenger service.

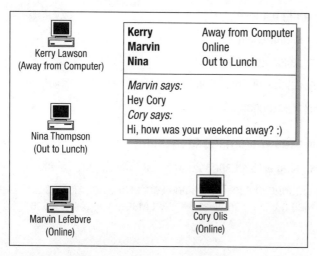

Figure 13.1   Example of Instant Messaging.

Exchange 2000 Instant Messaging

Exchange 2000 provides Instant Messaging services for both Internet and intranet users. Exchange 2000 uses *Internet Server Application Programming Interface (ISAPI)* server extensions running through Internet Information Services (IIS). Instant Messaging uses *Hypertext Transfer Protocol (HTTP)* to transfer messages. Instant Messaging uses an extended version of HTTP 1.1 over TCP port 80. Messages are formatted using *extensible markup language (XML)*.

Exchange 2000 Instant Messaging can be set up separately from other Exchange 2000 services. Exchange 2000 Instant Messaging, however, does require an Exchange organization to be present to function. The Exchange 2000 Instant Messaging service can be installed into a pre-Exchange 2000 organization. Before the Exchange 2000 Instant Messaging service is installed in a pre-Exchange 2000 environment, make sure the following requirements are met:

➤ At least one Exchange server in the organization must be running Exchange Server version 5.5 with Service Pack 3 or higher.

➤ The Exchange organization must be a member of an Active Directory domain.

➤ An Active Directory Connector connection agreement must be established between Exchange and Active Directory.

Instant Messaging Architecture

Exchange 2000 Instant Messaging has a separate and unique architecture from Exchange 2000 and Windows 2000. Instant Messaging servers can serve different roles. Instant Messaging servers and clients are members of domains. These domains may or may not have similar structures as Windows 2000 domains and Exchange 2000 organizations.

Server Roles

Exchange 2000 servers can serve two roles in Instant Messaging architecture; they can serve either role or both roles. These roles include Instant Messaging home servers and Instant Messaging routers:

➤ *Home Servers*—Each Instant Messaging client is associated with a single Instant Messaging home server. These home servers service clients' Instant Messaging requests.

➤ *Routers*—Instant Messaging routers refer intranet clients to their home server (see Figure 13.2). If an organization has more than one home server, it is recommended that they have at least one router. Routers can also proxy client requests to prevent Internet clients from directly communicating with their home server (see Figure 13.3).

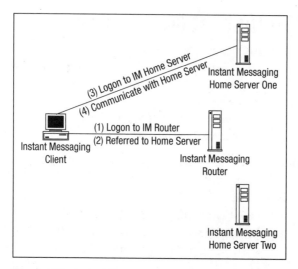

Figure 13.2 Instant Messaging router, intranet client referral.

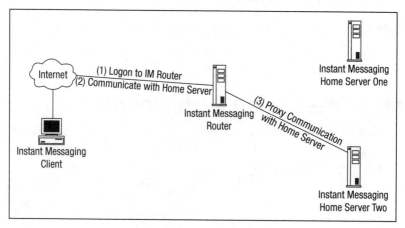

Figure 13.3 Instant Messaging router, Internet client proxy.

Domains

Each Exchange 2000 Instant Messaging server and client is a member of an Instant Messaging domain. These domains are DNS domains and represent a discrete namespace. Most organizations have one Instant Messaging domain for each email domain. The Instant Messaging domain can be separate from the email domain or the same. For example, a user named Cory Olis in the wrbaldwin.com email domain could be a member of the im.wrbaldwin.com Instant Messaging domain. If Cory's email address is **colis@wrbaldwin.com**, his Instant Messaging address would be **colis@im.wrbaldwin.com**. If his organization, however, decided to have *a unified namespace*, his email address and Instant Messaging address would both be **colis@wrbaldwin.com**.

For companies using separate namespaces, a host record should be defined with the host name of the Instant Messaging domain and the IP address of the Instant Messaging router. The *fully qualified domain name (FQDN)* is the Instant Messaging domain. For example, if a server with an IP address of 192.168.1.222 is the Instant Messaging router for the im.wrbaldwin.com domain, a host record for im in the wrbaldwin.com zone pointing to the IP address of 192.168.1.222 should be created. If multiple routers exist in the domain, multiple host records should be defined (see Figure 13.4).

Many organizations want to have email and Instant Messaging with a unified namespace. To configure a unified namespace for Instant Messaging, DNS *service locator (SRV) records* must be defined for each router in the domain. For example, to define the Instant Messaging routers Luke and Darth (from the example shown in Figure 13.5) as Instant Messaging routers in the **wrbaldwin.com** domain, the

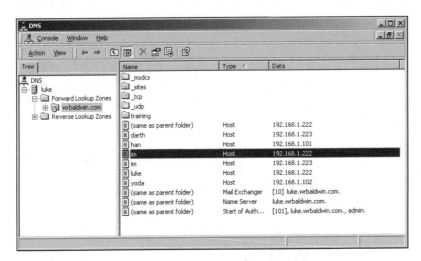

Figure 13.4 Setting up multiple host records for Instant Messaging routers.

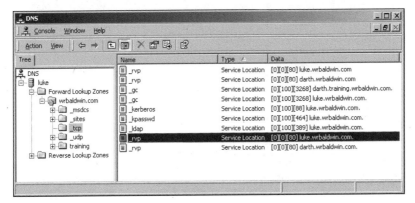

Figure 13.5 Setting up _RVP SRV records for a unified email and Instant Messaging domain.

_RVP SRV records must be defined (see Figure 13.5). Active Directory clients use this SRV record to locate Instant Messaging routers. Pre-Windows 2000 clients must be running the Active Directory client to find service records.

For the exam, remember that pre-Windows 2000 clients must be running the Active Directory client to find service records.

Instant Messaging (RVP) Virtual Server

Instant Messaging uses the rendezvous protocol (RVP). Adding a virtual server under the Instant Messaging (RVP) protocol in the Exchange System Manager enables Exchange 2000 Instant Messaging (see Figure 13.6). The Active Directory security of the virtual server can be configured using the Exchange System Manager. Configuration such as authentication must be configured using the Internet Services Manager.

The Instant Messaging virtual server does not support anonymous or basic authentication. By default, each virtual server is configured to accept both digest and Integrated Windows authentication. For Internet clients, it is recommended that only digest authentication be used.

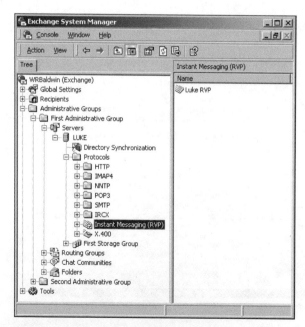

Figure 13.6   Instant Messaging (RVP) virtual server.

MSN Messenger

The Instant Messaging client included with Exchange 2000 is the MSN Messenger. The MSN Messenger supports communication with MSN and Exchange Instant Messaging. Once the MSN Messenger is launched and the client is authenticated, the client's status is automatically configured to online. After 20 minutes of computer inactivity, MSN Messenger changes a user's status to Away. MSN Messenger supports the following statuses:

➤ *Online*—You can send and receive messages. A flash appears when you receive new messages.

➤ *Invisible*—You are not seen on the system, but you are able to see the status of others.

➤ *Busy*—You receive messages, but they do not flash.

➤ *Be Right Back*—You receive messages and they flash.

➤ *Away*—You receive messages and they flash. This status is activated automatically after 20 minutes of inactivity. The amount of inactivity is configurable.

➤ *On the Phone*—You receive messages, but they do not flash.

➤ *Out to Lunch*—You receive messages and they flash.

➤ *Appear Offline*—You appear as Offline to others, but you are able to see the status of others.

Practice Questions

Case Study

General Information

You have been hired by Cheap Food, Inc. (CFI), to assist the company with its deployment of Exchange 2000 Instant Messaging servers.

CFI was created when five separate pre-packaged food manufacturers in Ohio merged. The five companies had approximately 5,000 employees each. These employees have offices in several cities around Ohio. CFI has consolidated its offices so that it now has one office in each major city in Ohio. This includes headquarters, two regional offices, and two local offices.

The board required that the five former technology groups be consolidated, and that a single messaging system be deployed. They have asked management to merge the five companies while ensuring the company put out the same award-winning products it always has.

Figure 13.7 shows the physical locations of CFI's offices.

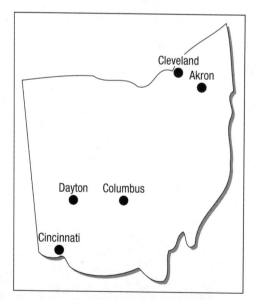

Figure 13.7 CFI's physical locations.

IT Environment

Each of the five companies that merged to create CFI used Exchange to provide email services. The five email systems have been migrated to a single Exchange 2000 organization.

Active Directory has been deployed across CFI. The existing Active Directory design includes a single Active Directory tree and forest. There are four domains: one root domain and one for each of the Ohio regions—Northeast, Central, and Southwest. Each location has two domain controllers, each of which is a Global Catalog server. The groups are structured to keep replication traffic to a minimum. The administrators of each domain can create domain global and local groups, but they are not allowed to create universal groups. Only the Enterprise administrator can create universal groups. The physical structure of the Active Directory is shown in Figure 13.8 and the logical is shown in Figure 13.9.

CFI has upgraded all messaging clients to either Outlook 2000 or OWA.

Requirements and Goals

CFI would like to deploy an Instant Messaging system across its organization. CFI would like all employees to have access to Instant Messaging.

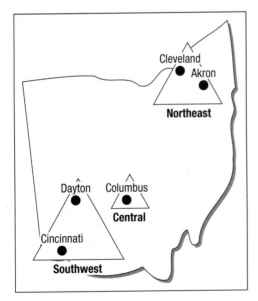

Figure 13.8 Physical Active Directory design.

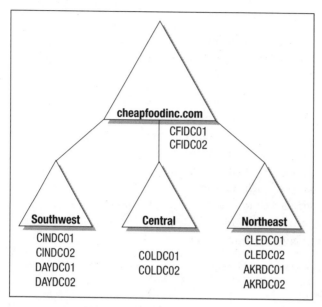

Figure 13.9 Logical Active Directory design.

Question 1

You have installed a pilot Instant Messaging system in a lab. You have two clients and a server. You would like to experiment with settings on the clients. What status or statuses could you set a client to, if you want that client to be able to see who is online, but not be seen by others?

○ a. Away

○ b. Appear Offline

○ c. Invisible

○ d. Shadow

Answer c is correct. Invisible status does not allow other users to see the client, but the client is able to see who is online. Answers a and b are incorrect, because the client would be seen by other users. Answer d is not a valid status.

Question 2

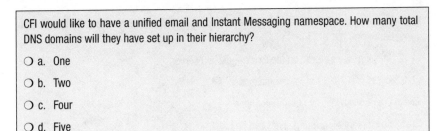

Answer c is correct. Even though Instant Messaging and email will both use **cheapfoodinc.com**, the three Active Directory child domains will each have a DNS domain associated with them. Answers a, b, and d are thus wrong.

Question 3

CFI would like to have separate email and Instant Messaging namespaces. The Instant Messaging router is called IM. Which of the following service locator records should they configure?

○ a. _rvp._tcp.cheapfoodsinc.com SRV 0 0 80 im.cheapfoodinc.com

○ b. _rvp._tcp.im.cheapfoodsinc.com SRV 0 0 80 im.cheapfoodinc.com

○ c. _rvp._tcp.cheapfoodsinc.com SRV 0 0 80 cheapfoodinc.com

○ d. _rvp._tcp.im.cheapfoodsinc.com SRV 0 0 80 cheapfoodinc.com

○ e. None of the above

Answer e is correct. When an Instant Messaging domain is in its own DNS namespace, service locator records do not have to be defined. A host record associated with the Instant Messaging domain should be configured. Answers a, b, c, and d are thus wrong.

Question 4

> Which of the following are characteristics of Exchange 2000 Instant Messaging? [Check all correct answers]
>
> ❑ a. Messages are stored on the Exchange 2000 server.
>
> ❑ b. Client use POP3 for communications.
>
> ❑ c. Client use HTTP for communications.
>
> ❑ d. Any Instant Messaging client can be used.

Answer c is correct. Exchange 2000 Instant Messaging uses HTTP for communications. Answer b is thus incorrect. Answer a is incorrect, because messages are not stored on any server. Answer d is incorrect, because not all Instant Messaging clients are compatible with Exchange 2000 Instant Messaging.

Question 5

> MSN Messenger clients can use which authentication methods? [Check all correct answers]
>
> ❑ a. Anonymous
>
> ❑ b. Basic
>
> ❑ c. Digest
>
> ❑ d. Windows Integrated

Answers c and d are correct. The Instant Messaging virtual server only supports digest and Windows Integrated authentication. Answers a and b are thus incorrect.

Question 6

Exchange 2000 Instant Messaging supports which of the following Instant Messaging clients? [Check all correct answers]

❑ a. Yahoo Messenger

❑ b. AOL Messenger

❑ c. IRC compliant client

❑ d. MSN Messenger

Answer d is correct. Exchange 2000 Instant Messaging supports only the MSN Messenger client. Answers a, b, and c are thus incorrect.

Question 7

If CFI uses a unified DNS domain for Instant Messaging, how many total DNS domains will they have?

○ a. 1

○ b. 2

○ c. 3

○ d. 4

○ e. 5

Answer c is correct. CFI has four DNS domains. When using a unified DNS domain for Instant Messaging, the same DNS domain used for email is used for Instant Messaging. Answers a, b, d, and e are thus incorrect.

Need to Know More?

 Shannon, Michael. *MCSE Exchange 2000 Design Exam Prep*. The Coriolis Group, Scottsdale, AZ, 2001. ISBN 1-58880-026-1. This book is good as both a study guide and reference.

 Read Chapter 19 of the *Exchange 2000 Server Resource Kit*.

 Read Chapter 11 of the *Microsoft Exchange 2000 Server Planning and Installation* located in the \Docs folder of the Exchange 2000 CD-ROM.

 Search **www.microsoft.com/technet** and the Exchange 2000 Server Help file using the terms at the beginning of the chapter.

 Search **www.Win2000mag.com** using the term "Exchange 2000" and the terms at the beginning of the chapter.

Sample Test

Case Study 1

WRBaldwin, Inc., will be deploying Exchange 2000 and Active Directory within one year.

Company Profile

WRBaldwin is a medium-sized consulting company based in Atlanta, GA. Its core business has always been professional services and staff extension. WRBaldwin has recently expanded into training in its Atlanta and Tampa locations. This business accounts for 15 percent of total sales but is currently losing money.

Business Plan

WRBaldwin would like to expand its training business to all six locations. WRBaldwin is not concerned with the training business making money, but it would like to break even. Internally, the training department is referred to as WRB Training. WRBaldwin would like the consulting and training businesses to collaborate, but remain separate entities.

IT Environment:

WRBaldwin and WRB Training are currently running Windows NT 4. Each unit has its own NT domain (WRBALDWIN and TR). A two-way trust has been established between the two domains.

WRBaldwin's existing network infrastructure is shown in Figure 14.1.

WRBaldwin, Inc., plans to have a single forest and tree with two domains (**ad.wrbaldwin.com** and **tr.ad.wrbaldwin.com**). Two domain controllers are to be placed in each location. The Atlanta and Tampa locations will each have a single Global Catalog server.

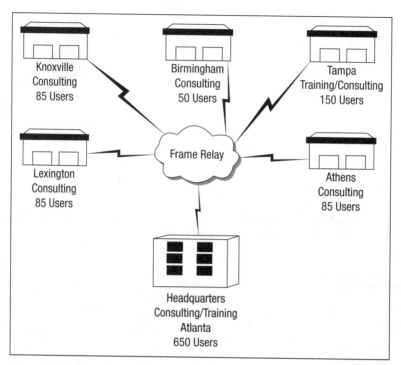

Figure 14.1 Physical network diagram.

WRBaldwin has two Exchange 5.5 organizations. WRBaldwin, Inc., is the organization for the consulting unit, and WRB Training is the organization for the training unit. The WRBaldwin, Inc., organization has six sites, one for each location. The WRB Training organization has two sites, one for each location. Both organizations have the Internet Mail Service configured for routing messages to the Internet and between organizations. WRBaldwin's Exchange servers are outlined in Tables 14.1 and 14.2.

Table 14.1 WRBaldwin, Inc.'s Exchange servers.				
Name	**Version**	**Service Pack**	**Mailboxes**	**Public Folders**
ATLEX01	5.5	4	Yes	Yes
ATLEX02	5.5	4	Yes	No
ATLEX03	5.5	3	No	Yes
ATHEX01	5.5	2	Yes	No
LEXEX01	5.5	3	Yes	No
KNOEX01	5.0	Unknown	Yes	No
BIREX01	5.5	4	Yes	No
TAMEX01	5.5	4	Yes	No

Table 14.2   WRB Training's Exchange servers.

Name	Version	Service Pack	Mailboxes	Public Folders
ATLEX04	5.5	4	Yes	Yes
ATLEX05	5.5	4	Yes	Yes
TAMEX02	5.5	4	Yes	Yes

Company Commentary

CEO: With all the money we're spending on these new systems, I want to know how we can find ways to save money. I heard Instant Messaging could reduce telephone charges. I want to see everyone have access to a reliable Instant Messaging solution. I don't want this to be some complicated system that no one uses; make it simple. No additional usernames or passwords to remember.

CIO: As we expand training to the other locations, I'll be hiring IT staff to handle the training computers. I feel that because the training computers may be exposed to students, it's important to have these in their own domain. As far as Exchange 2000 goes, I'd like to see Windows 2000 running on all member servers, then on all domain controllers. After all servers are running Windows 2000, then I'll approve the Exchange 2000 migration. I know WRB Training is itching to deploy Active Directory, so we'll upgrade as many of their servers as we can first, then focus on consulting.

Director of Consulting IT: As we deploy Active Directory and Exchange 2000, I'm concerned with additional traffic on our frame relay connections. I'd like to control traffic between sites and prevent users from having to cross the frame to get logged on, access their mailboxes, and access public folders. We should be ready to deploy Active Directory in about six months. Exchange 2000 will follow shortly after that.

Director of Training IT: We have discussed the possibility of making the training department its own forest. Unfortunately, this will not be the case. TRAINING will be a subdomain of the **wrbaldwin.com** domain. I will have full control over **training.wrbaldwin.com**, but the admins in **wrbaldwin.com** will also have administrative rights in my domain. We are ready to deploy Active Directory now. One big problem we have with our current Exchange organization is moving mailboxes. It's common for employees to move from between the consulting unit and training units. We want to be able to move mailboxes seamlessly between the two units.

Network Administrator: We are currently using **wrbaldwin.com** for our Internet presence. I'd like to see Active Directory use a subdomain, maybe **ad.wrbaldwin.com**. Consulting users have **wrbaldwin.com** for their email domain, but Training uses **tr.wrbaldwin.com**; we'd like to have everyone using **wrbaldwin.com**.

Email Administrator: We will be ready to deploy Exchange 2000 as soon as IT deploys Active Directory. I want to be able to let the trainers have total control over their Exchange servers. I plan on doing the Exchange 2000 server upgrades during off-hours in case I need to take any of the servers offline. I just got new Exchange servers six months ago, so I don't see having many new servers to use.

Exchange 2000 Requirements

Senior executives in Atlanta and the managers at the other locations should have the quickest restore time. All mailboxes should be backed up every night except those of the office personnel; their mailboxes will only be backed up on the weekends.

Remote clients should be able to check their Exchange 2000 email from home using a remote mail solution. Remote clients will be running either Windows 95 or Windows 98.

Question 1.1

For both units, WRBaldwin will use DNS domains for email, Active Directory, and Instant Messaging. Once WRBaldwin has completed its migration, how many DNS domains will it have?

○ a. 1

○ b. 2

○ c. 3

○ d. 4

○ e. 5

Question 1.2

Before upgrading to Exchange 2000, you need to design a strategy for migrating WRBaldwin's two NT domains to Windows 2000 Active Directory. You will also need to migrate member servers to Windows 2000. Place the following steps in order. You may use each step only once and you may not need to use every step.

Create a new Active Directory domain for wrbaldwin.com.

Create a new Active Directory domain for tr.wrbaldwin.com.

Use the Active Directory Migration Tool to migrate accounts from WRBALDWIN to wrbaldwin.com.

Use the Active Directory Migration Tool to migrate accounts from TR to tr.wrbaldwin.com.

Upgrade all Windows NT member servers in the TR domain to Windows 2000.

Upgrade the WRBALDWIN PDC to Windows 2000.

Upgrade the TR PDC to Windows 2000.

Upgrade all Windows NT member servers in the WRBALDWIN domain to Windows 2000.

Upgrade all WRBALDWIN BDCs to Windows 2000.

Upgrade all TR BDCs to Windows 2000.

Question 1.3

WRBaldwin's Active Directory is in place; now you will need to design a strategy for migrating the Exchange servers. Place the following steps in order. You may use each step only once and you may not need to use every step.

Update all Exchange servers in the WRBaldwin, Inc., organization to Exchange Server 5.5 with Service Pack 3 or higher.

Update all Exchange servers in the WRB Training organization to Exchange Server 5.5 with Service Pack 3 or higher.

Upgrade all Exchange servers in the WRBaldwin, Inc., organization to Exchange 2000.

Upgrade all Exchange servers in the WRB Training organization to Exchange 2000.

Create a new Exchange 2000 organization.

Move mailboxes from the WRBaldwin, Inc., organization to the new organization using the Exchange Server Migration Tool.

Move mailboxes from the WRB Training organization to the new organization using the Exchange Server Migration Tool.

Move mailboxes from the WRB Training organization to the WRBaldwin, Inc., organization using the Exchange Server Migration Tool.

Move mailboxes from the WRBaldwin, Inc., organization to the new organization using the Active Directory Connector.

Move mailboxes from the WRB Training organization to the new organization using the Active Directory Connector.

Move mailboxes from the WRB Training organization to the WRBaldwin, Inc., organization using the Active Directory Connector.

Question 1.4

WRBaldwin would like to provide remote clients with access to public folders. Which of the following messaging protocols will provide that functionality? [Check all correct answers]

❑ a. IMAP4

❑ b. SMTP

❑ c. POP3

❑ d. MAPI

❑ e. NNTP

Question 1.5

After WRBaldwin's Exchange 2000 deployment, a consulting user in Lexington is running Outlook 98 and creates a distribution list containing friends from both the training and consulting units. This user will have to cross a WAN link to accomplish this task.

○ a. True

○ b. False

Question 1.6

You are designing the hard disk configuration for ATLEX01. This server will contain three storage groups. The first storage group contains mailbox stores. The second storage group contains the default public folder tree. The third storage group contains a general-purpose public folder tree that is used to pull newsfeeds from the Internet. The server's disks have been configured as follows:

Drive C: (mirrored drive)

Drive D: (mirrored drive)

Drive E: (mirrored drive)

Drive F: (RAID 5 array)

Match the following files with the disks above

System/boot partition

Mailbox stores

Public folder store

News store

First storage group's transaction logs

Second storage group's transaction logs

Third storage group's transaction logs

Question 1.7

After WRBaldwin has migrated to Exchange 2000, all Exchange servers except ATLEX02 are running Exchange 2000. ATLEX02 is still running Exchange Server 5.5. How many administrative groups should WRBaldwin have at this point?

○ a. 1

○ b. 2

○ c. 4

○ d. 6

○ e. 7

○ f. 8

Question 1.8

After WRBaldwin has migrated to Exchange 2000, all Exchange servers except ATLEX02 are running Exchange 2000. ATLEX02 is still running Exchange Server 5.5. How many routing groups will WRBaldwin have at this point?

○ a. 1

○ b. 2

○ c. 4

○ d. 6

○ e. 7

○ f. 8

Question 1.9

After WRBaldwin converts its Exchange 2000 organization to native mode, its servers are consolidated into two administrative groups: WRB-AG and TR-AG. You would like members of the WRB-Admins security group to have total control over both administrative groups, and members of the TR-Admins group to have total control over the TR-AG administrative groups. Which of the following tasks must you perform? [Check all correct answers]

❑ a. Assign the WRB-Admins group the Exchange Full Administrator role at the organization level.

❑ b. Assign the WRB-Admins group the Exchange Full Administrator role at the TR-AG level.

❑ c. Assign the WRB-Admins group the Exchange Full Administrator role at the WRB-AG level.

❑ d. Assign the TR-Admins group the Exchange Full Administrator role at the organization level.

❑ e. Assign the TR-Admins group the Exchange Full Administrator role at the TR-AG level.

❑ f.   Assign the TR-Admins group the Deny Exchange View Only Administrator role at the WRB-AG level.

❑ g. Assign the TR-Admins group the Exchange View Only Administrator role at the organization level.

Question 1.10

Which of the following most affects WRBaldwin's routing group design once Exchange 2000 is converted to native mode?

◯ a. Existing messaging system

◯ b. Physical network topology

◯ c. Active Directory physical design

◯ d. Active Directory logical design

◯ e. Administrative model

Question 1.11

WRBaldwin has decided to allow POP3 clients to check their email from home. What options does WRBaldwin have for encrypting the remote data? [Check all correct answers]

❑ a. L2TP

❑ b. SSL

❑ c. Integrated Windows authentication

❑ d. Basic authentication

❑ e. PPTP

Question 1.12

WRBaldwin has decided to allow POP3 clients to check their email from home. Clients will be required to secure traffic using SSL. What port or ports would they have to open in the firewall? [Check all correct answers]

❑ a. 25

❑ b. 80

❑ c. 110

❑ d. 119

❑ e. 993

❑ f. 995

Question 1.13

WRBaldwin has decided to allow POP3 clients to check their email from home. Using Outlook Express and POP3, clients will have access to the default public folder tree, but not general-purpose public folder trees.

○ a. True

○ b. False

Question 1.14

You have decided to upgrade ATLEX01 to Exchange 2000. What steps must be performed before Exchange 2000 can be installed on ATLEX01? [Check all correct answers]

❏ a. ATLEX01 must be running Windows 2000 Server or Advanced Server.

❏ b. ATLEX01 must be running Windows 2000 Server Service Pack 1.

❏ c. The PDC in the WRBALDWIN domain must be running Windows 2000 Server or Advanced Server.

❏ d. The PDC in the WRBALDWIN domain must be running Windows 2000 Server Service Pack 1.

Question 1.15

During the migration, WRBALDWIN wants to maintain message routing between the WRBaldwin, Inc., organization and the old WRB Training organization. Which of the following tasks must be performed?

○ a. Create a routing group connector from a WRBaldwin, Inc., organization routing group to a WRB Training site. Create a site connector from a WRB Training site to a WRBaldwin, Inc., routing group.

○ b. Create a routing group connector from a WRBaldwin, Inc., organization administrative group to a WRB Training site. Create a site connector from a WRB Training site to a WRBaldwin, Inc., administrative group.

○ c. Create an SMTP connector using DNS to route messages.

○ d. Create an SMTP virtual server using DNS to route messages.

○ e. None of the above.

Case Study 2

North Coast Training will be upgrading from Exchange 5.5 to Exchange 2000.

Company Profile

North Coast Training is a small training center in Cleveland, Ohio. Its core business has always been Instructor-Led Training (ILT). Recently, due to the popularity of the Internet, North Coast has expanded into the eLearning business. This business accounts for 5 percent of total sales but 20 percent of total profits. North Coast also publishes a line of training material.

Business Plan

North Coast recently opened its third training center in the Cleveland area and has plans to expand throughout the Midwest. North Coast has been very successful recently and is resisting the temptation to expand too fast. The company would like to focus on eLearning and publishing, but not lose focus on the ILT business.

Existing IT Environment: Network Diagram

Figure 14.2 shows North Coast's network diagram.

Company Commentary

CIO: We have been growing faster than our IT department can handle. Our senior administrators spend too much time responding to help desk issues. We need to better delegate control to junior administrators. My hope is to maintain the current senior administrators and hire more junior administrators.

Director of IT: We know the current leased lines are overtaxed and need upgrading. Until we get the funds for this upgrade, we've got to control traffic between locations. I'd like to see traffic reduced as much as possible.

Email Manager: Our slow links have caused us to abandon MAPI clients in Mentor. Mentor clients use POP3 to access the email servers. We're uncertain when the new links will be available, so I've been toying with the idea of using Outlook Web Access in Mentor.

Messaging System

North Coast upgraded from Exchange 5.0 to 5.5 just over a year ago. The company has three Exchange servers. There is a server in each site except Mentor. Mentor

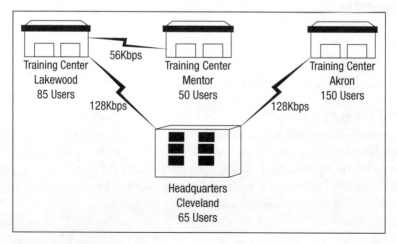

Figure 14.2 Network diagram.

clients use POP3 to access the server in Lakewood. All other clients use Outlook 98 with MAPI. Because users transfer frequently from location to location, all three servers are in the same Exchange site, NCT. The organization name is North Coast Training.

Hardware

All clients are currently running Window 2000 Professional.

North Coast currently has three Exchange servers and three domain controllers. The IT department has determined that each new Exchange server should have at least 256MB of RAM. The Cleveland server's RAM cannot be upgraded. Table 14.3 shows the server configurations.

Exchange 2000 Requirements and Goals

North Coast would like to upgrade its Exchange environment to Exchange 2000. It would like to have a server in each location except Mentor. These servers should all be administrated by a single group of users in the IT staff. The current email system must remain online during the upgrade.

Table 14.3	Server configuration.			
Location	Operating System	Service Pack	RAM	Function
Cleveland	Windows NT 4 Server	SP5	128MB	Exchange
Cleveland	Windows NT 4 Server	SP6	256MB	PDC
Akron	Windows 2000 Server	SP1	384MB	Exchange
Akron	Windows NT 4 Server	SP6	128MB	BDC
Lakewood	Windows 2000 Server	None	256MB	Exchange
Lakewood	Windows NT 4 Server	SP6	128MB	BDC

Question 2.1

While planning North Coast's Active Directory design, you have had suggestions about deploying OUs for various departments in the organization. You are not sure if the benefits of OUs outweigh the additional complication of setting them up and managing them. Which of the following can be achieved only by using OUs in Active Directory?

○ a. Delegation of control

○ b. Deploying software to users

○ c. Deploying software to computers

○ d. Deploying group policies

○ e. None of these

Question 2.2

After North Coast deploys Active Directory, if they decide to install a new Exchange 2000 server into the existing Exchange 5.5 organization, what task or tasks must be performed first?

○ a. Run ForestPrep.

○ b. Run DomainPrep.

○ c. Upgrade at least one Exchange 5.5 server to Service Pack 3 or higher.

○ d. Upgrade at least one Exchange 5.5 server to Exchange 2000.

○ e. Deploy the Active Directory Connector.

Question 2.3

How many routing groups should North Coast have in its new Exchange 2000 design?

○ a. 0

○ b. 1

○ c. 2

○ d. 3

○ e. 4

Question 2.4

After upgrading the first Exchange 5.5 server to Exchange 2000, how many administrative groups will North Coast have in its Exchange 2000 organization?

○ a. 0

○ b. 1

○ c. 2

○ d. 3

○ e. 4

Question 2.5

North Coast is concerned with security across the WAN link to Mentor. What encryption methods can the Mentor clients use? [Check all correct answers]

❑ a. L2TP

❑ b. IMAP4

❑ c. SSL

❑ d. PPTP

❑ e. None of the above

Question 2.6

North Coast has decided to upgrade its Mentor client to Outlook 2000. The Mentor clients will use Internet Mail to check their email across the WAN. Clients will be required to secure traffic using SSL. What port or ports would they have to open in the firewall? [Check all correct answers]

❑ a. 25

❑ b. 80

❑ c. 110

❑ d. 119

❑ e. 993

❑ f. 995

Question 2.7

North Coast has decided to upgrade its Mentor client to Outlook 2000. The Mentor clients will use Internet Mail to check their email across the WAN. Mentor clients will have access to the default public folder tree and general-purpose public folder trees when using Outlook 2000.

○ a. True

○ b. False

Question 2.8

North Coast would like its Exchange 2000 recipients to receive email from the Internet. What is the best way to accomplish this?

○ a. Create an SMTP connector on an Exchange 2000 server. Configure the connector to point to a same smart host.

○ b. Create an SMTP connector on an Exchange 2000 server. Configure the connector to use DNS.

○ c. Configure the default SMTP virtual server on an Exchange 2000 server to point to a same smart host.

○ d. Configure the default SMTP virtual server on an Exchange 2000 server to use DNS.

○ e. None of the above.

Question 2.9

North Coast is toying with the idea of using OWA at the Mentor location. If Mentor clients used OWA, they would not be able to manage tasks in Outlook.

○ a. True

○ b. False

Question 2.10

North Coast is toying with the idea of using OWA at the Mentor location. If Mentor clients used OWA, they would not be able to drag-and-drop messages between folders.

○ a. True

○ b. False

Question 2.11

North Coast is interested in deploying Instant Messaging shortly after the Exchange 2000 deployment. If Instant Messaging is deployed to a server called CLEEX01 and has a unified namespace, which of the following records must be added to DNS?

○ a. _rvp._tcp.northcoasttraining.com SRV 0 0 80 cleex01.northcoasttraining.com

○ b. _rvp._tcp.northcoasttraining.com RVP 0 0 80 cleex01.northcoasttraining.com

○ c. _rvp._tcp.northcoasttraining.com SRV 0 0 389 cleex01.northcoasttraining.com

○ d. _rvp._tcp.northcoasttraining.com RVP 0 0 389 cleex01.northcoasttraining.com

Question 2.12

Which of the following methods should North Coast use to migrate to Exchange 2000?

○ a. Perform an in-place upgrade of all its Exchange servers.

○ b. Install Exchange 2000 server into the existing organization. Move the current Exchange mailboxes to Exchange 2000 server.

○ c. Create a new Exchange 2000 organization and move mailboxes using the Exchange Server Migration Wizard.

○ d. Create a new Exchange 2000 organization and move mailboxes using the Active Directory Connector.

Question 2.13

North Coast would like to have three separate public folder hierarchies. Jim is going to be responsible for managing the hierarchies and he will use Outlook Express. How many public folder trees will need to be created?

○ a. None

○ b. 1

○ c. 2

○ d. 3

Question 2.14

You are designing the hard disk configuration for the three Exchange 2000 servers. Each server will contain one storage group and two stores. The server's disks have been configured as followed:

Drive C: (hardware RAID 1)

Drive D: (hardware RAID 5)

Match the following items with the disks above:

System partition

Boot partition

First storage group's transaction logs

Mailbox store

Public folder store

Question 2.15

After the Exchange 2000 migration, the IT department will need access to Exchange from their desktops. What steps will they have to perform before they can manage Exchange 2000 from their desktops? Choose only the correct steps and place them in the correct order.

Install Adminpak.msi

Install Srvtools.msi

Upgrade to Windows 2000 Server

Install Exchange System Management Tools

Install Exchange Messaging and Collaboration Tools

Install Exchpak.msi

Case Study 3

Cheap Food, Inc. (CFI), is migrating to Exchange 2000.

General Information

You have been hired by CFI to assist the company with its deployment of Exchange 2000.

CFI was created when five separate pre-packaged food manufacturers in Ohio merged. The five companies had approximately 5,000 employees each. These employees have offices in several cities around Ohio. CFI has consolidated its offices so that it now has one office in each major city in Ohio. This includes headquarters, two regional offices, and two local offices.

The board required that the five former technology groups be consolidated, and that a single messaging system be deployed. They have asked management to merge the five companies while ensuring the company put out the same award-winning products it always has.

Figure 14.3 shows the physical locations of CFI's offices.

IT Environment

Each of the five companies that merged to create CFI used Exchange to provide email services. Each of the five companies still has its own Exchange organization. Four of the organizations are using Exchange 5.5 while one is using Exchange 5.0. CFI has already upgraded all servers to Windows 2000 Server and all clients to Windows 2000 Professional. They have deployed Active Directory and are running in mixed mode. All client computers have Outlook 2000.

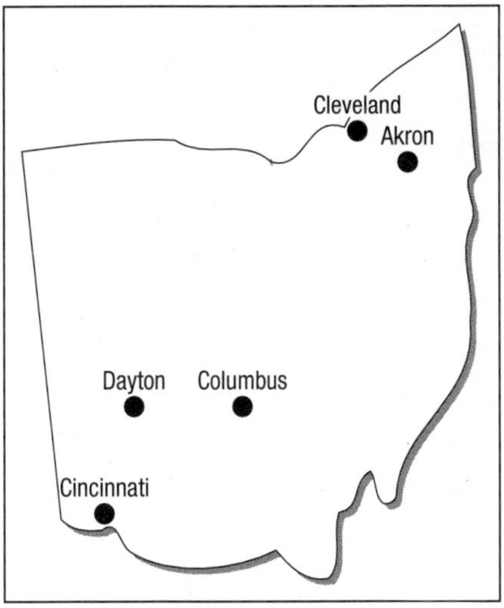

Figure 14.3   CFI's physical locations.

Active Directory has been deployed across CFI. The existing Active Directory design includes a single Active Directory tree and forest. There are four domains: one root domain and one for each of the Ohio regions—Northeast, Central, and Southwest. Every location has two domain controllers, each of which is a Global Catalog server. The groups are structured to keep replication traffic to a minimum. The administrators of each domain can create domain global and local groups, but they are not allowed to create universal groups. Only the Enterprise administrator can create universal groups. The physical structure of the Active Directory is shown in Figure 14.4 and the logical structure is shown in Figure 14.5.

Figure 14.4   Physical Active Directory design.

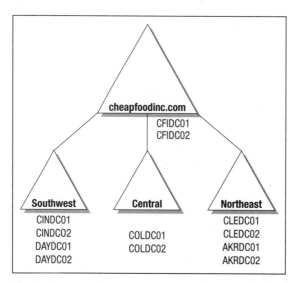

Figure 14.5 Logical Active Directory design.

CFI has upgraded all messaging clients to either Outlook 2000 or Outlook Web Access.

New Hardware

There will be two new servers per location. These servers will be used as Exchange servers. There are two server sizes: small and large. Large servers are quad-processor machines with 4 gigabytes (GB) of RAM and seven 18GB hard drives. Small servers are dual-processor machines with 2GB of RAM and six 9GB hard drives. Table 14.4 shows the locations of the new servers. Both server types have hardware RAID controllers.

Table 14.4 Exchange servers at each location.		
Location	**Name**	**Server Size**
Cleveland	CLEEX01	Large
Cleveland	CLEEX02	Large
Akron	AKRALLEX01	Large
Akron	AKREX02	Large
Columbus	COLEX01	Large
Columbus	COLEX02	Small
Dayton	DAYEX01	Small
Dayton	DAYEX02	Small
Cincinnati	CINEX01	Large
Cincinnati	CINEX02	Small

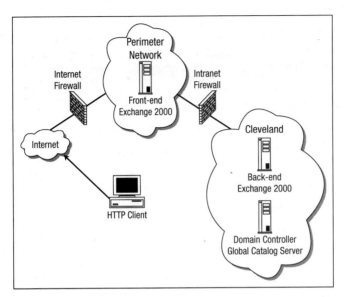

Figure 14.6   Cleveland perimeter network configuration.

Remote Client Access

The Cleveland location will have a perimeter network (see Figure 14.6). Remote users will be able to access their mailboxes over the Internet using Outlook Web Access. The traffic between the clients and the front-end server should be encrypted.

Requirements and Goals

CFI would like to provide all clients with access to their mailboxes.

CFI would like to have a single Exchange 2000 organization for the entire company.

CFI would like to deploy an Instant Messaging system across its organization. CFI would like all employees to have access to Instant Messaging.

CFI would like to provide Internet email for all users. Email sent from the company should be passed to the Internet and email from the Internet should be sent into the company.

CFI would also like to provide users with access to USENET newsgroups from an Internet feed. CFI would like clients to use Outlook MAPI access to these newsgroups. The internal WAN traffic should be limited. Users will frequently use the **alt.food** and the **alt.food.cheap** newsgroup.

Front-end servers will be deployed in pairs to provide load balancing. Exchange 2000 servers should not have processor utilization that ever exceeds 70 percent. All clients and servers should be protected from viruses with anti-virus software. Client will be educated not to open email attachments from unknown users.

Question 3.1

At what point during the migration can CFI convert its Exchange 2000 organization to native mode?

○ a. After the first Exchange 2000 server is installed in the organization

○ b. After the last Exchange 2000 server is installed in the organization

○ c. After all Exchange servers are running Exchange Server 5.5 with Service Pack 3 or higher

○ d. When no pre-Exchange 2000 servers exist in the organization

○ e. When no pre-Windows 2000 servers exist in the forest

Question 3.2

How should the disks on a small server be configured?

○ a. RAID 0 array for the system/boot partition; RAID 1 array for the transaction logs; RAID 1 array for the database files.

○ b. RAID 1 array for the system/boot partition; RAID 1 array for the transaction logs; RAID 1 array for the database files.

○ c. RAID 1 array for the system/boot partition; RAID 1 array for the transaction logs; RAID 5 array for the database files.

○ d. RAID 1 array for the system/boot partition and the transaction logs; RAID 5 array for the database files.

○ e. RAID 5 array for the system/boot partition and database files; RAID 1 array for the transaction logs.

Question 3.3

How should the disks on a large server be configured?

◯ a.   RAID 0 array for the system/boot partition; RAID 1 array for the transaction logs; RAID 1 array for the database files.

◯ b.   RAID 1 array for the system/boot partition; RAID 1 array for the transaction logs; RAID 1 array for the database files.

◯ c.   RAID 1 array for the system/boot partition; RAID 1 array for the transaction logs; RAID 5 array for the database files.

◯ d.   RAID 1 array for the system/boot partition and the transaction logs; RAID 5 array for the database files.

◯ e.   RAID 5 array for the system/boot partition and database files; RAID 1 array for the transaction logs.

Question 3.4

For the perimeter network at Cleveland, what messaging port or ports should be opened on the Internet firewall? [Check all correct answers]

❑ a.   25

❑ b.   80

❑ c.   110

❑ d.   443

❑ e.   995

Question 3.5

For the perimeter network at Cleveland, what port or ports should be opened on the Intranet firewall?

◯ a.   25

◯ b.   80

◯ c.   110

◯ d.   443

◯ e.   995

Question 3.6

After Exchange 2000 is deployed, if public folders were created on a public folder server in Columbus (COLEX01) in the default public folder tree, how would you replicate this folder to CINEX01? Place the correct steps in the correct order.

Create a public folder tree on COLEX01.

Create a public folder tree on CINEX01.

Create a public folder store on COLEX01.

Create a public folder store on CINEX01.

Add a replica to CINEX01.

Question 3.7

Remote clients in Dayton will be accessing the public folder support under the top-level public folder in Dayton using a Web browser. They will gain access through a front-end server (CLEEX09) in Cleveland. The public folder replicas will exist on the DAYEX02 and COLEX02 servers. If the administrator wanted to create a direct link to this folder on a Web page, what URL could he use?

○ a. **http://CLEEX02/public/dayton/support**

○ b. **http://DAYEX02/public/dayton/support**

○ c. **http://CLEEX02/exchange/dayton/support**

○ d. **http://DAYEX02/exchange/dayton/support**

○ e. **http://CLEEX10/public/dayton/support**

○ f. **http://CLEEX10/exchange/dayton/support**

Question 3.8

CFI would like to create public folder hierarchies for each location. A manager at each location will use the Exchange System Manager to manage his or her hierarchy. What type permissions should be assigned to grant these managers the rights they need?

○ a. Client permissions

○ b. Directory rights

○ c. Administrative rights

○ d. Exchange rights

○ e. Manager rights

Question 3.9

CFI would like to give customers the ability to send email to certain public folders. Internal users should not see these folders in the Global Address List in Outlook 2000. If CFI creates these folders before switching to native mode, what steps must be performed on these folders? [Check all correct answers]

❑ a. Hide from Exchange address list.

❑ b. Mail-enable the folders using the Exchange System Manager.

❑ c. Mail-enable the folders using the Active Directory Users and Computers.

❑ d. Nothing

Question 3.10

Which of the following methods should not be used by CFI to migrate to Exchange 2000? [Check all correct answers]

❑ a. Perform an in-place upgrade of all its pre-Exchange 2000 servers.

❑ b. Install Exchange 2000 servers into the existing organizations. Move pre-Exchange 2000 mailboxes to Exchange 2000 servers.

❑ c. Install Exchange 2000 servers into one of the existing organizations. Move pre-Exchange 2000 mailboxes to Exchange 2000 servers using the Active Directory Connector.

❑ d. Create a new Exchange 2000 organization and move mailboxes using the Active Directory Connector.

Question 3.11

If CFI deploys Instant Messaging, what authentication methods can be used? [Check all correct answers]

❑ a. Anonymous

❑ b. Basic

❑ c. Digest

❑ d. Integrated Windows

Question 3.12

The email administrator for one of the Exchange organizations would like to upgrade one of her servers, Exchange 5.0 to Exchange 2000, before the corporate migration. Which of the following steps must she perform before she upgrades the server? [Check all correct answers]

❑ a. Upgrade the Exchange server to Windows 2000.

❑ b. Upgrade the Windows NT PDC to Windows 2000.

❑ c. Upgrade the Windows NT BDCs to Windows 2000.

❑ d. Install Windows 2000 Service Pack 1 on the Exchange server.

❑ e. Install Windows 2000 Service Pack 1 on all Windows 2000 domain controllers.

❑ f. Install Exchange 5.5 Server with Service Pack 3 or higher on the Exchange server.

❑ g. Switch the Windows 2000 domain to native mode.

Question 3.13

Before deploying Exchange 2000, CFI has decided to upgrade all inhouse clients to the same messaging software. They want to make sure the new client will be able to access all current Exchange deployments. Clients will access the new Exchange 2000 organization using MAPI and the old organizations using IMAP4. What client software would you recommend they install?

○ a. Outlook 95

○ b. Outlook 97 version 8.03

○ c. Outlook 98

○ d. Outlook 2000

○ e. Outlook Express

Question 3.14

Before installing Exchange 2000 on a computer running Windows 2000 Server with Service Pack 1, which of the following protocols must be installed? [Check all correct answers]

❑ a. POP3

❑ b. NNTP

❑ c. IMAP4

❑ d. MAPI

❑ e. HTTP

Question 3.15

CFI would like to configure its clients and servers with IPSec. The following goals should be accomplished:

Windows 2000 domain controllers should use IPSec when communicating with other computers configured with IPSec.

Exchange 2000 servers should use IPSec when communicating with other computers configured with IPSec.

Exchange 2000 servers should be accessible by non-IPSec clients.

Internal Windows 2000 Professional computers running Outlook 2000 should use IPSec when connecting to Exchange 2000 servers.

Internal Windows 2000 Professional computers running Outlook 2000 should use IPSec when connecting to Windows 2000 domain controllers.

If CFI assigns the Secure Server rule to all servers and the Client rule to all clients, which of their goals were accomplished? [Check all correct answers]

❏ a. Windows 2000 domain controllers should use IPSec when communicating with other computers configured with IPSec.

❏ b. Exchange 2000 servers should use IPSec when communicating with other computers configured with IPSec.

❏ c. Exchange 2000 servers should be accessible by non-IPSec clients.

❏ d. Internal Windows 2000 Professional computers running Outlook 2000 should use IPSec when connecting to Exchange 2000 servers.

❏ e. Internal Windows 2000 Professional computers running Outlook 2000 should use IPSec when connecting to Windows 2000 domain controllers.

Answer Key

For asterisked items, please see textual representation of answer on appropriate page of this chapter.

1.1.	c	2.1.	e	3.1.	d
1.2.	*	2.2.	c	3.2.	b
1.3.	*	2.3.	d	3.3.	c
1.4.	a, d, e	2.4.	b	3.4.	b, d
1.5.	b	2.5.	a, c, d	3.5.	b
1.6.	*	2.6.	d, e	3.6.	*
1.7.	e	2.7.	a	3.7.	e
1.8.	f	2.8.	e	3.8.	c
1.9.	a, e, g	2.9.	a	3.9.	d
1.10.	b	2.10.	a	3.10.	a, b, c, d
1.11.	b, e	2.11.	a	3.11.	c, d
1.12.	c, f	2.12.	b	3.12.	a, b, d, f
1.13.	b	2.13.	c	3.13.	d
1.14.	a, b, c	2.14.	*	3.14.	b, e
1.15.	e	2.15.	*	3.15.	a, b, d, e

Question 1.1

Answer c is correct. Because WRBaldwin will not use **wrbaldwin.com** for its Active Directory domain, it will define a DNS subdomain (**ad.wrbaldwin.com**, for example). A subdomain (**tr.ad.wrbaldwin.com**) will be created for the Training domain. Email and Instant Messaging will both use the **wrbaldwin.com** DNS domain. That is a total of three DNS domains. Answers a, b, d, and e are thus incorrect.

Question 1.2

The correct answer is:

Upgrade all Windows NT member servers in the TR domain to Windows 2000.

Upgrade the WRBALDWIN PDC to Windows 2000.

Upgrade the TR PDC to Windows 2000.

Upgrade all WRBALDWIN BDCs to Windows 2000.

Upgrade all Windows NT member servers in the WRBALDWIN domain to Windows 2000.

Upgrade all TR BDCs to Windows 2000.

The first priority is to upgrade servers in the TR domain. Member servers in this domain can be upgraded first, but domain controllers will have to be upgraded after the PDC in WRBALDWIN is upgraded. Once the PDCs in WRBALDWIN have been upgraded, then the PDCs in the TR domain can be upgraded, followed by the BDCs in the TR domain. Finally, the member servers and the BDCs in the WRBALDWIN domain should be upgraded, per the CIO's request. There is no need to create new domains and use the Active Directory Migration Tool.

Question 1.3

The correct answer is:

Update all Exchange servers in the WRBaldwin, Inc., organization to Exchange Server 5.5 with Service Pack 3 or higher.

Upgrade all Exchange servers in the WRBaldwin, Inc., organization to Exchange 2000.

Move mailboxes from the WRB Training organization to the WRBaldwin, Inc., organization using the Exchange Server Migration Tool.

Because WRBaldwin, Inc., will use existing servers and perform the migration during off-hours, an in-place upgrade is the best solution. Before servers in the WRBaldwin, Inc., organization can be upgraded, they must be running Exchange Server 5.5 with Service Pack 3 or higher. WRBaldwin, Inc., would like to be able to move mailboxes easily throughout the company. A single organization facilitates this, so the WRB Training organization should be abandoned. Mailboxes from the WRB Training organization can be moved using the Exchange Server Migration Tool. The Active Directory Connector is used to copy and synchronize directory information, not mailboxes.

Question 1.4

Answers a, d, and e are correct. IMAP4, MAPI, and NNTP all can be used to read Exchange public folders. For remote clients to use MAPI, a VPN must be established. Answer b is incorrect, because SMTP is used to send email and cannot be used to access public folders. Answer c is incorrect, because POP3 can only be used to access a single folder and cannot be used to access public folders.

Question 1.5

> Answer b is correct. Pre-Outlook 2000 and legacy Exchange clients will query Exchange 2000 server for directory information and will not access Active Directory directly. The Exchange 2000 will send the request to an Active Directory Global Catalog server on the behalf (proxy) of the client. The Directory Service Proxy (DSProxy) service on the Exchange 2000 server will perform this action. DSProxy will also proxy Lightweight Directory Access Protocol (LDAP) queries made by IMAP4 and POP3 clients. If the client were running Outlook 2000, Outlook 2000 would access the Global Catalog server directly and hence would cross the WAN link. Outlook 2000 uses a referral process to access a Global Catalog server. An Exchange 2000 server will give the Outlook 2000 MAPI client a list of servers and the client will contact the server directly. Answer a is thus incorrect.

Question 1.6

> The correct answer is:
>
> > Drive C: (mirrored drive)
> >
> > > System/boot partition
> >
> > Drive D: (mirrored drive)
> >
> > > First storage group's transaction logs
> >
> > Drive E: (mirrored drive)
> >
> > > Second storage group's transaction logs
> >
> > Drive F: (RAID 5 array)
> >
> > > Third storage group's transaction logs
> > >
> > > Mailbox stores
> > >
> > > Public folder store
> > >
> > > News store
>
> Because transaction logs are written sequentially, it is most important to put transaction logs on their own spindle. It would be nice to separate the databases also; however, there are not enough disks. Because recovery and performance of the newsfeeds is less important, the transaction logs from the first and second stores are separated. Microsoft recommends using RAID 1 (mirroring) for system/boot partitions and for transaction logs. RAID 5 is recommended for databases.

Question 1.7

Answer e is correct. After WRBaldwin performs an in-place upgrade of the Exchange 5.5 server, the Exchange 5.5 sites will become Exchange 2000 administrative groups. The Training Exchange servers are to be controlled by the trainers, the Training servers should be in one administrative group, and all other Exchange servers should be in the other six administrative groups. Once the last Exchange 5.5 server is upgraded and the organization is converted to native mode, servers can be moved between routing groups. At that point, WRBaldwin would probably consolidate their servers into two routing groups. Answers a, b, c, d, and f are thus incorrect.

Question 1.8

Answer f is correct. To reduce WAN traffic, each location should have its own routing group. Because the Training Exchange servers are to be in their own administrative group and servers from different administrative groups cannot be in the same routing group, Atlanta and Tampa will each have two routing groups. Once the last Exchange 5.5 server is upgraded and the organization is converted to native mode, routing groups can contain servers from different administrative groups and WRBaldwin could reduce the number of routing groups to six. Answers a, b, c, d, and e are thus incorrect.

Question 1.9

Answers a, e, and g are correct. The Exchange Full Administrator role will give WRB-Admins full control over the entire organization. The TR-Admins will need at least Exchange View Only Administrator on the organization. TR-Admins will also need Exchange Full Administrator on the TR-AG administrative group. Answers b and c are incorrect, because the WRB-Admins role from the organization will be inherited from the organization to all administrative groups. Answer d is incorrect, because the TR-Admins only need read access on the organization. Answer f is incorrect, because there is no Deny role.

Question 1.10

Answer b is correct. WRBaldwin's message routing is dictated by its physical network topology. One of WRBaldwin's design goals is to reduce network traffic; an effective routing group design will reduce network traffic. Answer a is incorrect, because once WRBaldwin switches to native mode, the existing site topology will no longer dictate routing group design. Answers c and d are incorrect, because Active Directory design does not directly affect this design. Answer e is incorrect, because once in native mode, routing groups and administrative groups are no longer tied together.

Question 1.11

Answers b and e are correct. Clients could use a VPN with Point-to-Point Tunneling Protocol (PPTP) to connect to the WRBaldwin network. PPTP can be configured to encrypt traffic. Secure Sockets Layer (SSL) can be used to encrypt POP3 traffic. Answer a is incorrect, because remote clients are running Windows 95 or Windows 98 and these operating systems do not support Layer 2 Tunneling Protocol (L2TP). Answers c and d are incorrect, because authentication methods do not encrypt data. Integrated Windows authentication encrypts the username and password.

Question 1.12

Answers c and f are correct. POP3 uses port 110 for retrieving messages. When secured with SSL, POP3 also uses port 995. Answer a is incorrect, because port 25 is used by SMTP. SMTP can be used to send email; however, the question only wanted the users to check email. Answers b and d are incorrect, because port 80 is for HTTP and port 119 is for IMAP4. Answer e is incorrect, because port 993 is used by IMAP4 when secured with SSL.

Question 1.13

Answer b is correct, because POP3 clients cannot access any public folders. Outlook Express using IMAP4 can access both the default public folder tree and general-purpose public folder trees. Thus, answer a is incorrect.

Question 1.14

Answers a, b, and c are correct. Exchange 2000 must be installed on a computer running Windows 2000 Server or Advanced Server with Service Pack 1 or higher. Exchange 2000 requires Active Directory; therefore, the PDC in the WRBALDWIN domain must be running Windows 2000 Server or Advanced Server. Answer d is incorrect, because Exchange 2000 does not require the PDC to be running Windows 2000 Server Service Pack 1.

Question 1.15

Answer e is correct. There is an Exchange 5.5 server running the Internet Mail Service in each organization. During the migration, these services will still function. Once the Exchange server running the Internet Mail Service in the WRBaldwin, Inc., organization is upgraded to Exchange 2000, the Internet Mail Service will be upgraded to an SMTP virtual server and SMTP connector. No additional configuration is needed, and thus answers c and d are incorrect. Answers a and b are incorrect, because routing group connectors and site connectors only function within an organization.

Question 2.1

Answer e is correct. Although OUs make accomplishing all these tasks easier, none of these requires the deployment of OUs. Delegation of control can be accomplished on a per account basis. Group policies can be deployed at the domain level, then filtered using security. Software can be deployed to users or computers using group policies. Answers a, b, c, and d are thus incorrect.

Question 2.2

Answer c is correct. Exchange 2000 servers can join an Exchange 5.5 organization so long as at least one server is running Exchange 5.5 Server with Service Pack 3 or higher. Answers a and b are incorrect, because ForestPrep and DomainPrep can be run during the Exchange 2000 installation. Answer d is incorrect, because it is not necessary for an Exchange 5.5 server to upgrade to Exchange 2000. Answer e is incorrect, because Exchange will deploy the Active Directory Connector when it is installed into an Exchange 5.5 organization.

Question 2.3

Answer d is correct. Exchange 2000 servers will be deployed into three different locations and these locations are separated by WAN links. North Coast Training should deploy three routing groups. Answers a, b, c, and e are thus incorrect.

Question 2.4

Answer b is correct. North Coast's Exchange 5.5 organization has a single site. When one of the servers in the site is upgraded to Exchange 2000, it will still be in that site. Exchange 2000 refers to Exchange 5.5 sites as administrative groups. Answers a, c, d, and e are thus incorrect.

Question 2.5

Answers a, c, and d are correct. Clients could use a VPN with Point-to-Point Tunneling Protocol (PPTP) or Layer 2 Tunneling Protocol (L2TP) to connect to the Norh Coast network. Windows 2000 can be configured with both PPTP and L2TP. Secure Sockets Layer (SSL) can be used to encrypt POP3 traffic. Answer b is incorrect because IMAP4 is not an encryption method; it is a messaging protocol. Answer e is thus incorrect.

Question 2.6

Answers d and e are correct. Outlook 2000 can use either POP3 or IMAP4 for Internet mail. When both are available, it uses IMAP4. IMAP4 uses port 119 for retrieving messages. When secured with SSL, IMAP4 also uses port 993. Answer a is incorrect, because port 25 is used by SMTP. SMTP can be used to send email; however, the question only wanted the users to check email. Answers b and c are incorrect, because port 80 is for HTTP and port 119 is for POP3. Answer f is incorrect, because ports 995 is used by POP3 when secured with SSL.

Question 2.7

Answer a is correct. Outlook 2000 can use either POP3 or IMAP4 for Internet mail. When both are available, it will use IMAP4. IMAP4 can be used for accessing all public folder trees in Exchange 2000. When Outlook 2000 uses MAPI to access Exchange 2000, only the default public folder tree is accessible. Answer b is thus incorrect.

Question 2.8

Answer e is correct. When email is sent from the Internet, an MX record must be configured in DNS. This MX record points to the SMTP server and enables clients to receive Internet email. Answers a and b are incorrect, because SMTP connectors do not need to be created to receive email from the Internet. Answers c and d are incorrect, because no configuration is needed on the default SMTP virtual server to receive Internet email. Configuring an SMTP virtual server to use DNS or a smart host has to do with sending email to the Internet.

Question 2.9

Answer a is correct. Outlook Web Access (OWA) does not support task management. Answer b is thus incorrect.

Question 2.10

Answer a is correct. OWA only supports drag-and-drop with rich Web browsers. Because all clients are using Windows 2000, Mentor clients are using Internet Explorer 5.0 or higher. Internet Explorer 5.0 or higher is a rich browser. Answer b is thus incorrect.

Question 2.11

Answer a is correct. Instant Messaging clients find Instant Messaging services through the DNS service. Instant Messaging uses service (SRV) records for storing the location of the rendezvous protocol (RVP). The service locator (SRV) record _rvp must be added to the _tcp sub-domain. Instant Messaging uses port 80. Answers b, c, and d are thus incorrect.

Question 2.12

Answer b is correct. Installing a new Exchange 2000 server and moving mailboxes will maintain the existing organization and none of the servers will have to be taken down. Answer a is incorrect, because an in-place upgrade will cause servers to be taken offline. Answer c is incorrect, because even though creating a new organization is a valid option, the design does not require it. Answer d is incorrect, because the Active Directory Connector will not move mailboxes.

Question 2.13

Answer c is correct. The default public folder tree is created by default. Because Outlook Express can also access general-purpose public folder trees, two general-purpose public folder trees can be created for a total of three. Answers, a, b, and d are thus incorrect.

Question 2.14

The correct answer is:

Drive C: (hardware RAID 1)

System partition

First storage group's transaction logs

Drive D: (hardware RAID 5)

Boot partition

Mailbox store

Public folder store

Because transaction logs are written sequentially, it is more important to put transaction logs on their own spindle than database files. The Windows 2000 system partition contains the boot loader and must be on the active partition, which in most situations is C:. All other items can be put on the hardware RAID 5 array.

Question 2.15

The correct answer is:

Install Adminpak.msi

Install Exchange System Management Tools

The users will need both the Exchange System Management Tools and the Windows 2000 Administrative Tools to administer Exchange 2000. Both these tools require Windows 2000, but do not specifically require Windows 2000 Server. Adminpak.msi is the Windows 2000 installer package for the Windows 2000 Administrative Tools. The Windows 2000 Administrative Tools should be installed first. They will be extended by the Exchange System Management Tools when they are installed.

Question 3.1

Answer d is correct. Exchange 2000 mixed mode supports both Exchange 2000 and pre-Exchange 2000 servers. An organization should be upgraded only when no pre-Exchange 2000 servers are present in the organization. Answers a and b are incorrect, because this is no guarantee that all pre-Exchange 2000 servers have been upgraded or decommissioned. Answer c is incorrect, because Exchange 2000 native mode does not support pre-Exchange 2000 servers. Answer e is incorrect, because pre-Windows 2000 servers refer to upgrading a Windows 2000 Active Directory domain to native mode.

Question 3.2

Answer b is correct. This design will provide the greatest performance by having the transaction logs, database files, and system files each on their own spindle. Answer a is incorrect, because RAID 0 does not support fault tolerance. Answer c is incorrect, because small servers have six drives and two RAID 1 arrays, and a RAID 5 array would require seven disks. Answers d and e are incorrect, because the system files and either the transaction logs or the database files would be on the same spindle.

Question 3.3

Answer c is correct. This design provides the greatest performance by having the transaction logs, database files, and system files each on their own spindle. Microsoft recommends placing database files on RAID 5 if possible. Answer a is incorrect, because RAID 0 does not support fault tolerance. Answer b is incorrect, because this configuration would not yield as much disk space as RAID 5 would. Answers d and e are incorrect, because the system files and either the transaction logs or the database files would be on the same spindle.

Question 3.4

Answers b and d are correct. OWA uses the HTTP protocol that uses port 80. When using secure HTTP with SSL, port 443 is also used. Answer a is incorrect, because port 25 is used for SMTP. Answers c and e are incorrect, because POP3 uses port 110. When POP3 is secured with SSL, port 995 is also used.

Question 3.5

Answer b is correct and answer d is incorrect. The front-end server will relay the HTTP (port 80) packet to the back-end server but it will not use SSL (port 443 when used with HTTP) to communicate with the back-end server. Answer a is incorrect, because port 25 is used for SMTP. Answers c and e are incorrect, because POP3 uses port 110. When POP3 is secured with SSL, port 995 is also used.

Question 3.6

The correct answer is:

   Add a replica to CINEX01

Because the public folder is in the default public folder tree, there is no need to create an additional public folder tree or store. You should first add a replica to the CINEX01 server.

Question 3.7

Answer e is correct. OWA is installed by default and the public Web site is enabled for access to public folders in the default public folder tree. Because clients only have access to the CLEEX10 server, the URL must point to that server. The CLEEX10 server will then proxy requests to one of the servers that has a replica. Answers a and b are incorrect, because if the clients cannot gain access directly to the CINEX02 or CLEEX02 servers, they will access the CLEEX10 server. Answers c, d, and f are incorrect, because Public is an invalid folder under Exchange.

Question 3.8

Answer c is correct, because administrative rights are used to control access to public folder settings in the Exchange System Manager. Answer a is incorrect. Client permissions control how clients access the folders, including the ability to manage the folder using client software like Outlook. Answer b is incorrect, because directory rights can be assigned only to mail-enabled public folders. These permissions control access to the Active Directory object associated with the mail-enabled public folder. An example of a directory right is Send As. Answers d and e are incorrect, because Exchange rights and Manager rights are not valid types of permissions.

Question 3.9

Answer d is correct. In mixed mode, all new public folders are mail-enabled and hidden from the Exchange list by default. Answers a and b are thus incorrect. Answer c is also incorrect, because public folders are mail-enabled using the Exchange System Manager.

Question 3.10

Answers a, b, c, and d are correct. An in-place upgrade would not consolidate the organizations into one. Installing Exchange 2000 servers into the existing organization would not consolidate the organizations into one. The Active Directory Connector will not move mailboxes.

Question 3.11

Answers c and d are correct. The Instant Messaging virtual server only supports digest and Integrated Windows authentication. Answers a and b are thus incorrect.

Question 3.12

Answers a, b, d, and f are correct. Exchange 2000 Server must be installed on a computer running Windows 2000 Server or Advanced Server with Service Pack 1 that is a member of an Active Directory domain. The Exchange server that is being upgraded to Exchange 2000 has to be upgraded to Exchange Server 5.5 Service Pack 3 or higher. Answers c and g are incorrect, because Exchange 2000 does not have to be installed into a native-mode domain. Answer e is incorrect, because only the server running Exchange 2000 has to be running Windows 2000 Service Pack 1.

Question 3.13

Answer d is correct. Outlook 2000 support both MAPI and IMAP4. Answers a, b, and c are incorrect because these older versions are not the best options. Answer e is incorrect because Outlook Express is not a MAPI client.

Question 3.14

Answers b and e are correct. Exchange 2000 requires NNTP and HTTP be installed in IIS before it can be installed. Answers a and c are incorrect, because IMAP4 and POP3 are installed when Exchange 2000 is installed. Answer d is incorrect, because MAPI is the native Exchange client protocol and cannot be installed without Exchange 2000.

Question 3.15

Answers a, b, d, and e are correct. The IPSec rule Secure Server allows only IPSec secured communications with the server. The Client rule will respond with IPSec, but not request it. Answer c is incorrect, because for Exchange 2000 servers to communicate with non-IPSec computers, the Server rule would have to be assigned, instead of the Secure Server rule.

Index

Bold page numbers indicate sample exam questions.

A

Access Control List. *See* ACL.
Access restrictions, 170
ACID transactions, 107
ACL, 25, 83, 197
    updating, 234
    user SIDs in, 233, **265**
ACL mapping, **265**
Active Directory (AD)
    compatibility with NTDS, 24
    Configuration partition, 77–78
    data maintenance with, 235
    forest design, 52
    functionality of, 24
    installing. *See* Installation plan.
    LDAP access to, 30
    logical structure, 27–36
    migrating pre-Windows 2000
        domains to, 231–235
    physical structure of, 37
    schema, 26
    synchronizing Exchange 5.5. with,
        235–243
    upgrading to, **65**
Active Directory Cleanup Wizard,
    242–243, **260**
Active Directory Connector. *See* ADC.
Active Directory Display Name, 79
Active Directory Domains and Trusts, 32
Active Directory Migration Tool.
    See ADMT.

Active Directory objects, 24–26
    low-level management of, 79, **95**
Active Directory servers, 153–154
    discovery of, 157
    MAPI client access, 154
Active Directory Sites and Services, 61
Active Directory Tool, 79
    renaming administrative groups
        with, **95**
Active Directory Users and Computers,
    28, 79
    Advanced Features option, **45**
    for delegating administrative control,
        84–85
    extension for Exchange 2000, 61
    Full Name, 31–32
    moving mailboxes with, 246
    Security tab, **45**, 84
ADC
    connection agreements, 238–242
    for directory synchronization, 249
    disabled user account creation, **264**
    domain controllers, access to, 236
    Exchange 2000 version, 237
    Exchange servers, installing on, 236
    Exchange servers, reading from and
        writing to, 237
    Global Catalog servers,
        access to, 236
    Global Catalog servers,
        installing on, 236
    installing, privileges, 237
    mailboxes, moving with, **323**
    objects, creation of, 238

objects, synchronization of, 237–238
requirements of, 236–237
resource mailbox determination, **264**
service account for, 236
for synchronizing Exchange 5.5 and
 Active Directory, 235–238
versions of, 237
Windows 2000 version, 237
Address List container, 87
Address lists, 85–88
 All Address Lists, 86–87
 custom, 87
 default, 87
 filter rules for, 85–86
 Global Address Lists, 87
 mail-enabled folders hidden
  from, 193
 Offline Address Lists, 88
 permissions for, 86–87
 Recipient Update Service for, 88
Administrative control, delegation of,
 72–73, 80–85, **307**
Administrative groups, 29–31
 for administrator access
  restrictions, 170
 configuring prior to Exchange 2000
  installation, 81
 creating, 55
 for delegation of control, 80
 multiple groups, 73–74
 number of, **68**, 81, **93**, **306**, **312**
 permissions to, 74
 renaming, 81, **95**
 routing groups and, 128–129
 single group, 72
 when to create, 81, **95**
Administrative models, 72–75, **94**
Administrative rights, 197, **322**
Administrative roles, 75–77, **307**
 assigning, 82, **307**
Administrative tools, 60–61, 77–80, **316**
 installing, 61
Administrators
 delegation of control to, **44**
 for Exchange 2000, 53
 restricting access of, 170
Administrators local domain group,
 29–30, **42–43**
Administrators local group, 29–30
Adminpak.msi, 61
 installing, **66**

ADMT, 232–235
 Computer Migration Wizard, 234
 Exchange Directory Migration
  Wizard, 235
 Group Mapping and Merging
  Wizard, 235
 Group Migration Wizard, 234
 Reporting Wizard, 234
 Retry Task Wizard, 235
 Security Translation Wizard, 234
 Service Account Migration
  Wizard, 235
 SID history, 233–234, **265**
 Trust Migration Wizard, 235
 Undo Wizard, 235
 User Account Migration Wizard, 234
ADSI Edit, 61, 79–80
 address list permissions, assigning, 85
 administrative groups, renaming, **95**
 All Address Lists container,
  renaming, 87
All Address Lists, 86–87
All Contacts address list, 87
All Groups address list, 87
All Public Folders tree, 189
All Users address list, 87
Anonymous access, 214, 274, **281**
Application event log, 62
Atomic transactions, 107
Attributes, 26
Authenticated Users group, address list
 permissions, 86
Authentication, 132
 anonymous access, 274, **281**
 basic authentication, 275, **281**
 computer accounts for, 25
 digest authentication, 290, **296**, **323**
 by front-end servers, 157
 for IM, 290, **296**, **323**
 by independent software methods, **183**
 IPSec methods, 174
 MSN Messenger methods, **296**
 OWA, 273–275
 remote, 176
 for SMTP virtual service, **183**
 SSL method, 175
 verifying, 178
 virtual server requirements for,
  214–215, **296**
 Windows Integrated authentication,
  214–215, 275, **282**, 290, **296**, **323**

B

Back-end servers, 150–152.
See also Front-end/back-end server
configuration.
   placement of, 156
   protection behind firewalls, 151–152
   storage groups of, 151
Backup logs, verifying, 114
Backup utility, 114
Backups, 111–114
   brick-level, 112, 115
   full, 112–113
   types of, 112
   verifying, 114–115
Backward compatibility. *See* Mixed mode.
Basic authentication, 214, 275, **281**
BDCs (Backup Domain Controllers),
   upgrading, 231–232
Brick-level backups, 115
Bridgehead servers, 152–153
   with routing group connectors, 131
   with SMTP connectors, 132
   weak link detection, 135
   with X.400 connectors, 133
Bulk method upgrades, 247

C

Capacity planning
   mailboxes, number of, 148–149,
      162–163
   mailboxes, size of, 149, **162–163**
Centralized administrative model, 72–73
Certificate Authorities (CA), 174, 176
Certificate Service, 176
Certificates, 174, 176–177
   SSL use of, 175
   for virtual servers, 215
Chain topology, 136
Change Domain Controller dialog box, 78
CHAP (Challenge Handshake
   Authentication Protocol), 176
Chat servers, 155
Chat service, 56, 76, 275
   port for, 275
   securing, 275
Checkpoint files, 104–105
Child object classes, 26
Circular logging, 105
   enabling, 105
Client permissions, 196–197, **204**
   in EXIFS, 197

Client (Respond Only) security rule, 175
cn=Address Lists container, 85
Coexistence, 231, 249–254
   directory synchronization, 249–251
   message routing methods, 251
   public folder replication and access,
      251–252
   scenarios of, 252–253
Companies, administrative models of,
   72–75
Computer accounts, 25
Computer Migration Wizard, 234
Computer objects, 25
Conferencing servers, 155
Configuration connection agreements, 239
Configuration partition, 37, 77–78
Connection agreements, 238–242
   account creation, 241, **262–263**
   domain controller connections, 239
   Exchange connections, 239–240
   LDAP port settings, 241–242
   name of, 239
   objects, defining, 240
   objects, deleting, 240
   polling interval, 240
   primary, 240–241, **262–263**
   replication direction, 239, 242
   scheduling, 240
   server for, 239
   types of, 238–239
   user account for, 239
Connection control, for virtual servers, 216
Connector Properties page, 193
Connector servers, 152–153, **165–166**
   database locations, 152
   RAID 1 for, **166**
   separating folders on, 152, **165–166**
   transaction logs of, 152
Connectors, 127, 129–135
   bridgehead servers, 131.
      See also Bridgehead servers.
   cost values of, 134–135
   duplicating, 246–247
   encryption of, **143**
   folders used by, **165–166**
   for Lotus cc:Mail, 134
   for Lotus Notes, 134
   for MS Mail, 134
   for MS SchedulePlus FreeBusy, 134
   for Novell GroupWise, 134
   number of, 137

for PROFS, 134
public folder referrals from,
133, 192–193
routing group connectors,
130–131, **143**
security of, 131–132
SMTP connectors, 132–133
for SNADS, 134
X.400 connectors, 133
Consistent transactions, 107
Contact objects, 25
Containers, 27–28
Corporate Or Workgroup mail service, 270
CreateUnattended switch, 59
Custom recipients, 25, **266**

D

DAPI (Directory Access Programming
Interface), 251
Data
backing up, 111–114
encapsulated, 131–132
Data encryption. *See* Encryption.
Data management, 76
Data recovery
database file placement and, 109–110
transaction log placement and,
109–110
transaction logs and, 103–105
Data storage topology, 100
Data verification, 114–115
Database files, 101
placement of, 108–110
RAID 1 for, **320**
RAID 5 for, **321**
spindle for, 109
Database writes, 103
Databases
Configuration partition, 37
full-text indexing, 110–111
partitions in, 27, 35
RAID 5 for, 110, **121–123**
Default Offline Address Lists, 88
Default public folder tree, 189, **202, 315**
newsgroup folders in, 217, **227**
replication of, 251–252
Deleted item retention, 115
Deleted Item Retention option, 149
Demilitarized zone (DMZ), 156–157
DFS (Distributed File System), 37
DHTML (Dynamic Hypertext Markup
Language), 273

Digest authentication, 290, **296, 323**
Digital signatures, 177
Directories, synchronization of, 249–251
Directory
migrating, 230
in previous Exchange versions, 24
Directory lookups, 251
Directory rights, 197
Directory Service event log, 62
dir.edb
in previous Exchange versions, 24
dir.edb database, 249
Disaster recovery, 115–116
Disk mirroring, 110, **121**
Disk striping, 110
Disk striping with parity, 110
Distinguished names, 30–31
Distributed administrative model, 73–74
Distribution groups, 26
Distribution lists, 26
for public folder security, 252
synchronizing with security
groups, 252
DNS. *See also* MX records.
ports for, 158
round-robin process, 212, **224**
SMTP connector use of, 132–133, **145**
DNS lookups
reverse, 178
DNS namespace
contiguous versus non-contiguous, 28
number of, **302**
separate, for IM domain, 288–289, **295**
unified, for IM domain, 288–289, **295,**
297, 314
DNS service
SRV record configuration,
275–276, **314**
Domain Admins
running of DomainPrep, 53
Domain Admins global group, 29
Domain controllers, 27
adding, **42**
configuration data, access to, 78
Domain Naming Master, 35–36
FSMOs, 35
Global Catalog servers, 34–35
HTTP on, **222**
NNTP on, **222**
operation master roles, **46**
retrieving data from, 153
in same site, 37

Schema Master, 35–36
SMTP on, **222**
static entries for, 154
Domain local groups, 26
Domain Naming Master, 35–36, **46**
Domain structure
    upgrading, 231
DomainPrep
    unattended installation and, 60
DomainPrep switch, 53–55
Domains, 27, **41**
    FQDNs of, 33
    IM, 288–290
    logging on to, 33–34
    mixed mode, 27
    native mode, 27
    NetBIOS names of, 33
    permissions support, 52
DSAccess (Directory Service Access),
    153–154
DSProxy (Directory Service Proxy), 154
Duplicate accounts, 242–243, **260**
Durable transactions, 107

E

EAP (Extensible Authentication
    Protocol), 176, **183**
Email clients
    remote, **181**
    security for, 177
    virus protection on, 171–172
Email, Internet, 211–212, **223–225**, **314**
Encapsulated data, 131–132
Encryption, 131–132, **143**
    Exchange 2000 capabilities, 177
    of MIME content, 177
    by PPTP, **281**, **308**
    by SSL, 175, **281**, **308**
    for traffic between servers, 152
    by Windows Integrated
        authentication, 215
Enterprise Admins group, 29, **43**
    ADC installation by, 236
ESE (Extensible Storage Engine), 107
ETRN command, 212
EUSER_EXSTOREVENTS,
    creation of, 53
Exchange 5.5 servers and systems, 55.
    See also Pre-Exchange 2000 servers
    and systems.

backing up, 245
data maintenance with, 236
directory, migrating, 230
messaging system, migrating, 231
migrating from, 230–231, **304**
port configuration, 241
synchronizing with Active Directory,
    235–243
upgrade, verifying, 245
upgrading to Exchange 2000,
    244–245. *See also* Migration.
upgrading to Service Pack 3 or
    higher, **312**, **324**
Exchange 2000 Administrator Account, 53
Exchange 2000 Enterprise Server
    mailbox stores, 100
    service components, 56–59
Exchange 2000 Instant Messaging
    service, 286–287. *See also* IM.
Exchange 2000 Server
    mailbox store, 100
    service components, 56–59
Exchange 2000 servers and systems
    encryption capabilities, 177
    filtering, enabling, 173
    Global Catalog server requirements, **69**
    hardware requirements, 50–51
    installing, 55–60
    installing in Exchange 5.5 systems,
        81, **93**, 246–249, **261**, **312**, **315**,
        323. *See also* Coexistence;
        Migration; Mixed mode.
    installing in forests, 37, **43**
    IPSec security for, **184**. *See also* IPSec
        (IP Security).
    managing from desktop, **66**, **316**
    number of, **142**
    server requirements, 51, **324**
    shared directory with Windows
        2000, 24
    SMTP mail, pulling, 212
    storage groups, maximum number
        of, 103
    upgrading to, 243–249.
        See also Migration.
    upgrading to Windows 2000, **324**
    virtual SMTP servers on, 177
    Windows 2000 Service Pack 1 on,
        244, **261**, **324**
Exchange 2000 Setup program, 60
Exchange Administration Delegation
    Wizard, 82

Exchange Administrator, 82, **92**, **94**
Exchange Advanced Security, 61
Exchange Directory Migration Wizard, 235
Exchange Enterprise Servers global
    group, creation of, 54
Exchange Enterprise Servers local group,
    creation of, 54
Exchange Full Administrator role,
    82, **92**, **307**
Exchange Installable File System.
    See EXIFS.
Exchange Instant Messaging client, 275
Exchange Message Tracking Center, 61
Exchange Server Migration tool, 254–256
Exchange Server Migration Wizard,
    231, **259–260**
Exchange Setup program, 55
Exchange System Management Tool,
    60, **316**
    installing, **66**
    server management use of, 76
Exchange System Manager, 55, 77–78
    for address list management, 85
    administrative and routing group
        display, 56
    for administrative control
        delegation, 83–84
    domain controllers, contacting upon
        launch, 78
    enabling sites with, 195–196
    for front-end server configuration, 151
    for mail enabling public folders,
        193, **205**
    for OWA authentication settings
        configuration, 273, **282**
    for permissions assignment, 196
    for public folder creation and
        management, 188
    for replica creation, 190–191
    for replication configuration, 192
    for routing group creation, 126
    for RVP virtual server
        configuration, 290
    Security tab, 83
    for virtual server configuration, 176
    for virtual server management, 209
Exchange System (Manager), 61
Exchange View Only Administrator role,
    82, **92**, **307**
Exchsrvr folder, 61–62

EXIFS
    client permissions in, 197
    for public folder access, 194
Extensible Markup Language (XML), 273
    for IM message formatting, 287
External threats, 170, **181**, **184**

F

Fault tolerance, 212, **224–225**
    RAID configuration for, 110
    for transaction logs, 105
Filter rules, 85–86
Filtering, TCP/IP, 172–173
Firewalls, **184**
    back-end servers behind, 151–152
    configuring, 158, **164**
    configuring for remote access,
        181–182, **308**, **313**
    Internet, 157, **164**, **321**
    Intranet, 157, **164**, **321**
    for perimeter networks, **32**,
        156–157, **164**
    single firewall strategy, 158
First Administrative Group, 55, 81
First Routing Group, 56, 126–127
Flexible Single Master Operations.
    See FSMOs.
Folder Owner permission, 197
Folders, 61–62
    replicated folders, 150
Forest root domain, 29
ForestPrep, 81
    unattended installation and, 60
ForestPrep switch, 53
Forests, 28–30
    creating, 29, **41**
FQDNs, 33, **43**, 289
Front-end/back-end server configuration,
    150–152
    namespace, 151
    OWA deployment in, 153, 245
    performance of, 152
    scalability of, 151
    security of, 151–152
Front-end servers, 150–152
    Active Directory server discovery, 157
    authentication by, 157
    LDAP use, 157
    Outlook and, 152
    placement of, 156, 158
    proxy services of, 150–151

FSMOs, 35–36, **46**
Full Names, 31–32
Full-mesh topology, 137
Full-text indexing, 110–111
Fully qualified domain name.
   See FQDNs.

G

Gateway Address Routing Table.
   See GWART.
General-purpose public folder tree,
   189–190, **203**
     client permissions in, 197–198
     newsgroup folders in, 217
     replication of, 190, 252
Global Address Lists, 87, **323**
Global Catalog servers, 34
     access to, 35, **163**
     Active Directory data in, 154
     number of, **69**, 154, **167**
     placement of, 34
     retrieving data from, 153–154
     static entries for, 154
Global groups, 26, **42**
Group assignment, 26
Group Mapping and Merging
   Wizard, 235
Group Migration Wizard, 234
Group objects, 25–26
Group policies, for user account
   management, **44**
Group scope, 26
     domain local, 26
     global, 26, **42**
     universal, 26
Groups, 25–26
     administrative, 29–31
     distribution groups, 26
     security groups, 26
GWART, 135, 251

H

Hard disk configuration, **305**, **315**
     on large servers, **321**
     on small servers, **320**
Hardware requirements, of Exchange
   2000, 50–51
Home servers, IM, 287–288
Host names, 33
HTTP, 208
     Exchange 2000 requirement for, **324**
     IM use of, 287, **296**

for mailbox store access, 150
     ports for, 157, **164**, **321**
     for public folder access, 195–196
     SSL and, 175
HTTP virtual servers
     anonymous access to, 214
     configuration of, 176
HTTP-DAV, for mailbox store access, 150
Hub-and-spoke topology, 136, **142**
     multiple, 136
Hybrid administrative model, 74–75
Hypertext Transfer Protocol. *See* HTTP.

I

IIS, 51, 208–209
     additional protocols, 208–209, **223**
     core protocols, 208, **222–223**
     NNTP support, 216
IIS metabase
     backing up, 114
     SMTP settings in, **166**
     virtual server settings in, 209
IM, 275–276, **282**, 286, **314**
     architecture of, 287–290
     authentication methods for, **323**
     client statuses, 291, **294**
     domains, 288–290, **295**, **297**, **302**
     enabling, 290
     host records for domain, **295**
     HTTP server extensions use, 287, **296**
     ISAPI server extensions, 287
     MSN Messenger client, 291, **297**
     presence information, 286
     requirements for, 275
     RVP virtual server for, 290, **296**
     server roles, 287–288
IMAP4, 209
     for mailbox store access, 150
     Outlook 2000 use of, 270–271,
       313, **324**
     Outlook Express support for,
       271–272
     ports for, 157, **182**
     for public folder access, 196, **304**
IMAP4 virtual servers, **226**
IMC, 132, 255–256, **266**
In-place upgrades, 231–232, 244, **304**, **323**
Indexes, full-text, 110–111
Infrastructure Master, 36, **46**
Inheritance of permissions, 197
Install Adminpak.msi, **316**

Install Exchange System Management
Tools, **316**
Installation of Exchange 2000, 55–60
mixed/native mode, 59
services and dependencies, 56–59
unattended, 59–60
verifying, 61–62
Installation plan
ForestPrep for, 53
IIS installation, 51
permissions and, 52
verification of installation, 61–62
Windows 2000, preparing, 50–55
Instant Messaging, 76. *See also* IM.
Instant Messaging domains, 288–290
Instant Messaging home servers, 287–288
Instant Messaging routers, 287–288
Instant Messaging servers, 155
Interforest migrations, 234
Internal threats, 170
Internet connectivity
connection control, 216
planning for, 208
remote client connection via,
213–214
virtual server design and, 210
Internet email, 211–212, **223–225**, **314**
Internet Information Services. *See* IIS.
Internet Mail Connector. *See* IMC.
Internet Mail Service, **309**, **313**
duplicating, 246
Internet Message Access Protocol v4.
See IMAP4.
Internet messages, handling of, 51
Internet Only mail service, 270–271
Internet, ports open on, 157
Internet Services Manager
enabling sites with, 195–196
for HTTP virtual server
configuration, 176
for OWA authentication settings
configuration, 273, **282**
for virtual server management, 209
Intraforest migrations, 234
Intranets, ports open on, 157
IP addresses, multiple, configuring,
210, **226**
IPSec (IP Security), 132
authentication methods, 174
for communication in perimeter
networks, 157

security rules, 174–175, **184**, **325**
for server security, **184**
for TCP/IP packet security, 174–175
for traffic between servers, 152
IRC (Internet Relay Chat), 275
IRCX (Extended Internet Relay Chat), 275
ISAPI (Internet Server Application
Programming Interface), 287
Isolated transactions, 107

K

KCC (Knowledge Consistency
Checker), 245
Kerberos, 132, 174
ports for, 158
Key Management (KM) Server, 176–177

L

LANs
mailbox servers on, 155
newsgroup server connections over, 217
public folder servers on, 155
LDAP (Lightweight Directory Access
Protocol), 30–31
distinguished names, 30–31
front-end server use of, 157
ports for, 158
for queries to Global Catalog servers,
154, **305**
ldp.exe, 79
Link state table, 251
Link states, 135
Load balancing, 212, **224–225**
Local area networks. *See* LANs.
Log files, naming conventions, 104
Logon to domains, 33–34
Lotus cc:Mail, connector for, 134
Lotus Notes, connector for, 134
L2TP (Layer 2 Tunneling Protocol),
215, **312**

M

Mail exchanger records. *See* MX records.
Mailbox servers, 148–150
access protocols, 150
Deleted Item Retention option, 149
mailbox number and, 148–149,
162–163
mailbox size and, 149, **162–163**
mailbox stores, number of, 149
mailbox stores, storage groups of, 150
number of, **162–163**

placement of, 155
storage groups of, 150
Mailbox stores, 100, 148
access protocols, 150
number of, 149
placement of, **305, 315**
system policies for, 89
Mailbox-enabled objects, 37–39
Mailboxes, 76
backing up and restoring, 112
Deleted Item Retention option
for, 149
migrating to Exchange 2000 servers,
246–249, 254, **259–260, 304, 315**
number of, 148–149
restoring, 115
size limits on, 149
for user accounts, 242
MAPI, 101
for mailbox store access, 150
Outlook 2000 use of, 270, **324**
for public folder access, 194, 204, **304**
MAPI clients
Active Directory server access, 154
capabilities of, 270
connection to servers, 152
default tree access, 251–252
Global Catalog server access, **163**
mailbox server access, 155
pre-Outlook 2000, 271
public folder creation by, 189
public folder tree access, 189, **202**
reading data in stores, 101
MAPI tree, 189
Mesh topology, 126
Message routing, 251. *See also* Routing
groups.
routing groups for, 126–128
Message Transfer Agent. *See* MTA.
Messages
encrypting. *See* Encryption.
header storage, 101–102
restoring, 115
storage of, 107, 115, **123**
Messaging Application Programming
Interface. *See* MAPI.
Messaging protocols, for public folder
access, 194–196
Messaging systems. *See also* Connectors;
Routing groups.
backward compatibility, **144**
existing, 137–138

mixed mode versus native, 128–129
security for, 170. *See also* Security.
MetaEdit, **166**
Microsoft Management Console.
See MMC.
Migration, 230–231
from Exchange 5.5 to Exchange
2000, 230–231, 244–245, **304,
309, 315, 323**
Exchange Server Migration tool for,
254–256, **304**
interforest, 234
intraforest, 234
of mailboxes, from Exchange 5.5 to
Exchange 2000, 246–249, **304, 315**
from pre-Windows to Active
Directory, 231–235
reversing, 232
MIME (Messaging Internet Mail
Extensions), 101
Mirrored drives, 110, **121**
Mixed mode, 27, 59
administrative groups in, **306**
message routing in, 128–129
pre-Exchange 2000 sites and, 81, **93**
public folder creation in, 193
public folder tree, 252
public folders in, mail-enabled, **323**
routing groups and, 56, **306**
security settings in, 252
MMC, 60
ADSI Edit snap-in, 79
custom consoles, 79–80
Exchange System Manager snap-in, 78
Modified swing method upgrades, 248
MS Mail, connector for, 134
MS SchedulePlus FreeBusy,
connector for, 134
MS-CHAP (Microsoft Challenge
Handshake Authentication Protocol), 176
MS-CHAPv2, 176
MSN Messenger, 291, **297**
authentication methods for, **296**
user status management, 291
MTA, 251
folder used by, **165–166**
MTACheck utility, 245
MX records, 211–212, **223–224, 314**
priority of, 212

N

Namespace
   contiguous versus non-contiguous, 28
   number of, **302**
   separate, for IM domain, 288–289, **295**
   unified, for IM domain, 288–289, **295**,
      297, 314
Native mode, 27, 59
   mail enabling of public folders in,
      193, **205**
   message routing in, 129.
      See also Routing groups.
   migration to, **144**. *See also* Migration.
   routing groups and, 56, 76
   security settings in, 252
   switching to, **67, 320**
NetBIOS names, 32–33, **43**
netlogon, 157
   ports for, 158
Network adapters, TCP/IP filtering on, 173
Network infrastructure, routing topology
   and, 137, **144**
Network News Transfer Protocol.
   See NNTP.
Network security. *See also* Security.
   front-end/back-end server placement
      and, 156
Network traffic, server role separation
   and, 148
Networks. *See* Perimeter networks.
Newsgroup servers, LAN connections
   for, 217
Newsgroups
   accessing, 194–195
   Internet, 194–195
   remote access to, 217
   traffic generated by, 216–217, **227**
   transaction logs for, 217
   USENET, 216, **227**
NNTP, 208, 216–218
   Exchange 2000 requirement for, **324**
   installing, 51
   Outlook Express support for,
      271–272
   ports for, **68**, 157
   for public folder access, 194–195, **304**
   public folder server support of, 150
   verifying installation of, **68**
NNTP virtual servers, 194–195
   anonymous access to, 214
   newsfeed configuration, 216–217
   USENET newsgroup feeds on, 216

Novell GroupWise, connector for, 134
NTDSNoMatch, 242, **264**

O

Object classes, 26
Object mapping, ADC, 238
Objects, mailbox-enabled, 37–39
Offline Address Lists, 88
On-demand, in-memory content
   conversion, 101
Open Address List permission, 86
Operation masters, 35–36
   per domain, **46**
   per forest, **46**
Operations, 107
OUs (organizational units), 27–28, **44, 311**
   Security tab for, **45**
Outlook 9X, Internet Mail and MAPI
   configuration, 213
Outlook 2000, 270–271
   attachment warnings, 171
   backward compatibility of, **279, 305**
   configuring, 270
   Corporate Or Workgroup
      configuration, 270
   IMAP4 support, **324**
   Internet Mail and MAPI
      configuration, 213
   Internet Only configuration, 270–271
   MAPI support, **324**
   message storage, 101
   permissions assignment, 196
   pre-Outlook 2000 clients, 271, **305**
   public folder access, 194
   public folder creation by, 189
   scripts, restricted execution of, 171
   self-reconfiguration, 246
Outlook 2000 clients
   Active Directory server access, 154, **163**
   Global Catalog server access, **163**
Outlook Express, 271–272
   encryption of messages, **281**
   Internet Connection Wizard, 213
   Internet Mail configuration, 213–214
   as news reader, 214
   public folder tree access, **315**
OWA (Outlook Web Access), 208,
   272–275, **314**
   anonymous access, 274, **281**
   authentication, 273–275, **281**
   back-end servers, upgrading, 245
   basic authentication, 275, **281**

browser support, 273, **280**
disadvantages of, 272, **314**
email capabilities, 214
encrypting traffic, **227**
public folder access, 195, **204**
servers, 153, **164**
upgrading, 244–245
Windows Integrated authentication,
275, **282**

P

Packets
encrypting, 172, 177.
See also Encryption.
filtering, 172–173
headers of, 172–173
Parent object classes, 26
Partitions, 27, 35
Passwords, migration and, 232
Paths to server, determining, 134–135
PDC
ADMT installation on, 233
upgrading, 231, **309, 324**
PDC Emulator, 36, **46**
Performance
backup types and, 112–113
database file placement and, 109
transaction log placement and, 108
Perimeter networks, 156–157
port configuration, 157, **164, 321**
Permissions
for address lists, 86–87
for administrative groups, 55, 74
administrative rights, 197, **322**
client permissions, 196–197, **204**
directory rights, 197
inheritance of, 83–84, 197
pre-Windows-compatible, 52
for public folder access, 196–198,
204, 322
PKI (Public Key Infrastructure), 176–177
Point-to-Point Tunneling Protocol.
See PPTP.
Policies, 88–90
POP3, 208
encrypting traffic, **308, 313**
for mailbox store access, 150
Outlook 2000 use of, 270–271, **313**
Outlook Express support for,
271–272
ports for, 157, **182**
public folder access, 196, **201, 308**

Ports
for chat, 275
for Exchange 2000, 173
for messaging protocols, 157–158,
182, 308, 313, 321
perimeter network configuration of,
157, **164, 321**
for virtual servers, 209–210
Post Office Protocol. *See* POP3.
PPTP, 215, **227**
for message encryption, **281, 308**
Pre-Exchange 2000 servers and systems.
See also Exchange 5.5 servers and systems.
coexistence with Exchange 2000,
231, 249–254
domain users with multiple accounts,
242, **264**
IM service on, 287
mailboxes, moving to Exchange 2000
servers, 246–249
private information store, 101
public information store, 101
Remote Procedure Call
communication, 129
routing groups and, 128–129
upgrading to Exchange 2000, 81,
230–231, 243–249, **324**
versions of, 24
Presence monitoring, 286
Pre-shared string, 174
Pre-Windows 2000 designation, 27
Pre-Windows 2000 systems
in-place upgrades of, 231–232
migrating to Active Directory,
231–235
security, 52
service record location by, 290
User Logon Names, 32–33
Primary Domain Controller. *See* PDC.
Private stores, 76
in previous Exchange versions, 24
priv.edb database file, 101
in previous Exchange versions, 24
PROFS (Professional Office System),
connector for, 134
Properties page, of organization,
administrative and routing group
display configuration, 56–57
Property pages, object, 84
system policies and, 89
Protocols. *See also* Virtual servers.
virtual servers for, 209

Proxy services
  by DSProxy, 154, **305**
  of front-end servers, 151
pub.edb database file, 101
  in previous Exchange versions, 24
Public folder connection agreements, 239
Public Folder container, 191
Public Folder Instances container, replicas
  in, 191
Public Folder Properties page, 191
Public folder servers, 150
  general-purpose tree replication to, 190
  NNTP support, 150
  placement of, 155–156
  referrals to, 192–193
  replication of, 156
Public Folder Store Properties page, 190
Public folder stores, 100–101, **203**
  placement of, **305**, **315**
Public folder tree, 188–190
  accessing with IMAP4, **313**
  accessing with Outlook Express, **315**
  All Public Folders tree, 189
  default tree, 189, **202**
  general-purpose trees, 189–190
  permissions, assigning to, 197, **322**
  replication of, 190
Public folders, 76, 188
  accessing, 194–196, **201**, **204**, **304**, **308**
  administrative rights to, 197, **322**
  client permissions in, 197, **204**
  creating, 188
  directory rights to, 197
  email address of, 193, **205**, **322**
  mail-enabled, 193, **205**, **323**
  managing, 188
  moving from pre-Exchange 2000 to
    Exchange 2000, 248–249
  for newsgroups, 217
  permissions for, 196–198, **204**
  referrals, 133, 252
  replicas of, 190–192, **322**
  replicating, 188, 190–193,
    251–252, **322**
  security for, 238
Public Folders address list, 87
Public stores, 76
  in previous Exchange versions, 24
  system policies for, 89

R

RAID 1
  for connector servers, 152, **166**
  for database files, **320**
  for system/boot partition, **320–321**
  for transaction logs, 110, **121–122**,
    320–321
RAID 5, for database files, **321**
RAID arrays, 110, **121–122**
  for mailbox stores, 149, **305**
  software, 110
  for storage groups, 150, **305**
Reach browsers, 273, **280**
Real-time collaboration management, 76
Recipient connection agreements, 239
Recipient policies, 88–89
Recipient Update Service, 88
Recipients container, address lists in, 85
Recovering data to point of failure, 109
Redundant array of inexpensive disks.
  See RAID 1; RAID arrays.
Referrals
  for Active Directory server access, 154
  to public folder servers, 192–193
  transitive, 252
Relative Distinguished Name, 31
Remote access servers, 176
Remote authentication, 176
Remote client connectivity, 213–214
  security for, 215
Remote clients, newsgroup access, 217
Remote Procedure Calls. *See* RPCs.
Rendezvous protocol. *See* RVP.
Replicas
  adding, 191, **202–203**, **322**
  deleting, 192, **202**
  placement of, 192
Replicated folders, 150
Replication, 190–193, **202**
  configuring, 192
  by connectors, 192–193
  definition of, 239
  Message Priority setting, 192
  of newsgroup folders, 217–218, **227**
  of public folders, **322**
  of public folders, in coexistence state,
    251–252
  Replication Interval setting, 192
  Replication Size Limit setting, 192
Replication rings, 37
Reporting Wizard, 234

Reserved logs, 105
Resource mailboxes, 242, **264**
Restores, 115–116
    test restores, 115
Restoring data to point of failure, 105–106
Retry Task Wizard, 235
Rich browsers, 273, **280**
Rich text database file, 101–102
RID Master, 36, **46**
Routers, IM, 287–288
    SRV records for, 289–290, **295**
Routing group connectors, 130–131, **143**
    MTA use, **165–166**
    public folder referrals option, 133
    replication by, 192–193
    RPC use, 153
    security of, 131–132, **143**
Routing group master, 135
Routing groups, 37, 55–56, 126–128.
    See also Connectors.
    administrative groups and, 128–129
    displaying, 126–127
    First Routing Group, 126–127
    hub, 136, **142**
    message control between, 127–128
    multiple, 127–128
    number of, **67**, **306**, **312**
    SMTP for communications, 126
Routing management, 76
Routing topology, 135–137, **307**
    chain, 136
    design considerations, 137–138, **307**
    existing messaging systems and,
        137–138
    existing network infrastructure and,
        137, **144**, **307**
    full-mesh, 137
    hub-and-spoke, 136
    planning for growth and change, 138
RPCs
    ports for, 158
    for pre-Exchange 2000 site
        connectors, 131
    routing connector use of, 153
    security and, 131–132
    SRS use, 249
RVP, 275, 290
_RVP SRV records, 289–290

S

S/MIME, 177
    Outlook Express use of, 272
Schema, 26
    extending, 37
    modifying, 35–36, **43**, 53
Schema Admins group, 36, **43**
Schema Master, 35–36, **46**
    forest prep on, 53
Screened subnet, 156–157
Secure messaging, 177–178
Secure Multipurpose Internet Mail
    Extensions. *See* S/MIME.
Secure Server (Require Security) security
    rule, 175
Secure Sockets Layer. *See* SSL.
Security. *See also* Authentication; IPSec
    (IP Security).
    address list permissions, 86–87
    for delegating administrative
        control, 83
    of front-end/back-end server
        configuration, 151–152
    Internet connectivity and, **181**, **184**
    PKI for, 176–177
    pre-Windows 2000, 52
    remote access and, **181**
    remote authentication and, 176
    for remote client connectivity, 215
    of routing group connectors, 131–132
    secure messaging, 177–178, **181–182**
    for TCP/IP, 172–176
    threats to, 170
    for virtual services, **183**
    virus protection, 171–172
Security groups, 26
    Everyone group, 52
    synchronizing with distribution
        lists, 252
Security identifiers. *See* SIDs.
Security principals, 25
    copying between domains, 232
    migrating, 234, **265**
    SIDs of, 233, **265**
Security rules, 174–175, **325**
Security tab (Active Directory Users and
    Computers), 84
Security tab (Exchange System
    Manager), 83
Security Translation Wizard, 234
Server management, 76

Server (Request Security) security rule, 175
Server roles, 148–155
    Active Directory servers, 153–154.
      See also Active Directory servers.
    chat servers, 155
    conferencing servers, 155
    connector servers, 152–153
    front-end/back-end servers, 150–152
    in IM architecture, 287–288
    Instant Messaging servers, 155
    mailbox servers, 148–150
    OWA servers, 153
    public folder servers, 150
    separating, 148
Servers
    host system drive configuration, 116.
      See also Hard disk configuration.
    placement of, 155–158
    requirements of, 51
    restoring, 116
    virus protection on, 172
Service account, for ADC service, 236
Service Account Migration Wizard, 235
Service level agreements, 150
Service locator (SRV) records, 289–290, **295**
Service (SRV) records, 275, **282**,
    289–290, **314**
Services
    availability after failure, 150
    dependencies of, 58–59
    failures of, 62
    installing, 57–58
    reliability of, 150
Services console, 57–58
setup.exe/DomainPrep, 53–55
setup.exe/ForestPrep, 53
Shares, 62
SIDs
    of moved users, 233–234, **265**
    of security groups, 26
    of security principals, 26
Simple Mail Transfer Protocol. *See*
    SMTP.
SIS (Single Instance Storage), 107
Site links, 37
Sites, 37
Smart hosts, 132, **145**, 211, **225**
SMTP, 208
    Outlook 2000 use of, 270–271
    Outlook Express support for, 271–272
    ports for, 157
    for routing group connectors, 131

settings in IIS MetaBase, **166**
    use within routing groups, 126
SMTP connectors, 132–133
    address space setting, 212
    for communicating with pre-
      Exchange 2000 systems, **145**, **266**
    content restrictions setting, 212
    delivery restrictions setting, 212
    DNS lookups, 132–133, **145**, **225**
    encryption capabilities, **143**
    for Internet mail transmission,
      211, **225**
    local bridgeheads setting, 211
    public folder referrals option, 133
    replication by, 192–193
    scheduled delivery setting, 212
    smart hosts with, **145**, **225**
    SMTP service use, **166**
SMTP virtual servers, 177–178, **183**
    anonymous access to, 214
    for Internet email transmission,
      211–212, **223**
SNADS (SNA Distributed System),
    connector for, 134
Software deployment, group policies for, **44**
Software RAID, 110. *See also* RAID 1;
    RAID arrays.
Spindle failures, recovering from, 109
Spindles, 108
SRS (Site Replication Service), 249
SSL, 175, 208, **227**, **280**, **308**
    for communication in perimeter
      networks, 157
    firewall support for, 215
    Outlook Express use of, 272, **281**
    for security across WAN links, **313**
    for server security, **184**
Storage group topology, 106, **305**
Storage groups, 103
    of back-end servers, 151
    backing up, 111–113
    circular logging for, 105
    of mailbox stores, 150, **305**
    number of stores in, 103, **120**
    number per server, 103, **119–120**
    of public folder servers, 150
    transaction log sharing, 103, **305**
Stores, 100–103
    backing up, 112
    data in, 101–102
    maintenance of, 107
    mounting and unmounting, 107

number of, 103, **120**
restoring, 115
SIS in, 107, **123**
topology design, 103
Streaming database file, 101–102, **123**
Subnets, 37
Super-servers, 148
Swing method upgrades, 247–248
Synchronization
  definition of, 239
  of directories, 249–251
  of Exchange 5.5 and Active
    Directory, 235–243
System/boot partition
  placement of, **305**, **315**
  RAID 1 for, **121–122**, **320**
  RAID 5 for, **122**
System event log, service errors in, 62
System policies, 89–90
System Policy container, management of, 89

T

TCP/IP filtering, 172–173
TCP/IP networks
  security for, 172–176
  X.400 connectors on, 133
Test restores, 115
Threats, 170, **181**, **184**
TLS, 132, **143**, 177
Traffic, routing groups and, **67**
Transaction logs, 103–106
  backing up, 111–112
  checkpoint files, 104–105
  circular logging of, 105
  of connector servers, 152
  deleting, 104, 112
  naming conventions for, 104
  for newsgroups, 217
  placement of, 108–110, **121**, **305**, **315**
  RAID 1 for, 110, **121–122**, **320**
  reserved logs, 105
  sequential writing of, 108, **305**
Transactions, 107
  processing of, 108
  rolling forward and back, 104
Transport Layer Security. *See* TLS.
Trees, 28–30
Trust Migration Wizard, 235
Trust relationships
  creating for ADMT use, 233
  in-place upgrades and, 232

U

Undo Wizard, 235
Universal groups, 26, 34, 252
  AD support of, 238
Upgrades. *See also* Migration.
  in-place, 231–232
UPN suffix, 32
UPN (User Principal Name), 32
USENET newsgroups, 216, **227**
User Account Migration Wizard, 234
User account names, 31–32
User accounts, 25
  custom recipients for, **266**
  duplicate, 242–243, **260**
  mailbox-enabled, 37–39, **266**
  organizing into OUs, **44**
  single mailbox for, 242, **264**
User authentication. *See also* Authentication.
  Global Catalog server functions in, 34
User Logon Name, 32–33
User management, 75–76
  Active Directory Users and
    Computers for, 79
User objects, 25
  as security principals, 25
User roles, 72
Users
  administrative roles of, 75–77
  incremental migration of, 232
  viruses, educating about, 171

V

Verification of data, 114–115
Virtual Private Networks. *See* VPNs.
Virtual servers, 209–211
  anonymous access to, 214
  authentication requirements, 214–
    215, **296**
  basic authentication for, 214
  certificates for, 215
  configuration of, 176, 210–211
  connection control, 216, **226**
  digest authentication for, **296**
  IMAP4, **226**
  IP address and port configuration
    for, 209–210, **226**
  multiple per protocol, 209–210, **226**
  NNTP, 194–195, 214, 216–217
  RVP, for IM, 290, **296**
  SMTP, 177–178, **183**
  SSL configuration, 215

Windows Integrated authentication
for, 214–215, **296**
Virus protection, 171–172
client-side, 171–172
server-side, 172
Virus protection software, 172
Virus signatures, 172
VPNs, 215, **227**, **308**

W

WAN links, 155
public folder replication over, 192
public folder server access over,
155–156
security across, **313**
Web browsers
Outlook capabilities through, 272.
See also OWA (Outlook Web
Access).
OWA support for, 273
reach browsers, 273, **280**
rich browsers, 273, **280**
WebDAV, 273
Wide Area Networks. *See* WAN links.
Windows 2000 Delegation of Control
wizard, 82
Windows 2000 Professional
IPSec security for, **184**
upgrading to, **66**
Windows 2000 servers and systems
Administrative Tools, 60–61, **66**, **316**
Backup utility, 114
HTTP on, **222–223**
IIS on, **223**

IMAP4 on, **223**
IPSec security for, **184**
migration between, 232
mixed mode, 59
NNTP on, **222–223**
POP3 on, **223**
shared directory with Exchange
2000, 24
SMTP on, **222–223**
user management, 75–76
Windows 2000 Support Tools
Active Directory Tool, 79
ADSI Edit, 61, 79
Windows Explorer, permissions
management with, 197
Windows Integrated authentication,
214–215, 275, **282**, 290, **296**, **323**
Windows NT 4 Directory Service
(NTDS), 24
security principals in, 25
Windows NT 4 Remote Access Service
(RAS) Servers, 52
Windows NT domains, upgrading to
Windows 2000, **65**, 246, **261**, **303**, **324**

X

X.400 connectors, 133
MTA use, **165–166**
public folder referrals option, 133
replication by, 192–193
X.25 networks, X.400 connectors on, 133
XML, 273
for IM message formatting, 287